The Amidah

ISBN: 9780990667315

Cover Design: **Levi Blumenfeld**

Book Layout & Printing:

Tomer Naftali - TNT Design Group

Tomer@tntDesignGroup.com • 845-826-0484

Printed in USA

Dedicated as a

Zehut for Klal Yisrael

לעילוי נשמת

רבי עמרם בן דיוואן

In honor of my wife

Sally Cohen

In memory of

Toby Genud ע"ה

שינדל טויבא בת אשר לעמל ע"ה

In memory of our son
Michael M. Kameo A'H

By his parents
Keren and Mordi Kameo

MICHAEL KAMEO
F O U N D A T I O N

לעילוי נשמת

יוסף בן אסתר

In honor of my father
Sean Jacobi

•

**Dedicated to the safety
of Eretz Yisroel**

**Refuah Shelema to
Yehoshua ben Miriam**

•

In honor of my wife
Shanie Souid

**Dedicated in honor
of our Grandparents**

Amir and Nicole Benisti

לז"נ

רחל בת סול

עלי בן שמחה

ישראל בן רחל

In blessed memory of
our Great Grandfather
Chacham Yaakov Kassin –

**Chief Rabbi
Jacob S. Kassin ZT"L**

Sarah and Isaac J. Kassin

In honor of
**Rabbi Eli J.
and Rebbetzin Sandra
Mansour**

Dedicated in honor of
Frieda Kameo

**A shining example of love,
devotion, and strength
for our family.**

By Her Loving Husband & Children

In honor of my father

**Nissim Cohen
ben Ovadya Cohen**

In memory of
Rachel bat Esther Alta

לעילוי נשמת
מיכאל דוד בן חנה

In honor of our daughter
Pauline - Mazal bat Sarah
for always making Tefilah a
priority

**Dedicated for the
safe return of the soldiers
and protection of Klal Yisrael**

**For Zechut for Am Yisrael around
the world, all the soldiers
on the front lines.
Refuah Shelema to the victims
and the injured.
Leilui Nishmat to all the Holy
Neshamot taken away from us.**

The לימוד of this ספר and the תפילות
made, by all of those on the spiritual
front lines should be for the זכות of
עם ישראל and the צה"ל fighting
on the physical front lines

לעילוי נשמת
ר' דוד בן ר' משה • ר' צמח בן ר' יוסף
וכל הנשמות הקדושות שאבדנו

In honor of
Sol and Rita Wahba
&
Avi and Marlene Ben-Dayan

By their children and
grandchildren

לעילוי נשמת
משה אהרן יהושע בן אליעזר זוסמאן
•
שרה בת אשר

הרב עובדיה יוסף
הראשון לציון ונשיא מועצת חכמי התורה

מכתב ברכה

הובאו לפני גליונות ספר פסקי הלכות שכתב וערך ידידנו הדגול, איש חי רב פעלים, זך השכל והרעיון, חריף ובקי, משנתו זך ונקי, מרביץ תורה בישראל, פה מפיק מרגליות, דורש כתרי אותיות, הרה"ג רבי אליהו מנצור שליט"א, וכתב וערך הכל לפי הפסקים שכתבתי בס"ד בספרי שו"ת יביע אומר ושו"ת יחוה דעת ועוד, וסידר הכל בסדר ישר ונכון, בשפה ברורה ונעימה, דבר דבור על אופניו, תפוחי זהב במשכיות כסף, וזה מכבר יצא שמו לפניו למרחוק אשר הוצק חן בשפתותיו וזכה ללמד רבים מאהב"י תורה בשיעוריו הרבים, ולזכות את הרבים ולקרב רחוקים, ובפרט בקרב בני ק"ק יוצאי ארם צובא אשר בניו יורק, ולפעלא טבא אמינא איישר חיליה לאורייתא.

והנני מתכבד לברך את הרב המחבר שליט"א שיזכה עוד רבות בשנים להמשיך להפיץ מעינותיו חוצה ולהרביץ תורה בישראל, ולהיות ממצדיקי הרבים ככוכבים לכולם ועד, מתוך נחת ושלוה ואורך ימים ושנות חיים ושובע שמחות ונחת מכל יוצאי חלציו אמן.

בברכת התורה

עובדיה יוסף

Rabbi Ovadia Yosef

RISHON LE'TZIYON AND PRESIDENT OF THE COUNCIL OF TORAH SAGES

JERUSALEM, 18 ELUL 5768

I have seen the manuscripts of a book of halachic rulings written and prepared by our esteemed friend, a man of great achievement, of pristine intellect and thought, an erudite and knowledgeable scholar, whose teaching is clear and lucid, a disseminator of Torah in Israel, whose mouth speaks pearls of wisdom and expounds upon the "crowns of the letters," **HaGaon HaRav Eliyahu Mansour** *shelita*. He wrote and prepared everything according to the rulings I wrote with the Almighty's help in my works *Yabia Omer, Yehaveh Da'at* and others. He arranged it all in a proper, straightforward manner, in a clear and accessible style, each matter clearly elucidated, "golden apples in silver coverings." His reputation has long ago spread to vast distances for his masterful oratory skill, and he has been privileged to teach Torah to many among our fellow Jews through his many classes, and to bring merit to the public and bring Jews close to observance, particularly among the Aram Soba community in New York. I extend to him my sincere wishes for his admirable work.

It is my honor to bless the author *shelita* that he should be privileged to continue pouring forth from his fountains of wisdom for many years to come and disseminate Torah in Israel in peace, tranquility and long life, and he should be blessed with many years of life, joy and pride from all his offspring, *Amen.*

With the blessings of Torah,

Ovadia Yosef

עובדיה יוסף

Harav SHMUEL PINHASI
26 Hakablan St. Jerusalem
Tel: 524244

הרב שמואל פנחסי
רח' הקבלן 26 ירושלים
טל: 524244

בס"ד, תאריך __כח תמוז תשמ"ח__

דברי ברכה

בהגלות נגלות אור יקרות, עדיות ואגדות,
בפני הלכות, שנאמרו תעמוד כהוגן, אלופות מפי בוקי'ם
ורבנן, על פי שיטת מרן, הגאון הגדול מעוז ומגדול
פאר הדור, הרב עובדיה יוסף שליט"א בשפה האמיתית
מפי אחד המאמר רבה בצמיה, ומהכינא רהיטאמ"ה,
יהיגי הקר והעולה, כגול מרבבה, הרב אליהו מנצור שליט"א,
אשר הלבן הן הסאתנו, לקבץ רחוקים בשיטתנו, ומקדש שם
שמים בפולרבנ"ס. ואלץ טובת תליה כבנוי"דו.
הנני לתרבו מקרב לב, וני רצון שקבה עוד ורב ויא"ש
מאן, ויפולו מעיינו הלה להתגדל תורה להגבירה, יתק
נחת ונולה ושמחת עולם עד עולם.

ברכה והצירא האריאל

שמואל פנחסי

שמואל פנחסי
רב שכונת "מחנה-יהודה"
רח' יוסף בן מתתיהו 3
ירושלים - תובב"ה

Harav Shmuel Pinhasi
26 Hakablan St. Jerusalem

I would like to extend words of blessing on the occasion of the publication of this precious, illuminating work, halachic rulings that were presented each in their proper time, gleaned from the writings of our Rabbis and *poskim*, based upon the rulingsof our great Rabbi, the glory of our generation, Rav Ovadia Yosef *shelit"a*, in the English language. They were presented by one of the great figures of the nation, one of the leaders of the people, my dear, esteemed and distinguished friend, Rav Eliyahu Mansour *shelit"a*, who has been graced with the gift of speech with which to draw Jews near through his lectures, and who sanctifies the Name of God with his speeches, and "a precious stone hangs around his neck" to inspire those near and far.

I would like to bless him from the depths of my heart that it may be God's will that he reaches even greater heights, and his fountains shall continue to pour forth that he may elevate and glorify Torah with peace, serenity and endless joy forever.

With great honor and esteem for the Torah,
Shmuel Pinhasi
Rabbi of Mahane Yehuda
3 Yosef Ben Matityahu St.
Jerusalem

Foreword

"הריני מקבל עלי מצות עשה של "ואהבת לרעך כמוך", והריני אוהב את כל אחד מישראל כנפשי ומאודי, והריני מזמן פה שלי להתפלל לפני מלך מלכי המלכים הקב"ה."

Rabennu HaArizal advised that before one begins the service of prayer, he must accept upon himself the Misva of "Love Thy Neighbor" and proclaim his love and admiration for every Jew. This might be the deeper explanation of תפילה בציבור. Certainly, the Halacha advises that we pray in a Minyan of at least 10 men. The Arizal introduces that one must include himself and his prayer with the entire ציבור of Israel. Even those that are not present. David HaMelech A"H, alluded to this at the end of Chapter 72 of Tehillim when it says "כלו תפלות דוד בן־ישי". "כלו" is an acronym for "ואהבת לרעך כמוך". As if to say, the prerequisite to *Tefila* is "ואהבת לרעך כמוך".

The question is why?? A Minyan is necessary to recite דברים שבקדושה. After all, neither Kaddish, Nakdishach, Birkat Kohanim, or repetition of the *Amidah* can be recited without a ציבור. But, why did the Arizal require a second ציבור? A prayer that is connected to all of ישראל? Why must a Jew connect himself through "ואהבת לרעך כמוך" to all the ציבור of Israel before he can pray?

One answer may be that we are including in our prayers a special כונה for all those Jews who cannot or are not praying. We accept upon ourselves to pray on their behalf. After all through prayer, we are granted Life, Health, Teshuba, Wisdom, Parnasa, and more. Why should any Jew be deprived from these blessings? This might explain

why all the Berachot in the *Amidah* are in plural, for example; השיבנו,
חננו, ברך עלנו, רפאנו, etc. Prayer is a personal as well as a communal
service. Our prayers are intended to benefit all of כלל ישראל.

Unfortunately, the reality is that many Jews have never been
introduced to *Tefila* . They never experienced a שחרית, מנחה, or ערבית.
A siddur or מחזור can not be found in their libraries, and if by chance
they stumbled upon a Siddur, they would not know what to do with
it. To many, the closed Siddur has been relegated to nothing but a
good luck charm, an oversized amulet, something to keep in the
glove compartment of a car for protection. Until those Jews become
enlightened we have them in mind with our prayers. That is why the
Ariza"l mandates us to accept ואהבת לרעך כמוך before we begin the
service of prayer.

There is another reality that in my opinion is no less unfortunate
than the former. It is what I call the "Chinese Newspaper Syndrome".
People pray 3 times a day, 4 times on Shabbat and on Yamim Tobim,
and even 5 times on Yom Kippur. To these people, the Siddur is
open. Its pages are turned and worn out. The text is recited with all
the proper pronunciation and grammatical rules. What is missing?
MEANING!! What do the words mean? To many, the Siddur has just as
much meaning as the Chinese Newspaper (to someone who doesn't
speak Chinese.) The exercise of prayer becomes monotonous at
best, boring at worst. The Siddur becomes a 'book' that arouses in
a person feelings of irrelevance, purposelessness, routine, and Has
VeShalom what the Mishna in Avot calls קבע, a 'burden'. It would take
a great discipline and persistence to recite words for hours every
day, weeks on end, that the reader has no clue what they mean!!

"תפילה בלא כונה כגוף בלא נשמה" A prayer without 'meaning' is tantamount
to a body with a soul- lifeless!! It lacks the energy and lift to reach its
full potential. Although Hashem answers the prayers of every mouth
"כי אתה שומע תפילת כל פה", even if it is only from the mouth lacking

intent and meaning. However, for prayer to be fully effective it needs meaning. When we pray with meaning we have in mind to include not only those who do not pray, but those who do pray but without meaning.

This may shed light on a Mishna in פאה;

"אלו דברים שאדם עושה אותם, אוכל מפירותיהם בעולם הזה, והקרן קימת לו לעולם הבא. ואלו הן: כיבוד אב ואם, וגמילות חסדים, וביקור חולים, והכנסת אורחים, והשכמת בית הכנסת, והבאת שלום בין אדם לחברו, ובין איש לאשתו. ותלמוד תורה כנגד כולם."

"The following are things that a person who performs them benefits of their fruits in This World, yet the principal remains intact for him for the World to Come. And they are: Honoring one's father and mother; bestowing kindness; visiting the sick; hospitality to guests; arriving early at the synagogue; bringing peace between a man and his fellow; and between a man and his wife; and the learning of Torah is equivalent to them all."

All these Misvot have one common denominator. They are all acts of Hessed. How does attending the Synagogue fit this model? When we pray we are doing a Hessed because we are praying not only for ourselves but for all of עם ישראל. This is a pure Hessed where we benefit total strangers and don't ask for anything in return.

The purpose of this book is to provide "MEANING" to our *Tefila* . Not to give a literal interpretation to the words, but to tell the story of each Beracha of the *Amidah*. To add the נשמה to the *Tefila* . To remove the rote and mechanical element of prayer and replace it with freshness and excitement. To trade in the "Chinese Newspaper" for the word of a living God, "דברי אלוקים חיים."

At this point, the reader may feel very hopeful that maybe

something in the coming pages will awaken and kindle the bright flame that lies in the words of the *Amidah*. Like the Baal Shem Tov said: "צהר תעשה לתיבה", 'bring light into the Teba - "the word". The siddur must be illuminating and inspiring. At the same time feelings of despair may set in. What about all the hundreds or even thousands of Tefilot that were uttered without 'meaning'? Did I waste my time? Was it all futile? To address this reaction I direct you to the words of the Kav Hayshar in the eighth chapter: "הרי לך חסד גדול מהבורא יתברך שבתפילה אחת נתקן הכל" With one *Tefila* He can fix everything.

When a person is awakened to start praying with כונה something magical happens. Not only does Hashem answer his first *Amidah* that is recited with "meaning", but all past Tefillot that were uttered without meaning are also accepted at this point and delivered in front of הקב"ה himself.

"...ומכאן ולהבא הוא מתפלל בכוונה היטב-אזי תפילות ראשונות שהן ביד הממונה סהדיא"ל, עולה עם תפילה ראשונה שהתחיל להתפלל בכונה, וההוא ממונה בעצמו נוטל התפילות הפסולות ומעלה אותם מעלה-מעלה, עד שבאה התפילה לפני הקב"ה בעצמו, ונעשית עטרה עם שאר תפילות ישראל הכשרות. הרי לך חסד גדול מהבורא יתברך, שבתפילה אחת נתקן הכל."

"...and from here on in he prays with concentration, then the first Tefillot who in the hands of 'Sahadiel', go up along with the first Tefila he prayed with concentration, and he himself takes the blemished Tefillot and raises them all the way to God's throne, and it becomes a crown for all the previous Tefillot of Am Yisrael. This is a tremendous Hessed from Hashem, that with one Tefillah, all other Tefillot are fixed."

The Angel 'Sahadiel' who holds all the blemished prayers declares all of them from one level to the next until they reach הקב"ה himself and before a crown to him with the rest of the kosher prayers of Israel".

This amazing phenomenon takes place as the first *Tefila* with meaning is offered. So please don't worry about the past. Let this book help you move forward in a meaningful prayer and at the same time assist to recoup old meaningless prayers as well.

I am well aware of the Gemara in Berachot: אין עומדים להתפלל אלא מתוך כובד ראש" - Rashi's meaning - One must stand in prayer with total effacement and humility in front of Hashem yitbarach. As our Rabbis taught: "דע לפני מי אתה עומד" Know in front of whom you stand in prayer. I apply this rule as well as I stand to publish insights on the *Amidah*. The *Amidah* which is a product of אנשי כנסת הגדולה the men of the Great Assembly, was written by great personalities who possessed רוח הקודש, Divine inspiration and some even prophecy.

Far be it from me to even think for a moment that we have done the *Amidah* the justice that it deserves. Only men on the caliber of those who instituted it can truly expound on the endless waters that are within these blessings. It is for this reason that I embark on this "mission of meaning" with כובד ראש.

My gratitude is to the Boreh Olam. "מודה אני לפנך מלך חי וקיים" for placing my share in the walls of the Bet HaMidrash, for sharing his infinite wisdom with mortal human beings, and for allowing me to disseminate his holy word.

This project is the brainchild of Dr. Eric BenTollila הי"ו. He approached me and requested that I deliver shiurim on the *Amidah*. He suggested it be a series of lectures covering the entire Shmoneh Esreh. "גדול המעשה יותר מן העושה" "Greater is the motivator than the doer". May Hashem answer all your prayers לטובה and the זכות stand for you and your family Amen! At his request these shiurim were given לע"נ the sadik R' David U'Moshe זצוק"ל.

A special thanks to The Edmond J Safra Synagogue of Brooklyn where I serve as Rabbi and its president **Morris A Dweck** הי"ו and the Board of Directors for creating and maintaining our venue, so we have a base from where we can spread Torah.

To **Rico Toussoun** הי"ו, silent hero and innovator of Torah CDs and videos, for being the driving force behind this project.

To **David Silverberg** הי"ו from Israel who transcribed the oral word to the written word.

I am very grateful to **Adam Azrak** for his devotion in giving hundreds of hours in editing and perfecting this work. Adam has labored over every word of this Sefer. Yeshalem Hashem Paolech.

To **Tomer Naftali** הי"ו and his staff at TNT Design Group for putting these papers into book form. Excellent service!

To my parents **Joe and Rochelle Mansour** הי"ו, certainly deserve more than a few lines for me to express how indebted I am for giving me and my siblings the proper Torah Hinuch. I pray that they should continue to see much נחת from all their offspring Amen!

"אחרון אחרון חביב" My dear "אשת חיל" **Rebbittsen Sandra** מב"ת. 'What's mine is yours.' This book is not mine, but ours. May Hashem bless you with continued strength and health in raising our children and family. I couldn't have done it without you. It is my fervent prayer that all of our Tefillot should be answered.

תקובל תפילתנו ברצון, אמן

Rabbi Eli J Mansour, 5775

The Amida is this very moment of closeness with H. Unfortunately it is easy to fall in the routine when praying it.

We should all give a great Hakarat Hatov to Rabbi Mansour for giving us, with his work, special Kavanot. This help all the readers with new uplifting emotions when praying the Chmone Essre.

May H., bless and protect Rabbi Elie Mansour and his family. May H. Give him the strength to continue to spread the words of Torah the way he does. In good health, bryout, success for 120 years with more and more followers.

May the Zekhout of Rabbi David ou Moche protect him and his family. It is at the site of the graveside of Rabbi David ou Moche, in Morocco, that this project started.

May H. Listen to all the readers prayer.
Amen

From the contributors of this book

Dedicated in Honor of our Father

Marc Mizrahi

He has taught us that a little step each day
goes a long way. His growth in Torah, and
Midot have been inspiring and this book
will BH only add to that.

May Hashem bless him to see the marriage
of his children, and continued joy from his
children and grandchildren.

Donated with love by
JEANNIE AND MARSHALL MIZRAHI

In Memory of our Mother

Diane Azrak a"h

דינה בת שרה

23 Tevet 5774

By
VICTOR AND CHERYL
ELLIOTT AND ANNIE
ADAM AND FRIEDA

In Memory of

Rimon ben Gelson

In Honor of My Mother

Yaffa bat Sara

She should live a long healthy life

In Honor of our Parents:

Esther & David Jemal

By their children:

GAIL AND RALPH SHAMAH

ELI AND STACIE JEMAL

LESLIE AND ZACKO SHEHEBAR

ALAN AND SOFIA JEMAL

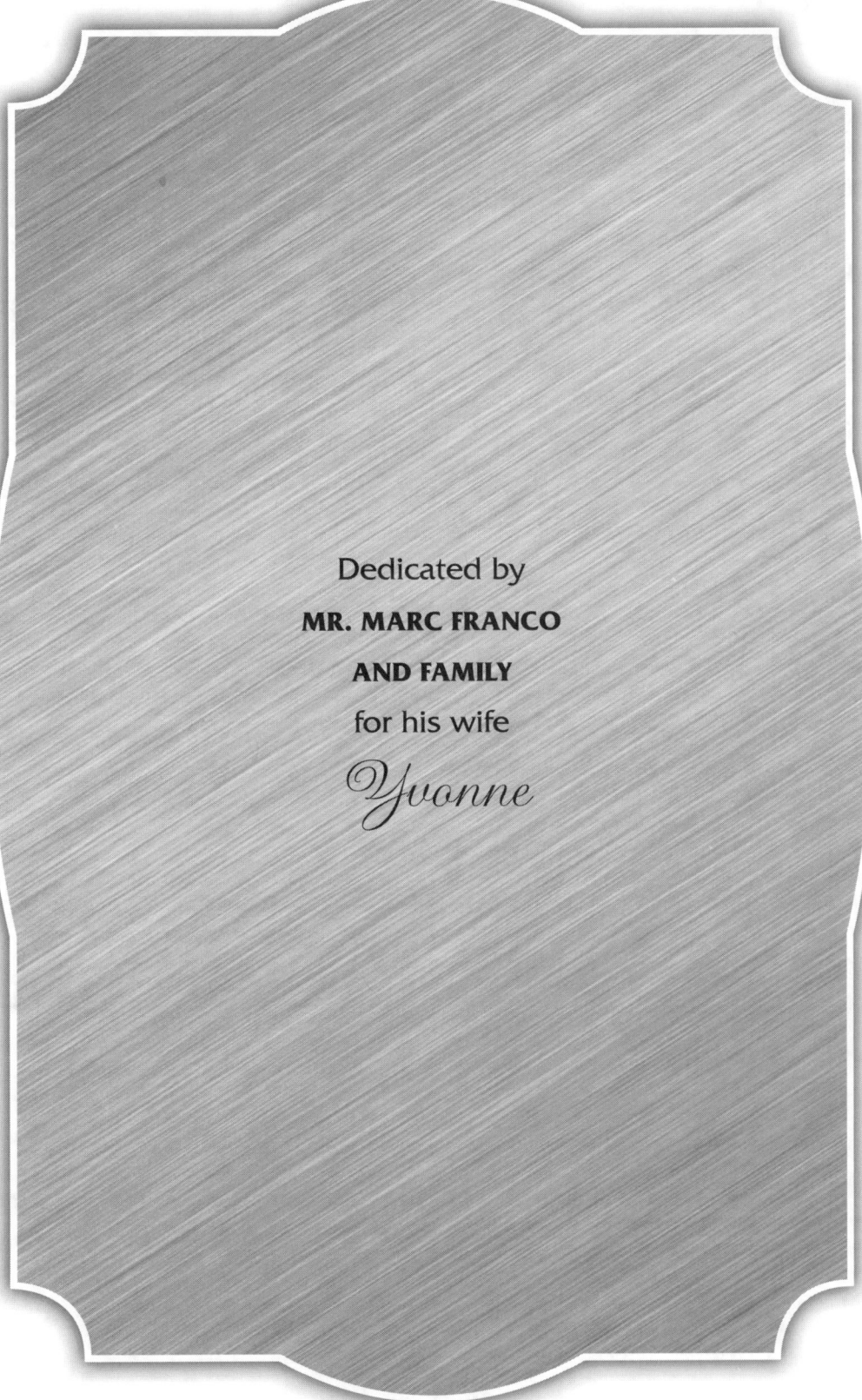

Dedicated by

MR. MARC FRANCO

AND FAMILY

for his wife

Yvonne

In Memory of

Albert R. Nackab

אברהם בן פולין

BY HIS FAMILY

For the
Beraja, Hatzlaja and Shalom
of

Jose ben Elvira

DEDICATED BY HIS SONS

In Honor and Memory
of our Parents

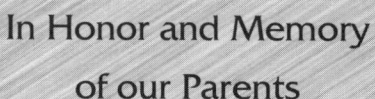

Chaim and Irene Orfali a"h
Zev and Sarah Finkelstein a"h

CHABY AND NICOLE ORFALI

In Honor of our Parents
and Grandparents

Farrokh & Shahla Ebrani

Yusef & Delaram Deil

By

DAVID AND GHILA EBRANI

ELIYAHU, ELIANNA,

SHIRLY AND YOEL

In Memory of my Beloved Father

Elyakim ben Mendel Hakohen

"Be bold as a leopard, light as an eagle, swift
as a dear and strong as a lion to carry out the
will of your Father in Heaven." (Ethics of the Fathers 5:23)

The Light of your Neshama continues
to illuminate our lives.
We remember your loving kindness.
We miss you and we love you

Your loving son and daughter in law,
MARK AND TSIPPI HERSH
and Grandson
JONAH ISAAC HERSH

L'iluy Nishmat

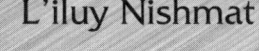
Isaac ben Camila Z"L

10 Elul 5774

Father, Teacher and Guide

Dedicated By
**JOEL AND BELA ABBO
AND FAMILY**

Panama

Dedicated for
the wellbeing of my father BH

רפואה שלמה

למשה בן רמו

CHAIM ELKAIM

In Honor of our Children

Jared, Daniel and David

May Hashem always answer your prayers together and provide you a life of Health, Happiness, Shalom and Family

DONNA AND EDWARD STROH

The Amidah

By Rabbi Eli J Mansour

Elucidated by David Silverberg

Table of Contents

Hanukah and Purim 342
על הנסים

In Everlasting Memory of

Hacham Baruch Refael ben Miriam ז״ל

Hacham Ovadia Yosef ben Gorgia ז״ל

The Purpose of Prayer

Why do we pray? What goal are we trying to achieve through our prayers?

At first glance, the answer seems simple: we pray to get the things we want. We pray because we want God to cure the family member who has taken ill, Heaven forbid, or because the business is struggling and only God can get it back on its feet. Prayer is, at first glance, simply one of the strategies we employ in trying to obtain what we want and need in life.

But this understanding of prayer is fundamentally incorrect and misguided. In fact, it is childish. It turns us into whiny toddlers tugging at God's clothes asking Him to give us the "toys" and "treats" that we crave. This is not what prayer is. Prayer is not about getting what we want, but about changing ourselves by building a close relationship with God.

We can easily prove this explanation of prayer by examining the word *tefila*. After the birth of a son to Bilha, Rahel's maidservant, Rahel declared, נפתולי אלקים נפתלתי עם אחותי (Bereshit 30:8). Loosely translated, this means that Rahel "wrestled", or was "knotted" in confrontation, with her sister. Similarly, the knotted seal covering a utensil is referred to in the Torah by the term פתיל (Bamidbar 19:15). *Tefillin* are so named because they are tied to our bodies. *Tefila* means a "knot". Through prayer, we bind ourselves to the Almighty; we form a relationship and bond with our Creator. It says in Tehillim (145:18), קרוב ה' לכל קוראיו – "God is close to all who call to Him". By calling to God in prayer, we draw close to Him, and this is the purpose of prayer.

In the Book of Debarim (3:23), Moshe recalls his prayer to God begging for permission to cross into the Land of Israel together with the rest of the nation. He describes his petition with the word ואתחנן, which has the numerical value of 515. The Sages teach that Moshe recited 515 prayers in an attempt to have the decree against him repealed. After the 515th prayer, God ordered him to stop praying. One might wonder why Moshe continued praying until God commanded him to stop. Once he did not receive a favorable response after, let's say, the 300th prayer, he must have realized that his request is not going to be granted, and yet, Moshe persisted. He continued praying, undeterred, until finally God had to tell him to stop. What purpose did his prayers serve once he realized the answer was "No"?

The answer is that, as mentioned, the value of prayer does not lie in the granting of one's request, but rather in the experience itself. Having one's prayer answered is a perk, the icing on the cake. The real benefit offered by *tefila* is the closeness with God, the bond that one creates with Hashem. When a person meets and speaks with a *sadik*, he senses the sanctity and spiritual energy emanating from him. All the more so, then, speaking directly to God, the experience of standing in Hashem's presence, injects a person with spiritual energy, uplifting him to great heights of *kedusha*

The Sages noted (Gemara Yebamot 64a) that three of the four matriarchs – Sara, Ribka and Rahel – were infertile for extended periods before they conceived. The reason, the Rabbis explained, is that God "desires the prayers of the righteous". In other words, God denied these righteous women the joy and privilege of children for many years because He wanted to hear them pray. At first glance, this sounds like sheer selfishness. Is it fair to deny people something they want and deserve, just to hear them ask, plead and beg for it for many years?

The answer, of course, is that God wanted the matriarchs to pray for their sake, not for His sake. God wants to give the *sadikim* the opportunity to advance and develop their relationship with Him. It wasn't the prayers that He desired, but rather the close relationship with the righteous patriarchs and matriarchs. In fact, this is the reason why He does not always give us exactly what we want or need right away. If He would do so, we would never feel the need to pray, and we would never have the opportunity to bond with Him, to enhance our relationship with Him. God specifically created us and our lives in such a way that we always need His assistance. Nobody is without problems, without worries and concerns. We all have needs and wants that have yet to be fulfilled, and this is how it is meant to be. This reality is to our advantage, as it forces us to turn to God in prayer, and thereby forge a relationship with Him. This privilege is granted especially to the *sadikim*, whom God invites to develop a particularly close bond with Him. For this reason, the righteous matriarchs were barren – as God's personal invitation to them and their husbands to come before Him in prayer.

It thus emerges that we do not pray because we need something; we need something so that we will pray.

This also explains the peculiar punishment God decreed upon the snake after Adam and Hava's sin. In the aftermath of the sin of the forbidden tree, God declared a series of curses that would befall Adam, Hava and the snake that had lured them into partaking of the fruit. Among the curses placed upon the snake was ועפר תאכל כל ימי חייך – that it would feed off "dust of the earth" (Bereshit 3:14). One might wonder, at first glance, why this should be a curse. After all, the snake would never again have to worry about its livelihood; its food would now be readily accessible anywhere in the world. Rav Simha Bunim of Peshischa, one of the legendary Hassidic masters, explained that in truth, there can be no greater curse than having all of one's needs immediately met all the time. God essentially declared that the snake would never have any relationship with its Creator; that He will never have any interest in hearing from the snake.

Rav Simha Bunim drew an analogy to a wealthy father who had an obedient, loyal son, and a rebellious, defiant son. He told the defiant son to come once a year, and at each annual visit he will give him enough money with which to support himself until the next year. When it came to his beloved, faithful son, however, he decided to give him only two weeks' worth of provisions at a time. If he would give him an annual lump sum, the son would only come visit him once a year. The father very much wished to see this son regularly, and so he supported him in small, biweekly installments, thereby ensuring to maintain a close, ongoing relationship with the son.

This should be our outlook on prayer, and, in truth, our outlook on life. We often ask ourselves, why does God make things so difficult? Why is it so hard to make a living? Why is child-rearing so complicated? Why must so many people deal with ill family members and financial hardships? Why can't God just make life simple and straightforward?

The answer is that God does not want us to be like the snake. He wants to forge a close, meaningful relationship with us; He wants to become an important part of our lives. He made it that we would need to approach Him several times a day to ask for health and financial stability. This way, we have the opportunity to speak with Him, to bond with Him, and make Him an integral part of our lives. The problems we confront are the "excuses" that we use to go to God, talk and connect with Him.

It occasionally happens that a wife phones her husband from a store while he is at work, asking for his advice regarding a purchase she is considering.

The husband, pressured at the office, hurriedly replies, "You can buy whichever one you want, thanks for asking. I'll see you later".

The husband thinks he is being considerate, allowing his wife the option to choose and not making any demands of her. The wife, however, feels slighted. She is angry at the husband for rushing off the phone without giving an opinion.

The husband's mistake in this situation is failing to understand the true purpose of the phone call. The wife did not call because she could not decide for herself which size bowls she should buy. Rather, she called because her question offered the opportunity to speak to her husband. During his long day at work, she thinks of him and wishes to continue nurturing their relationship. She thus finds opportunities to call him and speak to him.

The wife did not want to hear the husband answer the question and then say "Bye, have a nice day". She wanted to hear him say, "So how is your day going? Did you get done what you needed to do? How did the appointment go?" The question about the kitchenware was just her way of initiating a conversation to further develop her relationship with her husband.

Yeshiva students frequently employ this tactic, as well. Seeking a close relationship with their Rabbi, they often think of a question that does not really weigh too heavily – or at all – on their minds, as an excuse to approach the Rabbi and engage him in conversation. They aren't necessarily interested in an answer. To the contrary, if the Rabbi gives a clear, succinct answer to their question, they walk away disappointed. They want to develop a relationship, and the question is the means by which they hope to achieve that goal.

The same applies to *tefila*. The problems we confront in life are simply "excuses" for cultivating our relationship with the Almighty. Whether or not He grants our requests is far less important than the goal we achieve through heartfelt prayer – developing our connection to God. This is why we must not feel discouraged when our prayers aren't answered.

It often happens that women assemble for a special Tehillim recitation on behalf of a gravely ill patient, and despite their sincere, heartfelt and impassioned prayer, the patient does not survive, Heaven forbid. The death of an ill patient is certainly a tragedy, but it does not mean that the prayers were meaningless. We cannot and will not know why God chose to take the patient from this world, but we do know, with full confidence, that every person who prayed for that patient enhanced his or her relationship with the Almighty. Having our prayers answered is simply the icing on the cake. What we really gain from prayer is the opportunity to connect with God. As the verse states in Tehillim (105:3), ישמח לב מבקשי ה' – "Those who seek Hashem shall be joyful". Happiness does not come from God answering all our requests, but rather from making the requests. When we "seek Hashem", when we bring Him our בקשות, our lives are enriched as a result of the connection we've established with our Creator.

King David exclaims in Tehillim (116:1-2), אהבתי כי ישמע ה' את קולי תחנוני כי הטה אזנו לי – "I love it when God listens to the voice of my supplication, when He turns His ear to me". Regardless of whether or not God answered his prayer, David celebrated the very fact that "He turns His ear to me", that he is given an audience with the Almighty. This itself is cause for rejoicing. Prayer is a privilege and a most rewarding experience irrespective of the outcome of our requests. Even if the answer is "No", the encounter with God is itself a precious and invaluable opportunity.

In the *Shema Kolenu* blessing of the *Amidah (the 16th Beracha)*, we describe God as שומע תפילת כל פה – "who listens to the prayer of every mouth". God does not necessarily grant every request; we have never received such a guarantee. We are guaranteed, however, that God listens to every prayer, that He pays attention to us when we pray and cherishes each and every word. This is the most important and central purpose of the experience of prayer.

A person should also never be deterred by the difficulty of a situation. The Gemara teaches, אין מזל לישראל – the Jewish people are not subject to the same strict rules that govern over nations. *Tefila* has the power to overcome our מזל, the destiny determined by the various natural forces in the world. This concept is alluded to by the names of Yishak and Ribka, which have a combined numerical value of 515[1] – the same numerical value as the word תפלה. Yishak and Ribka epitomize the power of prayer, as their prayers for a child prevailed over Ribka's natural inability to conceive. The story of Ribka's conception, which was made possible only through prayer, teaches us the power of *tefila* , and that in all situations we can and must turn to prayer with complete and confident faith in its ability to help us.

Finally, God's office is open not only at all hours, but for all people. We should never feel too ashamed to approach God, and we should never feel as though we do not deserve an audience with Him. No matter who we are or what we have done, God lovingly waits for us in His "office", and eagerly anticipates our prayers.

The Mishna (Berachot 30b) teaches regarding prayer, – ואפילו המלך שואל בשלומו לא ישיבנו ואפילו נחש כרוך על עקבו לא יפסיק "Even –

---

1. יצחק = 208; רבקה = 307, for a total of 515 (208+307).

if the king greets him, he does not respond, and even if a snake is wrapped around his heel, he does not interrupt". The simple meaning of the Mishna is that we should aspire to a level of intense concentration while praying where no external factors are capable of distracting us, even clear and present risks such as a king or a snake. On a deeper level, however, our Sages here are teaching us that prayer is for everybody. "Even if the king greets him" – even if somebody has an especially close relationship with "the King", the Almighty, such that God comes to "greet him", as it were, he must still pray and continue building his connection to Hashem. Our spiritual work never ends until our final moments of life, and thus even the greatest sadikim must continue coming before Hashem in prayer. "Even if a snake is wrapped around his heel" – even if a person is caught by the snare of the "snake", the evil inclination, and is mired in sin, he should not abstain from prayer. He must never think that God is not interested in hearing from him. God's door is open to each and every one of us, and is eager to welcome us, listen to us, and accept our prayers.

No one should ever feel unworthy of the great blessing of prayer. It is an opportunity granted as a gift to one and all, and an opportunity which we should all seize and be sure never to squander.

In Honor of our Parents

Rachel & Avi Uziel

and

Sara & Adam Ash

In appreciation for their daily sacrifices
for the well being of our families

Violet and Judah Uziel

The Door is Always Open

Since *tefila* is about developing a relationship with God, and God wishes for each of us to develop such a relationship, He keeps His "door" open at all times. Even though the formal, fixed prayer services must be recited in a particular text according to a particular schedule, we are always invited and welcome to speak to God. The Torah (Debarim 4:7) teaches that God is receptive בכל קראנו אליו, whenever we call to Him. We have a standing invitation to come and bring Him our requests, however trivial they may be, because He wants us to build a special, personal connection with Him.

This is a special privilege given specifically to us, because of the Almighty's infinite love for us and His desire for us to nurture our relationship with Him. In the י ה-רבון hymn sung in the Friday night *bakashot*, we sing, שבחין אסדר צפרא ורמשא – "I shall arrange praises morning and evening". Morning is called צפרא because it is then when the birds (צפורים) begin to chirp, and evening is called רמשא because it is then when the small reptiles (רמשים) emerge from their lairs. Each creature has its designated time to praise God; some in the morning, some in the evening. Our Sages tell us that the angels, too, have specific times when they are allowed to come before God to sing His praises, and some angels are given this privilege only once in their existence. We, however, are able to come before the Almighty צפרא ורמשא, anytime day or night. For us, the door is always open; there are no special "office hours".

Nor are there any limitations on the kind of requests we may make of Him. If we are eager to establish a relationship with somebody, then we are thrilled anytime that person speaks to us, no matter how trivial the purpose – even if it was just to ask us the time. This is how God treats our prayers. He invites us to speak to Him at any time, for any kind of request. It is advisable to grow accustomed to speaking to God several times a day, in whatever language, asking Him whatever it is that we need, whether it is a good parking spot, success in an interview, or any other request. God always wants to hear from us, no matter the subject matter of our "phone call".

The story is told of Rabbi Nahum of Chernobyl, who once, in the middle of his learning session in the *bet midrash*, suddenly stood up, went to the corner of the room, and began praying with intense emotion. The Hasidim curiously stood near their Rabbi to hear what he was saying. It turned out that he was praying that his housekeeper would not quit her job. His wife was very anxious because the housekeeper mentioned that she was considering quitting, and the Rabbi pleaded with God to arrange that the housekeeper would stay on the job.

When his Hassidim asked why he would pray for something so trifling, he explained, "I try to find excuses to speak to God. I want to develop my relationship with Him, so I find any reason that I can to talk to Him!"

We can – and should – pray for anything. Any excuse we can find is good enough, and offers us a valuable opportunity to further develop and enhance our relationship with God.

Nourishing the Soul

R' Yehuda Halevi, in his *Sefer Hakuzari*, writes that prayer is to the soul what food is to the body. It is what nourishes, sustains and fortifies the soul. Just as the human body cannot endure without the nourishment of food, similarly, the human soul cannot survive without regular bonding with God. Just as spoiled food can cause illness, a "rotten" prayer is detrimental to the soul. Prayer sustains and nourishes the soul only if it is "wholesome", if it is recited meaningfully, with proper concentration. Mechanical, lifeless prayer cannot serve the goal of sustaining the soul; it leaves the soul "sick" and undernourished.

This is why the Mishna in *Pirkei Abot* (1:2) refers to prayer with the term *aboda*, which literally means "work" or "service". Other areas of religious life, such as Torah study and acts of kindness, also demand hard work and effort. But only prayer is called "work", because proper, "healthful" prayer is especially difficult to achieve and for good reason. The more valuable something is, the more difficult it is to obtain. For example, raising a child is a far more demanding undertaking than caring for a goldfish, because childrearing offers infinitely greater rewards. Likewise, caring for our souls, our most precious commodity of all, is especially challenging – because it is especially rewarding. Just as human food costs more than fish food – since nourishing a human being is a far more meaningful goal than nourishing a fish – similarly, nourishing one's soul is more "expensive" and demanding than nourishing the body. The challenges are immense – because so are the rewards.

In a similar vein, Rav Nosson Wachtfogel commented that prayer is what lends something *kiyum* – endurance. When something is achieved through עבודה שבלב, through serious prayer and an investment of emotional and spiritual energy, it will last.

The Gemara in Masechet Berachot (31b) tells that when the prophet Shemuel was a youngster, he issued a halachic ruling in the presence of his mentor, Eli HaCohen, and Eli HaCohen sentenced him to death.[2] Shemuel's mother, Hanna, who was childless for many years before Shemuel's birth, pleaded with Eli to spare the child. She begged, אל הנער הזה התפללתי – "I have prayed for this lad" (Shemuel I 1:27). She was saying to Eli HaCohen, "This child is the product of my heartfelt *tefillot* – and thus he must endure and live". Something which we achieve through prayer, rather than being given to us "free of charge" without this emotional investment, will last forever.

Anyone who knows anything about Jewish history cannot but marvel at the miracle of our nation's survival. How is it possible

---

2. As the Gemara explains, somebody who is מורה הלכה בפני רבו – who brazenly rules on halachic matters in his Rabbi's presence, is liable to capital punishment.

for such a tiny nation to survive for so many centuries among hostile enemy nations many times its size? How did a nation dispersed throughout the world without a home of its own, outnumbered and despised by the host nations, continue to exist for millennia?

The answer is that our nation's existence came about through prayer. ויעתר יצחק לה' לנכח אשתו כי עקרה היא – "Yishak prayed on behalf of his wife because she was barren" (Bereshit 25:21). Ribka was naturally unable to have children, and it was only through Yishak's prayers that she conceived. The Jewish nation would never have come into existence without prayer; the covenant with Abraham would have ended a generation later, with the death of Yishak and Ribka. It is only as a result of prayer that the Jewish people exist in the first place. Therefore, as prayer is what produced Am Yisrael, our kiyum is guaranteed, and we will forever endure because our existence was made possible by tefila.

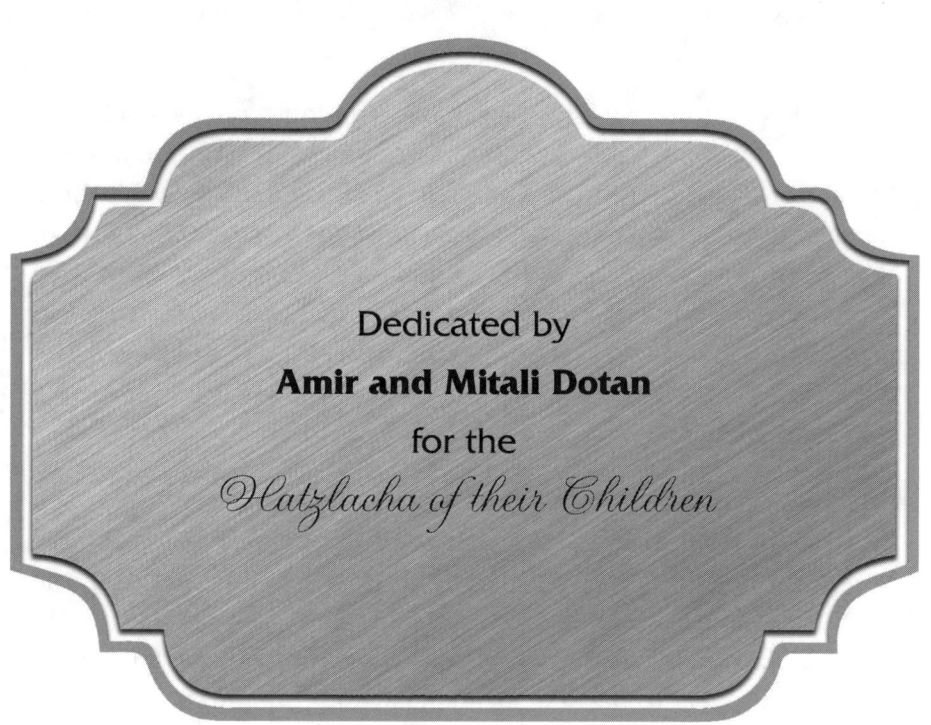

Dedicated by

Amir and Mitali Dotan

for the

Hatzlacha of their Children

The Unique Opportunity of Every Prayer

The Arizal noted that no two prayers are ever alike. The power, effect and result of every prayer depend on a wide range of factors, many of which relate to the spiritual, cosmic state of the person praying, as well as of the universe in general. Every prayer is unique because every prayer is recited under a different *mazal*, under a different set of circumstances. Hence, every prayer is uniquely suited to achieve a specific result; the prayer that a person recites at any given moment has the potential to accomplish what no other prayer recited by any other person could possibly achieve.

Every time we pray, we have a unique, once-in-a-lifetime opportunity, one which we will never have again. We should never think to ourselves before praying, "What's the big deal? I did this three times yesterday, I will be doing it three times today, so it's okay if I rush through it once in a while". If we squander an opportunity to pray properly, if we don't capitalize on the potential benefits of any given prayer, we will never get that opportunity back; it is lost forever. The prayer that we can recite now has unique powers which tomorrow's prayers do not have.

Even though we pray three times each day, we must approach each and every prayer as a precious opportunity. We can never grow bored of the experience, because each prayer is different from the next. If we approach prayer with this mindset, then we will remain focused and enthusiastic every time we begin to pray, and never allow our prayers to become mechanical and robotic.

Imagine if God had assigned us only five minutes every year to pray, and forbade us from praying at any other time. How would we pray during those five minutes? How would we anticipate and prepare for those five minutes? Without doubt, we would review our prayers weeks in advance and count down the days to our annual chance to speak with God. Many of us would probably find it difficult to think about anything else during the day before those precious moments.

If we can imagine such a situation, then we can begin to understand the proper approach we should have toward prayer. Each prayer we recite is an opportunity we will never be given again. How can we not approach every *shaharit*, *minha* and *arbit* with excitement, enthusiasm, emotion and feeling? How could we possibly squander such an invaluable opportunity?

Appending "Wings" Onto Our Prayers

A certain Rosh Yeshiva once walked into the study hall of his yeshiva, and announced, "This room is filled with Torah!" The students looked at one another proudly, assuming they had just received a compliment for the intensity of Torah study felt in the *bet midrash*. But then the Rosh Yeshiva moved to the front of the room and clarified his statement.

"This room is filled with Torah because the Torah isn't rising to the heavens like it's supposed to!"

Ideally, every *misva* we perform, whether it is prayer, learning, acts of kindness, or any other *misva*, should rise straight to God in the heavens. Often, however, we fail to perform *misvot* with the appropriate level of enthusiasm and emotion, and this lack of feeling prevents our good deeds from ascending to the heavens and having the effect we hope for.

The *Zohar* finds an allusion to this concept in the Torah's discussion of *kan sipor*, the obligation to send away a mother bird before taking her eggs or chicks (Debarim 22:6-7). The Torah describes a situation where a person encounters a nest with "chicks or eggs" ("אפרוחים או ביצים"). The *Zohar* comments that the image of a nest containing "*efrohim*" or "*besim*" is symbolic of two different kinds of *misvot*. Some *misvot* are like "*besim*", chicks that have just been formed and have yet to grow wings. They cannot fly; they have no choice but to remain here on earth, unable to ascend upward to the heavens. The *efrohim*, by contrast, are young birds capable of flying. The word *efro'ah* stems from the Hebrew root פ.ר.ח., which means "fly". The *efrohim* thus symbolize the *misvot* with "wings" that can fly straight to the heavens, where they are lovingly accepted by God.

How do we append "wings" to our *misvot*, and to our prayers? What must we do to ensure that our prayers reach the Divine Throne, so that they can have the desired effect?

The *Zohar* writes that the two "wings" with which our *misvot* ascend to the heavens are "*dehilu*"(דחילו) – fear of God – and "*rehimu*" (רחימו) – love of God. The feelings of fear and love invested into our prayers are what bring them to the heavens and before God's Throne. If our prayer experience is cold and emotionless, the prayers will remain in the synagogue; if our prayers are accompanied by sincere feelings of fear and love of God, then they will break through the roof and "fly" directly to God.

Many people have the custom to sway back and forth while

praying, and the question regarding the propriety of this practice is discussed and debated by the halachic authorities. The *Kaf Ha'haim* (Rav Yaakov Haim Sofer, Baghdad-Israel, 1870-1939) held that one should not sway while praying, just as one would never think to sway while speaking to a human king. Indeed, a number of prominent rabbis, including the Hatam Sofer (Rabbi Moshe Sofer of Pressburg, 1762-1839) and, more recently, Rabbi Moshe Feinstein (Russia-New York, 1895-1986), would stand straight and upright like a soldier throughout the recitation of the *Amidah*. However, many others were accustomed to sway during prayer, on the basis of a verse in Tehillim (35:10), "כל עצמותי תאמרנה ה' מי כמוך" – "All my bones shall declare: Hashem, who is like You!" King David describes how all his bones took part in exalting the Almighty, suggesting that he moved his body as an expression of praise. Still, the question arises, what is the particular significance of moving one's body back and forth – forward and backward – during prayer? What specific emotion and feeling does this back-and-forth motion symbolize?

Rav Shimon Schwab (Germany-New York, 1908-1993) explained that this motion expresses the two feelings that form the "wings" through which our prayers ascend to the heavens. Moving one's body forward represents *ahabat Hashem*, love of God, the desire to draw as near to Him as possible. But as a person approaches God, he is suddenly overcome by *yirat Hashem*, awe and dread. He then immediately recoils and retreats, distancing himself from God's presence just as quickly as he had approached the divine presence. This, Rav Schwab explains, is the meaning of swaying. True, as the *Kaf Ha'haim* noted, nobody would ever sway while speaking with a mortal king. But when we speak to God, we speak with intense feelings of love and trepidation, and this causes us to sway back and forth. We move forward out of love, and then move back out of fear. These are the two "wings", the two conflicting yet parallel emotions, which must accompany our prayers and which help ensure that they come before the Almighty.

The Power of Praying with a Minyan

How important is it to pray with a *minyan*? Doesn't God hear our prayers wherever or whenever we pray? Does it really matter whether I pray privately at home, or together with a *minyan* in the synagogue?

The Talmud in Masechet Berachot (8a) teaches us that, in fact, prayer with a *minyan* differs fundamentally from – and qualitatively more effective than – private prayer: בשעה שהקב"ה בא בבית הכנסת ולא" "מצא בה עשרה מיד הוא כועס שנאמר מדוע באתי ואין איש קראתי ואין עונה "When the Almighty comes to the synagogue and does not find ten [men],

He immediately grows angry and says, 'Why have I come but there is no man; I have called, but nobody answers?' (Yeshayahu 50:2)".

If the Almighty grows angry when there is no *minyan*, then the converse must also be true: He rejoices and looks kindly upon us when there is a *minyan*. The presence of a *minyan* has the capacity to transform God's disposition from one of anger to one of kindness. It is the difference between meeting God in a state of anger, and meeting God in a state of kindness and compassion.

Indeed, prayer is always a powerful and effective tool. But the presence of a *minyan* transforms the whole experience by enabling us to transform divine anger into divine mercy. When the tenth man arrives in the synagogue, it is a moment to celebrate. At that instant, God leaves behind His anger, so-to-speak, and looks upon us with benevolence.

In Memory of

Joseph & Mollie BenHaim

**Jody and Zvi BenHaim
and Family**

The Power of 'Ish'
אִישׁ

The Hachamim teach us that the divine Name of *El* (אל) refers to God's attribute of kindness, His desire to bestow goodness upon His creations and it is this particular quality that makes prayer possible. We are able to pray because God wants to treat us kindly. He invites us to come before Him in prayer because He is (אל) *El*, He is benevolent, and in His infinite kindness He wants us to bring our requests to Him so he can fulfill them.

Each Jew who walks into the synagogue to pray connects to this divine attribute of (אל) *El*. The word (אל) *El* has the numerical value of 31, and thus when ten people assemble to pray, each bringing the quality of (אל) *El*, we have a total of 310. God Himself joins the *minyan*, bringing the total to 311, the numerical value of the word "*ish*" (איש – "man").

The Gemara, as cited above, teaches that when the Almighty finds fewer than ten men in the synagogue, He exclaims, "מדוע באתי ואין איש?" ("Why have I come but there is no man"?) He bemoans the absence of "*ish*" – the assembly of ten Jews invoking the divine attribute of (אל) *El*, God's quality of kindness, which has the cumulative value of 311 – "*ish*".

If only nine men assemble in the synagogue with the divine attribute of (אל) *El*, they combine for a total of 279, to which we add God Himself for a final sum of 280. This number is the combined numerical value of the letters מנצפ"ך, the five letters of the Hebrew alphabet that assume a special form when they appear at the end of a word (ם-ן-ץ-ף-ך). In Jewish thought, these letters signify the divine attribute of *din*, strict judgment. The appearance of one of these letters at the end of a word precludes the possibility of adding more letters. They therefore symbolize restriction and confinement, like the divine attribute of judgment which does not allow for the kind of flexibility mandated by the attribute of kindness.

Thus, when only nine people arrive in the synagogue, they must pray within the attribute of judgment represented by the number 280. They are not granted the kindness of "*ish*", the power of the attribute of (אל) *El*. They must appeal to God's system of justice, which is less flexible and yielding.

This is why Judaism has always afforded such great importance to *tefila be'sibur*, praying specifically with a *minyan*. Of course, as mentioned earlier, prayer is always effective and beneficial, in all settings and under all circumstances. But without a *minyan*, our prayers are confined to the rigid system of divine judgment. It is only when we pray with a *minyan* that we tap into the remarkable power source of (אל) *El*, God's boundless reservoir of kindness, thus making our prayers qualitatively more effective.

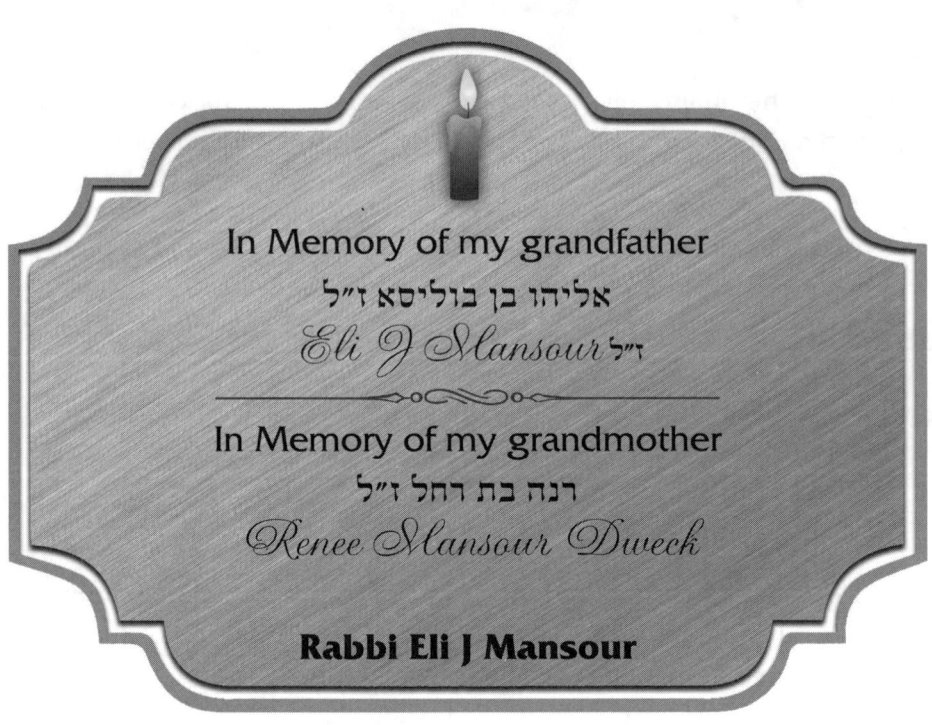

In Memory of my grandfather

אליהו בן בוליסא ז״ל

Eli J Mansour ז״ל

In Memory of my grandmother

רנה בת רחל ז״ל

Renee Mansour Dweck

Rabbi Eli J Mansour

Invoking a Gezera Shava

From where does this power of a *minyan* evolve? What makes the presence of ten Jews capable of transforming the divine attribute of justice into the divine attribute of kindness?

The answer lies in the Biblical source of the entire concept of a *minyan*. The Talmud (Megillah 23b) raises the question of where the Torah indicates that ten people comprise a *minyan* for prayer, and it responds by citing a verse in the Book of Vayikra (22:32): "I shall be sanctified among the Israelites"- ונקדשתי בתוך בני ישראל The Torah speaks here of God's sanctification בתוך "be'toch" ("among", or, literally, "in the midst of") the Jewish people. As the Gemara demonstrates, the word תוך "*toch*" is associated elsewhere in the

Torah with the ten spies, who rebelled against God by discouraging *Beneh Yisrael* from entering the Land of Israel. The Sages applied here the principle of *gezera shava*, which states that an unusual term found in two contexts in the Torah indicates a halachic association between those two subjects. The fact that תוך *toch* is used in reference to the ten spies, as well as in the context of God's sanctification among the Jewish people, suggests that this sanctification occurs specifically in the presence of ten Jews. On the basis of this *gezera shava*, the Talmud derives the notion of ten people comprising a *minyan*.

Gezera shava is the second of the thirteen "*midot she'ha'Torah nidreshet bahen*" – the exegetical tools conveyed to the Sages through which they extracted halachic concepts from the Biblical text. We recite the list of these thirteen *midot* in the morning prayer service, just before *Pesukeh De'zimra* ...רבי ישמעאל אומר בשלש עשרה מידות ("*R' Yishmael omer bi'shlosh esreh midot...*"). The Rabbis teach us that these thirteen exegetical principles correspond to the thirteen divine attributes of mercy which are listed in the Book of Shemot (34:6-7) and which we recite as part of *tahanunim* at *shaharit* and *minha*. Each of the thirteen exegetical principles parallels and relates to the corresponding attribute of mercy. As such, *gezera shava*, the second of the thirteen "*midot she'ha'Torah nidreshet bahen*", corresponds to "*rahum*" ("merciful"), the second of the divine attributes of mercy. Therefore, when ten men enter the synagogue to pray together with a *minyan*, in accordance with the *gezera shava* surrounding the word "*toch*", they invoke the divine attribute of *rahum*. They gain access to God's attribute of compassion through the power of this *gezera shava*.

This concept, too, is alluded to in the Gemara cited above. The three patriarchs – Abraham, Yishak and Yaakob – represent the three qualities of *hesed*, *gebura* and *tif'eret*. *Hesed* refers to kindness, *gebura* means strength and judgment, and *tif'eret*, which is also called *rahamim* (mercy), denotes the perfect balance between *hesed* and *gebura*. The Sages (Zohar A, 119; Bereshit Rabba 76) speak of Yaakob as the "*behir ha'abot*", the "choicest" of the three patriarchs (Tehillim 135:4), because he embodied the pristine equilibrium that should be maintained between the qualities represented by Abraham and Yishak. This is why the Jewish people are referred to as "*Benei Yisrael*" – the children of Israel, Yaakob, because we too must maintain a proper balance between kindness and strict justice. For the same reason, we are often described as an "עם סגולה" (literally, "treasured nation"). This term alludes to the vowel *segol*, which is formed by two adjacent dots with a third dot positioned in between the two. The segol represents the balancing of two opposing forces, finding the midway point between the two "dots" of hesed and gebura. The formation of the *segol* thus symbolizes the way *Am Yisrael* is supposed to conduct itself – in accordance with the attribute of *rahamim*, the "midway point". We are thus called the "עם סגולה", the nation that maintains the balance signified by the *segol*.

"מדוע באתי ואין איש?" When God enters a synagogue and finds that there is no *minyan*, He laments that there is no "*ish*". The letters that comprise this word (ש,י,א) also serve as an acrostic for the words, אמצע ימין שמאל ("middle, right, left"). Without a *minyan*, we forfeit the power of *rahamim*, the attribute of mercy represented by the *segol* – ("middle, right, left"). We lose the power of the *gezera shava* which invokes the divine attribute of mercy, and find ourselves subject to God's attribute of strict judgment.

L'iluy Nishmat
Nissim Cohen ben Ovadya Cohen

(ניסים הכהן בן עובדיה הכהן)

From his loving wife,
**Miriam Cohen, and Children
Sharona, Moshe, Tomer,
and Leeor Cohen**

The Spark Within Every Jew

There is yet another, particularly powerful aspect of this *gezera shava* from which *tefila be'sibur* draws its incomparable strength. As mentioned earlier, the concept of *minyan* emerges from the word "*toch*" used in both the context of prayer ("I shall be sanctified among the Israelites") and the ten sinful spies. Remarkably, the "model" *minyan* is a group of ten sinners. The *meragelim*, the ten spies who rejected God and led the entire nation astray, and who (according to one undisputed view in the Mishna of Mesechet Sanhedrin) lost their share in the eternal life, are the source from which we derive the concept of praying with a *minyan*.

Interestingly enough, this *gezera shava* yields important halachic implications. The *Shulhan Aruch* (*Orah Haim* 55:11) rules that non-observant Jews count toward the required quorum for a *minyan*. Even if sinners are included in the group of ten men, the group constitutes a full-fledged *minyan* and they can recite all the prayers that require the presence of ten men. (The exception to this rule is an individual whom the community consigned to *herem*, formal excommunication, as a means of legal enforcement, and who may not be counted toward a *minyan* due to his state of excommunication.) The *Mishna Berura* adds that this applies even to sinners who have committed capital crimes. As the entire notion of *minyan* originates from the ten *meragelim*, it naturally extends to all members of *Am Yisrael*, regardless of their spiritual stature. If even the ten wicked spies qualified as a *minyan*, then all sinners are likewise eligible for inclusion in a *minyan*. The *Mishna Berura* appropriately cites in this context the famous adage, "ישראל אף על פי שחטא ישראל הוא" – "A Jew, even though he has sinned, is a Jew".

Why are sinners invited to join a *minyan*? Why do they deserve access to the unique powers of *tefila be'sibur* and inclusion in the sacred assembly of a *minyan*?

The answer stems from the *gezera shava* that forms the basis of the halachic institution of *minyan*. This *gezera shava*, as we saw, surrounds the word "*toch*", which literally means "inside". The association between the ten spies and public prayer lies in the concept of "*toch*", the spark of holiness embedded deep within each and every Jew. "A Jew, even though he has sinned, is a Jew". Although a Jew commits grievous sins, they result from the exterior elements of his soul. Deep inside, there is a spark of purity and sanctity, a holy essence which remains untainted. That spark makes every Jew eligible to participate in a *minyan*, regardless of his spiritual past – and regardless even of his spiritual present.

When a *minyan* assembles to pray, they awaken this quality of "*toch*", they ignite a raging flame from the sparks of holiness lying deep within the soul of every participant. *Tefila be'sibur* allows us to pray to God with that inner spark of sanctity within us, the pure essence that lies in the depths of our souls. The prayers recited in a *minyan* emanate from a source of sanctity and purity, and are therefore qualitatively more powerful than any prayer we could recite in private.

The Obligations of a Sadik

There is one final aspect of *tefila be'sibur* alluded to by the Gemara's description of God coming into a synagogue that does not have a *minyan*. The Gemara (Berachot 6b) tells us that "מיד הוא כועס" – God "immediately" grows angry when He finds fewer than ten people assembled in the synagogue. How are we to explain the Gemara's emphasis on the immediacy of God's anger?

Elsewhere, the Talmud (Niddah 30b) teaches that before an infant exits the womb, he swears to grow to become a *sadik* (righteous person). The Rabbis explain that the word *sadik* (צדיק) in this context actually refers to the respective numerical values of the four letters צ-ד-י-ק. The letter צ, ninety, alludes to the requirement to answer ninety "amen" responses over the course of every day. *Dalet* ד, which equals four, indicates that one must recite, "*Kadosh kadosh kadosh*" four times each day – once during *Yoser* (before *shema*), once in *U'ba Le'sion*, and during *Nakdishach* in *shaharit* and *minha*. *Yod* י has a value of ten, referring to the ten *kaddish* recitations to which one must respond each day. Finally, the letter *kof* ק, one hundred, alludes to the obligation to recite one hundred *berachot* over the course of every day.

When a child enters the world, he promises to observe the four obligations of צ-ד-י-ק, to make these recitations as required.

Of these four obligations, two require participation in a *minyan*: *kaddish* and *nakdishach* may not be recited without a *minyan*, and, therefore, one cannot fulfill the requirements of "*kadosh kadosh*" or *kaddish* without praying together with a *minyan*. By contrast, answering "*amen*" and reciting *berachot* can be done even privately, and do not depend upon the presence of a *minyan*.

Returning to the Gemara, when God sees that fewer than ten men have assembled for prayer, He grows angry מיד ("immediately") – on account of י"ד, the ten and the four. His fury is aroused by the fact that the community will necessarily be unable to fulfill the requirement of *yod* – the ten *kaddish* responses – and the requirement of *dalet* – the four recitations of "*kadosh kadosh*". These recitations are so critical and so central to our religious obligations as Jews that our failure to attend the *minyan*, which guarantees our failure to fulfill these requirements, constitutes a breach of our basic commitment to God and arouses divine anger.

Then, *Tefila be'sibur* is much more than simply the preferred mode of prayer. It is an entirely different experience, one which not only grants us access to the greatest manifestations of divine mercy and kindness, but also relates to some of our most basic obligations as Torah Jews. We must view public prayer as not just a "nice thing" or added level of piety, but, rather, as part of our daily religious responsibilities, and as an invaluable opportunity to appeal to God's unlimited benevolence and bring His endless blessings upon us, our families and the entire Jewish nation.

The Power of Praying in the Synagogue

Besides the importance of praying together with a *minyan*, the Sages (Berachot 6a) have also taught us the vital importance of praying specifically in a synagogue. Indeed, *Halacha* (Shulhan Aruch 90:9) states that even if a person, for whatever reason, missed the *minyan* and must pray privately, it is preferable for him to go to the synagogue to pray, rather than pray at home. Despite the fact that he will not have a *minyan* in the synagogue, he should go there to pray.

Why is it so important to pray in a synagogue? If a person in any event must pray privately, why can't he pray in the comfort of his own home? What difference does it make if he prays privately in his basement or alone in the synagogue?

The answer is rooted in a seemingly perplexing passage that appears in the Gemara in Masechet Berachot (8a). R' Yohanan, a famous Rabbi in *Eretz Yisrael*, heard that there were elderly Jews living in Babylonia and that some people in the Babylonian Jewish community reached advanced ages. The Gemara relates that R' Yohanan was initially very surprised to hear of the Babylonians' longevity. He noted that in the Book of Debarim (11:21), the Torah exhorts us to observe the *misvot* "in order that your days and the days of your children shall be many upon the land that Hashem has promised…" This verse promises longevity "upon the land that Hashem has promised" – meaning, specifically in the Land of Israel. R' Yohanan thus wondered how it was possible that some Babylonian Jews earned long life despite living far away from *Eretz Yisrael*.

R' Yohanan quickly solved the mystery, the Gemara tells, when he was told that the Babylonian Jews attend the services in the synagogue each morning and night. At that point he understood why these Jews could achieve longevity despite living in the Diaspora.

Quite simply, going to the synagogue helps one earn long life. Of course there are exceptions, and, due to reasons known only to God, there are some people who regularly attend synagogue services who do not earn longevity. But as a rule, the Gemara teaches, attendance in the synagogue is a means of extending our stay here on earth.

What gives synagogue attendance this power? How does coming to the synagogue each day help extend a person's life?

Convincing the Soul to Stay

The Midrash Tehillim (150) comments that the human being's soul constantly seeks to exit the body. The soul, which originates from the Heavenly Throne, feels uneasy trapped inside a physical body. Its "natural habitat", so-to-speak, is the pure, pristine, spiritual existence in the heavens. The soul has been brought into the body against its will, and its nature is completely at odds with the realities of physical existence. Each time we use the restroom, we recite the *beracha* of *asher yasar* which concludes by describing God as "*mafli la'asot*" – "Doer of wonders". The Rabbis explain that this refers to the "wonder" of the soul's existence inside the body. The combination of flesh and spirit is like the merging of fire and water. The two constantly struggle against one another. It is truly a *pele*, a wonder, that the human being can live with a body and soul working in tandem for so many years. The body wants physical gratification, while the soul wants holiness and spirituality. Understandably, the soul is constantly trying to escape the suffocating confines of the human body.

What prevents the soul from leaving the body? How do we survive if the soul always tries to leave and return to its source?

The answer, the Midrash writes, is that the soul sees the Almighty, whose presence fills the world, and it then decides to remain in the body.

Rav Moshe Alshich (Israel, 1508-1593) explained that when the soul sees God Himself residing here in the physical earth, it decides that it, too, can remain inside a body. If the Almighty, whose glory and sanctity far exceeds anything that could be imagined, decides to have His presence fill the lowly earth, then the soul, which is but a minuscule spark of God, can certainly reside in a human body.

What keeps the soul inside the body, then, is exposure to *Shechina*, to the Divine Presence. We are always at risk of losing our souls, because our souls are constantly trying to escape. The soul decides to remain only when it beholds the *Shechina*, when it sees God's presence in the world, which reminds it of its role to remain inside a body. To achieve longevity, then, we must expose our souls to the *Shechina* on a regular basis. Certainly, we must also ensure that the body remains healthy enough to function; maintaining a healthy lifestyle and consulting with medical professionals is undoubtedly crucial for enabling the body to work as it should. But in addition, we must ensure that the soul encounters The Divine Presence each day so it will want to stay. Otherwise, Heaven forbid, it will "escape" and return to where it came from.

This concept formed the basis of the insidious plan devised by Bilam, the gentile prophet, to lead *Beneh Yisrael* to sin. As the Sages (Sanhedrin 106a) teach, Bilam understood that God despises immorality and would refuse to reside among *Beneh Yisrael* if they engaged in illicit relations. Therefore, as we read in the Book of Bamidbar (Chapter 25), Bilam advised the nation of Moab to send women to lure *Beneh Yisrael* to immorality. When this happened, the Torah relates, 24,000 members of the nation perished in a devastating plague. Once the Divine Presence left, *Beneh Yisrael's* souls no longer wished to remain within physical bodies, and they departed en masse.

For the same reason, the Sages (Shabbat 12b) teach that the *Shechina* hovers over the head of an ill patient. When a person takes ill and his soul begins the process of leaving the body, God comes near the person so that the soul would see the *Shechina* residing on earth. The *Shechina's* presence is the protection that God provides to a patient to help him survive his illness. Likewise, the Sages advise that when a person experiences pain somewhere in his body, such as a headache or stomachache, he should study Torah. Pain indicates that the soul has begun to leave that part of the body, causing it to ache. Besides taking painkillers and consulting with physicians when necessary, a person should also respond to his pain by learning Torah, which, as the Mishna teaches in *Pirkeh Abot* (3:7), brings the Divine Presence. The soul will then see the *Shechina* and decide to remain within the body.

When *Beneh Yisrael* stood at Mount Sinai, the Sages teach, they rose to a level of spirituality where they became immune to the *Mal'ach Ha'mavet* (Angel of Death). They returned to the level of Adam before the sin, and were thus destined to live forever. The sin of the golden calf, however, which occurred just weeks after the Revelation at Sinai, brought them down from this exalted level, and they became once again exposed to the *Mal'ach Ha'mavet*. When God descended upon Mount Sinai, the people experienced such an intense, close encounter with The Divine Presence that their souls decided to permanently remain inside their bodies. They overcame the curse of death through their direct exposure to the *Shechina*. But the Divine Presence departed in the wake of the golden calf, thus allowing for the possibility that their souls would depart, and they therefore became susceptible to death once again. In response, God commanded *Beneh Yisrael* to construct a *Mishkan*, a residence for the *Shechina*, so that they would be able to experience The Divine Presence in a manner resembling the experience of the Revelation at Sinai. The way to return to the level achieved at the Revelation was to build a site where the people could encounter the *Shechina* and thus help ensure that their souls would remain inside their bodies.

Nowadays, of course, we do not have a *Mishkan* or a *Bet HaMikdash*. Nevertheless, we are still able to experience the Divine Presence by coming to the synagogue. The Talmud (Megillah 29a) teaches that when the prophet (Yehezkel 11:16) declares in God's Name, "I shall be for them a small Temple", he refers to the synagogues constructed after the Temple's destruction. They take the place of the *Mikdash* as the site of the Divine Presence, the place where a person can encounter the *Shechina*. By frequenting the synagogue, we show our souls the Divine Presence, and thus ensure they will choose to remain inside our bodies. This is how R' Yohanan explained the phenomenon of longevity in Babylonia, in the Diaspora, far from the Land of Israel, where the *Shechina* resides. The Babylonian Jews earned long life through their diligence in praying in the synagogue, which has the effect of keeping one's soul in the body and thus ensuring long life.

Of course, there are exceptions. We are all aware of devoted Jews who came to the synagogue every day and are, unfortunately, no longer with us. Ultimately, God is the Supreme Judge of the universe, and we cannot expect to understand all His decisions and decrees. What we do know, however, is that coming to the synagogue, exposing our souls to the *Shechina*, is a significant measure we can take to help earn long life. Synagogue attendance is much more than a social event, and even more than an enjoyable religious experience. It is an opportunity to directly experience the *Shechina*, and reinforce the bond between body and soul, thereby helping to extend our lives.

Dedicated in Loving Memory of our Dear Father
Elie V. Esses
אליהו בן אלגרה ז״ל

Dedicated in Honor of our Devoted Mother
Rita Esses

Donated by their children

**Victor, Adam and David Esses
and their families**

The Hazan

What exactly is the role of the *hazan* in the prayer service? Does he simply set the pace of the service? Is he there to perform and entertain?

The *hazan* is more than a "cantor" or a conductor. His job is to inspire the congregation and motivate them to pray with concentration. Just as the service in the *Bet HaMikdash* was accompanied by the beautiful music of the *Leviyim* which inspired the visitors, similarly, the *hazan*'s voice is to uplift and motivate the congregation. The *teba* where the *hazan* stands may be compared to an engine. The *hazan*'s job is to ignite the engine and carry the congregation with him on a journey to the highest level of prayer.

This job requires a good deal of passion and energy. All too often, people suddenly become humble when they serve as *hazan*, they feel intimidated and anxious, and speak softly, in an inaudible whisper or mumble. Serving as *hazan* is an occasion that demands "*ga'ava di'kdusha*" – "holy arrogance". A person who agrees to be the *hazan* must see himself as playing a crucial leadership role in the synagogue, bearing the responsibility of motivating and uplifting the rest of the congregation.

It is customary for people to serve as the *hazan* when observing a *yahrtzeit* for a departed family member, to provide an additional source of merit for the deceased's soul. This is certainly an admirable practice, but one must realize that to bring merit to the soul, he must fulfill the role properly. He must ensure to pronounce all the words correctly and clearly, and to pray with vigor and enthusiasm, in a manner that arouses the congregation to higher levels of concentration and feeling. A *hazan* who adorns the prayers with beautiful and heartfelt singing effectively places crowns atop each word of the prayer service, helping to ensure the prayer's loving acceptance by the Almighty.

A striking illustration of the importance of the *hazan* can be found in the Book of Melachim I (chapter 21), which tells the tragic story of a man named Nabot. The palace of the idolatrous King Ahab overlooked Nabot's vineyard, and the king saw the vineyard and wanted it for himself. He approached Nabot and offered to purchase the property, but Nabot refused. Ahab's wife, Jezebel, hired two men to falsely testify that Nabot committed treason, and then had him executed. Ahab thereupon seized Nabot's vineyard as he had wanted.

The Sages address the question of why Nabot was deserving of such cruelty. They explain that Nabot, who was graced with a beautiful voice, had made it his practice to visit the *Bet Ha'mikdash* during each of the three pilgrimage festivals (Pesah, Shabuot and Sukkot), and sing praises of God. His singing drew large crowds of people and inspired them with the love of God. One year however, Nabot decided it was time to "retire" from this role of serving as the *hazan* for the pilgrims in Jerusalem, denying them the inspiration and spiritual encouragement that his singing provided. As he had sinned with his voice by failing to use it for the sake of glorifying God's Name, he was punished by falling victim to false witnesses, who used their voice to have him convicted of treason.

Serving as a *hazan*, inspiring one's fellow Jews to draw closer to their Creator through sincere and heartfelt prayer, is a privilege and an opportunity that must not be squandered. The tragedy of Nabot demonstrates just how seriously the Almighty treats this role. True, *halacha* requires one to initially hesitate when asked to serve as *hazan*, as an expression of humility. However, *halacha* also requires one to proudly accept the job if he is asked repeatedly, and, in fact, if the Rabbi asks a congregant to serve as the *hazan*, then he should go immediately, without hesitation. The job of *hazan* is a great *misva* and privilege, and thus a role which one should be eager to accept.

The Status of Shali'ah

The Sages (Berachot 34b) teach: יחיד שטעה, סימן רע לו, שליח צבור שטעה, סימן רע לו ולשולחיו – "If an individual makes a mistake [in his prayer] – it is a bad omen for him; if a *hazan* makes a mistake – it is a bad omen for him and for those who sent him". Whereas a mistake made by an individual during his private prayer bodes negatively for him, a mistake made by the *hazan* during the public prayer is an inauspicious omen for the entire congregation.

The explanation of this concept lies in the term שליח צבור which is used here (and in other contexts) in reference to the *hazan*. The term literally means "messenger of the congregation", and denotes the *hazan*'s status as the congregation's agent, or representative.

A famous halachic principle establishes that שלוחו של אדם כמותו –
a person's agent has the status of the person himself. A man can
commission another person to betroth a woman in a different
country. When the agent places the ring on the woman's hand, that
act is akin to the groom himself placing the ring on the finger. The
agent is viewed as an extension of the person who commissioned
him.

This principle has implications beyond the realm of formal
legalities. For example, it helps explain how the *meragelim*, the
scouts whom Moshe sent to explore *Eretz Yisrael*, could have
sinned so severely by dissuading the nation from entering the land.
Tradition teaches that the scouts were righteous men (see Rashi,
Bamidbar 13:3), yet they eventually became corrupt and conspired
to lead the people to betray God. This occurred because the
meragelim saw themselves as having been sent by the nation, by
Beneh Yisrael, rather than having been sent by Moshe. The people
wanted to send scouts because of their deficient faith in God; Moshe,
however, wanted to send scouts to endear the land to *Beneh Yisrael*.
The scouts' mistake was a reflection of the people who sent them.
שלוחו של אדם כמותו – the messenger is an extension of the person who
sent him. Once the messengers saw themselves as messengers of the
nation, their faith was diminished, in accordance with the people's
lack of faith. Had they seen themselves as messengers of Moshe,
they would have completed the mission properly in the manner that
Moshe had intended.

This applies to the *shali'ah sibur* as well. He stands at the
teba as a representative of the congregation. His mistake therefore,
is their mistake. If he fails in his role, then this is a reflection of a flaw
in the people who sent him. The congregation must therefore not
berate a *hazan* who errs. If their representative did not fulfill his duty
properly, then this reflects poorly on them. It thus behooves the
congregation to improve themselves in order that they be worthy of
a flawless *hazan*.

Men as Messengers of God

This concept of *shelihut* bears relevance not only to the *hazan*, but to each and every individual as well. The Gemara teaches that just before an infant exits the mother's womb, God has the child swear that he/she will act righteously during his/her stay on earth. From the moment we are born we are in God's service, having been dispatched directly by Him to this world for the purpose of observing the *misvot*.

It thus emerges that each and every individual is a *shali'ah* of the Almighty, His "messenger". He has sent us here for a purpose, which is to fulfill His will. When we consider this in light of the principle of שלוחו של אדם כמותו, we arrive at an astonishing conclusion: to one extent or another, we have the status of God. We are like Him! If an agent assumes the status of the one who sent him, then we each assume the status of God Himself, who sent us to this world for a purpose. Therefore, nobody has the right to say that Torah observance is too difficult, since we all act on God's behalf. Just as nothing is too difficult for the Almighty, so too, the job He assigned us cannot possibly be too difficult for us.

The Talmud teaches, גדול המצווה ועושה משאינו מצווה ועושה. This means that performing a *misva* which one was commanded to do is greater than performing a voluntary *misva* which was not commanded. While this may at first seem counterintuitive, it follows directly from the concept of *shelihut* discussed in this section. When we perform a *misva* which God commanded us to do, then we perform the act as His agents, as His representatives, and we therefore perform the act with all the powers of the Almighty Himself. However, when we perform a voluntary *misva*, we only represent ourselves, and we therefore bring to the *misva* only our limited concentration, feelings and devotion. But when we act as God's agents, we bring to the *misva* everything that God could bring into a *misva*. Such a *misva* is therefore on a much higher level than a *misva* performed voluntarily.

Before one begins praying, it is advisable to declare in his mind that he prays in order to fulfill God's commandment to pray. Once we recite our prayers in fulfillment of the divine command, as faithful servants and "messengers" of God sent to fulfill this mission, then we assume His status. Our prayers become even more powerful than prayers recited with all the Kabbalistic intentions of Rav Shalom Shara'abi; they are considered as recited by God Himself, whom we proudly represent as we pray in fulfillment of His command.

Yehushoa ben Moshala

Dedicated by
Fred Zaghi

Praying in a Room With Windows

The Gemara, in two places in the fifth chapter of Masechet Berachot (31 and 34), establishes that one should pray specifically in a room that has windows. This *halacha* is codified by the *Shulhan Aruch* (Orah Haim 90:4). The *Mishna Berura* clarifies that this requirement applies both in the synagogue as well as in one's home. Regardless of whether one prays in the synagogue or in the privacy of his home, he should endeavor to pray in a room with a window. The *Mishna Berura* adds that it is customary to construct a synagogue with twelve windows, at least some of which face toward Jerusalem.

Why is it important to specifically pray in a place with windows?

Several answers are given by the *Rishonim*. Rabbenu Yona explained this requirement as intended to ensure a pleasant environment in the room. A room without windows is generally dark and dreary, and it is very difficult in such an environment to achieve the peace of mind necessary to properly concentrate on one's prayer. For this reason, Rabbenu Yona claimed, *halacha* requires praying in a place that has windows.

Rashi, in his commentary to the second instance where this *halacha* appears (Berachot 34), gives a different reason. In his view, windows are needed so that a person can look up to the heavens during his prayer, and thereby feel humbled and subdued. The sight of the vastness of the sky leaves a person awe-inspired, and one should therefore pray in a room with windows so he could see the sky and feel a sense of awe and dread as he stands before the Almighty in prayer.

The practical difference between these two opinions is whether the windows must be situated in the direction where a person faces as he prays. According to Rabbenu Yona, the concern is simply that light enters the room. It makes no difference where the windows are positioned; so long as the room has windows that allow light to enter, the room is suitable for prayer. Rashi however, would presumably require that the windows are situated in the part of the room that faces Jerusalem, the direction one faces during prayer. Since the windows are needed to give a person a view of the heavens as he prays, it stands to reason that the windows must be positioned in the direction one faces. (The *Shulhan Aruch* (90:4) indeed rules that there must be a window facing Jerusalem.)

The *Bet Yosef* questions Rashi's view in light of a different comment of the Gemara (Masechet Yevamot 105b) requiring one to look downward during prayer to avoid distractions. If one must keep his eyes facing downward as he prays, then how does the sight of the heavens through the synagogue's windows help inspire a person? He is required to look downward to the floor, not upward! The *Bet Yosef* comments that this question is likely what led Rabbenu Yona to offer a different reason.

Others however, defended Rashi's explanation noting a distinction between consistent gazing and a brief glance. Although *halacha* requires one to look downward as he prays, on occasion, it is permissible and even admirable to look upward to the heavens during prayer to gain inspiration and humble himself. Thus according to Rashi, one should pray in a room with windows so that he will be able to glance at the heavens from time to time during his prayer.

This understanding of Rashi's view helps explain why he commented only on the second instance in the Gemara where this *halacha* appears. At first glance, we would have expected Rashi to provide us with his explanation already the first time this *halacha* is mentioned. (A similar question may be asked regarding the Rif and the Rosh, both of whom codify this *halacha* in their discussion of the second passage in the Gemara, and not the first) The reason perhaps, is that Rashi understood these two passages as referring to two different *halachot*. In the first instance, the Gemara writes לעולם יתפלל אדם בבית שיש בו חלונות ("A person should always pray in a room that has windows"), whereas in the second passage, it formulates the *halacha* differently: אל יתפלל אדם אלא בבית שיש בו חלונות ("A person should only pray in a room that has windows"). The different formulations indicate that these two comments refer to two different *halachot*. Likewise, in the first context the Gemara cites as the source for this *halacha* a brief, three-word phrase from the Book of Daniel (6:11) that describes the prophet Daniel praying in a room with windows – וכוין פתיחן ליה ("and windows were open for him"). In the second passage, by contrast, the Gemara cites the complete clause – וכוין פתיחן ליה בעליתה נגד ירושלם ("and windows were open for him in his attic, facing Jerusalem"). Additionally, the Gemara cites the *halacha* in the first context in the name of R' Hiya bar Abba speaking in the name of R' Yohanan, whereas in the second passage, this *halacha* is simply cited in R' Hiya bar Abba's name, without any mention of R' Yohanan.

It would thus seem that Rashi understood these two Talmudic passages as expressing different opinions. In the second passage, the Gemara requires praying in a room with windows for the purpose of gaining inspiration from the sight of the heavens. The Gemara therefore cited the complete clause from Daniel, which emphasizes that the windows were "facing Jerusalem". Since one must be able to look through the window as he prays, the windows must be positioned in the direction one faces during prayer – toward Jerusalem. In the first passage however, R' Hiya cited his teacher R' Yohanan, as requiring windows for the reason mentioned by Rabbenu Yona – to allow light to enter the room. R' Yohanan formulated this *halacha* by emphasizing, לעולם יתפלל אדם בבית שיש בו חלונות "A person *should always* pray in a room that has windows". This means that one should pray in a room with windows even in a situation where we might have thought otherwise – specifically, in a room where the windows are behind the person, where he cannot see them. Even such a room is suitable for prayer, because according to R' Yohanan, windows are necessary simply to allow light to enter, and not to enable one to see the sky during prayer. Rashi (as well as the Rif and Rosh) declined commenting on this *halacha* stated by R' Yohanan, because he followed the view of R' Hiya who required windows so that one will be able to see the heavens during his *tefila*. Therefore Rashi presented his explanation later, in the context of the *halacha* stated by R' Hiya.

Yet a third explanation for this *halacha* appears to emerge from the Rambam's formulation in codifying this requirement (Hilchot *Tefila* 5:6): וצריך לפתוח חלונות או פתחים כנגד ירושלים כדי להתפלל כנגדן – "And one must open windows or entrances facing Jerusalem, so he can pray facing them". It appears from the Rambam's wording that *halacha* requires not only the presence of windows in the room, but also that the windows be open. And, like Rashi, the Rambam requires that the windows face the direction of Jerusalem. The ב"ח explains the Rambam's view based on a comment by the *Zohar,* that all of our prayers first travel to Jerusalem, to the Western Wall, which is called the שער השמים (gateway to the heavens), and from there our prayers ascend to the heaven. Accordingly, one must pray in a room with open windows so that his prayers can leave the room and make their way to Jerusalem and then to the Almighty in the heavens.

A possible precedent for this notion is the *halacha* requiring that the gates of the Temple be open during the *aboda* (ritual service). Each ritual in the *Bet HaMikdash* had the power to bring blessing to the entire world. The gates of the Temple thus had to remain open during the service to allow the spiritual force of the *aboda* to burst forth from the *Bet Hamikdash* and spread throughout the world. Similarly, we must have an open window in the room as we pray, so that our prayers can leave and reach their desired destination.

We might also suggest a fourth explanation. *Halacha* perhaps requires praying in a room with windows so that a person will look beyond himself and his own personal needs as he prays. Before one comes before God to pray, he must look outside and realize that there are many people in need of the Almighty's mercy and assistance. Our instinctive tendency as we pray is to focus our own problems and concerns and bring them before God. The Sages wanted to broaden our frame of reference, so that we look beyond the narrow confines of our lives and experiences, and realize that when we pray we represent the entire Jewish Nation. Indeed, all of our prayers were written in plural form. In the *beracha* of רפאנו, for example, we pray not only for our personal health and the health of our loved ones, but for the health of all Jews. We must not be thinking only about ourselves as we pray, but rather about the needs of every Jew in the world.

This is one of the reasons why one should not pray in front

of a mirror. Besides avoiding giving the appearance of praying to oneself, this *halacha* also helps ensure that prayer does not become a self-centered activity. During prayer, a person should not be looking at himself or at his problems and concerns. His mind should be focused outward to all Jews throughout the world, and have all their many needs in mind as he prays.

For this reason perhaps, we must pray in a place with windows, which remind us that we stand before God as representatives of all *Am Yisrael*. Our minds must not remain confined to our immediate surroundings, and must rather be focused upon the needs of the Jewish nation at large.

Dedicated by
Gil Ovadia

For the Refuah and Hatzlaha
of the Ovadia Family

Conversations During the Prayer Service – A Sin "Too Great to Bear"

How important is it to refrain from socializing and conversing during the prayer services? A number of sources indicate that this is at least as important as any other religious obligations.

The *Zohar* comments (Parashat Teruma), "One who engages in idle talk in the synagogue – woe unto him, for he has no share in Israel!" According to the Zohar, a person who converses during the prayer service displays a lack of religious faith. If one truly believes that God exists and comes to listen to our prayers, he would not dare socialize in the synagogue. After all, he would certainly never think of chatting with his fellow in the presence of a mortal king or ruler. A person visiting the White House or even the local library, ensures to remain quiet and respectful. If one chats in the synagogue, then it must mean that he does not see himself as being in the presence of God, and that he views the synagogue as less sacred than his local library!

The *Hatam Sofer* (Rabbi Moshe Sofer of Pressburg, 1762-1839), in one of his published *derashot* (sermons), writes that when congregants converse with one another in the synagogue, the synagogue comes under the domain and possession of the *Satan*. Speaking during the prayers has the effect of transferring the synagogue from the realm of sanctity, from the property of the *Shechina*, into the hands of the *Satan*.

The Talmud teaches in Masechet Megila (29a) that a synagogue has the status of a "*Mikdash Me'at*" – a "Miniature Temple" – as described by the prophet (Yehezkel 11:16), and therefore in the times of *Mashiah* all synagogues will be brought to the Land of Israel. Just as the Temple can be built only in the sacred territory of *Eretz Yisrael*, similarly every synagogue which is considered a "Miniature Temple" must eventually be moved to the holy land. However, when people use the synagogue for idle chatter, *lashon ha'ra* and frivolity, rather than as a place for prayer and Torah, it loses this status. It is overrun by the evil spiritual forces, and it cannot be transported to *Eretz Yisrael*. Decorum in the synagogue is critical for maintaining its intrinsic status of *kedusha*, which ensures the ongoing presence of the *Shechina* between its walls. By speaking during services we not only forfeit the invaluable opportunity offered by the synagogue prayers, but also undermine its capacity to offer this opportunity in this future.

The *Magen Abraham* (Rabbi Avraham Gombiner of Poland,

1637-1682), in his commentary to the laws of the synagogue, makes the following chilling comment: *"Synagogues in which people do not refrain from idle chatter or arguments become houses of idol worship. As a result of our many sins, we see that this has been fulfilled in the fullest sense of the word"*. The *Magen Abraham* testifies to the fact that synagogues where talking and fighting were widespread ultimately became churches. Speaking during prayers drives away the divine presence and invites the presence of *Satan*, thus resulting in the building's transformation from a place of sanctity to a place of impurity and foreign worship.

Unfortunately, speaking during the service is all too common in many communities, particularly during the Torah reading and the *hazzan*'s repetition of the *Amidah*. It is worthwhile, if not obligatory, for every Jew to learn and regularly review the stern words of the *Shulhan Aruch* in this regard (*Orah Haim* 124:6): "One should not engage in mundane conversation during the time of the [*hazzan*'s] repetition [of the *Amida*]. If he does converse, he is a sinner, and his iniquity is too great to bear, and he should be reprimanded". In expressing the gravity of this sin, the *Shulhan Aruch* uses the expression, גדול עוונו מנשוא – "his iniquity is too great to bear". Those familiar with the Humash will immediately shudder upon reading these words. This expression is taken from Kayin, who turned to God after murdering his brother, shamefaced, and bitterly cried, "גדול עווני מנשוא" ("My iniquity is too great to bear!" – Bereshit 4:13). Difficult as it may be for us to comprehend, the *Shulhan Aruch* describes the gravity of speaking during prayers in the same terms used by Kayin in reference to his act of murder!

The *Shulhan Aruch* also writes that one who speaks during the service "should be reprimanded". This should not be understood as encouraging self-appointed "policemen" to hush people during the prayer service or to humiliate them. It goes without saying that we must not compromise people's dignity or the cohesiveness of a community in our efforts to maintain synagogue decorum. Certainly though, congregations bear the responsibility to make decorum a high priority, and find the appropriate means of ensuring a proper, reverent atmosphere in the synagogue.

In the years 1648-9, tens of thousands of Jews were brutally murdered in Eastern Europe by the Kozacks. Entire communities were lost, and untold numbers of religious books and articles were burned. In the aftermath of this unfathomable tragedy, the leading Rabbis, who saw the massacres as a call for retrospection, searched for areas of religious observance in need of improvement. Rabbi Yom Tov Lipman Heller (1579-1654), author of the *Tosefot Yom Tov* commentary to the Mishna, singled out the lack of synagogue decorum as a possible cause of the calamity. In his efforts to improve decorum, he formulated a special "*Mi Sheberach*" prayer to be recited publicly each week in the synagogue, asking God to bless all those who refrain from speaking during the synagogue service. This prayer is recited in some Ashkenazic communities to this very day.

It is obvious to all that we live in very dangerous times, when the forces of evil threaten us at all levels. Rabbi Yom Tov Lipman Heller's suggestion that the lack of synagogue decorum could have been the cause of the massacres of 1648-1649 is nothing short of frightening. As the threats to the Jewish people mount, we must double our efforts to maintain proper decorum in the synagogue, to treat our sacred buildings with the respect and reverence they deserve. Even if one completes the *Amidah* before the *hazzan* he must refrain from talking. He should stand silently in his place, or quietly recite Tehillim or study. We must be cognizant at all times of the *Shechina*'s presence in the synagogue, and conduct ourselves accordingly.

Praying with Concentration

All too often, we pray precisely the way the Sages admonished us *not* to pray: mechanically, robotically, without feeling, as drudgery that we would like to finish as quickly as possible.

Contrast this experience with the description given by R' Yehuda Halevi (1075-1141) in his *Sefer Hakuzari* of the attitude we should have toward prayer: "That moment in which a person prays should be the heart of his time and his achievement [literally, 'fruit'], and all his other moments should be like paths leading to that moment". Remarkably, the Kuzari speaks of prayer as the centerpiece, the "heart", of our lives, around which all our other activities revolve. Ideally, we should approach the prayer services as the primary moments of our day, and everything else as subordinate to *Tefila*. In reality however, we often do just the opposite, viewing prayer as a cumbersome burden that we shoulder begrudgingly, waiting anxiously to return to our "regularly scheduled program".

Many people are unfortunately unaware of the fact that this understanding constitutes a halachic requirement – at least for part of the *Amidah* prayer. The *Shulhan Aruch* (*Orah Haim* 101) explicitly rules that one who does not concentrate on the meaning of text while reciting the first *beracha* of the *Amidah* does not fulfill his obligation of prayer, and must therefore repeat the *Amidah*. It should noted that the Rama writes in his glosses to the *Shulhan Aruch*, that nowadays one should not repeat the *Amidah* in this case because in all likelihood he will fail to properly concentrate the second time around as well. However, Hacham Ovadia Yosef *zt"l* ruled (Yabia Omer 3:8) that if a person feels confident in his ability to concentrate on the meaning of the words while repeating the *Amidah*, then he must repeat the prayer and make every effort to recite at least the first Beracha with concentration.

In any event, all agree that we bear a halachic obligation to concentrate on the meaning of the words in the *Amidah*, and that without this concentration during the first blessing one does not fulfill his requirement of prayer.

Furthermore, praying without concentration can jeopardize the entire enterprise and render our prayers invalid. We can appreciate the importance of concentration more fully when considering the close connection between the prayer service and the *korbanot*, the sacrifices offered in the Temple. The Gemara in Masechet Berachot (26a) comments that the three daily prayers correspond to the three sacrificial rituals in the *Bet Hamikdash*. The morning prayer parallels the *tamid* offering that was brought each morning, the afternoon *minha* prayer represents the daily afternoon *tamid*, and the evening prayer, *arbit*, corresponds to the burning of the various limbs and fats of the sacrifices that lasted throughout the night. One of the laws that apply to the sacrifices in the *Bet HaMikdash* is פיגול, whereby a sacrifice is disqualified if a *kohen* prepared the sacrifice with the wrong intention or thought. Specifically, if the *kohen* performed the rituals with the intention of eating the sacrificial meat after the final time when eating the meat is permissible, or in a place where eating the meat is forbidden, the sacrifice is invalid.

As the prayers correspond to the sacrificial rituals, the law of פיגול applies to prayer as well. If a person prays with "foreign thoughts", thinking of matters that have no place during the *tefila*, then his "sacrifice", his prayer, is invalid. Just as the sacrificial rituals must be performed with the correct intention, similarly we must recite our prayers with the proper mindset and level of concentration.

Concentration during *Amidah* is not only a Halachic requirement, but also an invaluable tool for bolstering the power of one's prayer. The efficacy of *tefila* stems from the combined force of the intrinsic quality of the words, and the feeling and emotion of the worshiper.

The text of the *Amidah* as mentioned earlier, was composed by the sages and prophets of the Great Assembly, and each word and letter is intrinsically sacred and powerful. One must therefore ensure to pronounce each letter and vowel sound carefully, with precision, without swallowing, skipping or mispronouncing even a single syllable of the *Amidah*.

This power of the words is multiplied exponentially when a person prays with concentration and feeling. The *Sefer Hasidim* tells the story of an illiterate shepherd who did not know the text of the *Amidah*. Unable to recite the standardized prayer text, he prayed each day the following prayer: "Master of the world! I am a shepherd, I take care of sheep for a living. If You would give me Your sheep to care for, I would care for them without pay, because I love You so much!"

The shepherd recited this short, simple prayer each day, until finally one day a Rabbi passed by and heard the prayer. He decided he would teach the shepherd the text of the *Amidah* prayer so he could pray properly.

The shepherd quickly learned the text and began reciting the *Amidah* each day in place of the informal, personal prayer that he had been accustomed to reciting. With time, however, he forgot the text of the *Amidah*. He felt that after he had learned the *Amidah* prayer, he could no longer return to his short personal prayer, and so he simply stopped praying altogether.

God appeared to the Rabbi in a dream, and reprimanded him for disrupting the shepherd's prayer.

"You cannot imagine what a stir that shepherd's simple, heartfelt prayers created in the heavens", the Rabbi was told. "You should not have interfered".

Even a simple, two-sentence prayer formulated by an ignorant shepherd succeeded in penetrating the heavens because of the feeling and emotion with which it was recited. We cannot even imagine how meaningful and effective *tefila* prayer could be if one recites the sacred text composed by the Men of the Great Assembly with sincere concentration. When our feelings and concentration combine with the intrinsic sanctity of the words, our prayers become a remarkably powerful force that can have a profound effect upon ourselves and the world at large.

Alas, as anyone who takes prayer seriously knows that it is extremely difficult to pray with proper concentration. Almost invariably, our minds wander far away from the prayer text onto matters that are not even remotely related to the *tefila*.

The reason why this happens is fairly simple. If we were given a five-page Chinese text and told to recite it precisely, word for word, three times a day, every single day for the rest of our lives, we would hardly be enthusiastic about this exercise. We would find it tedious and boring, and we would rush through it as quickly as we could so we could get on to more enjoyable and worthwhile activities.

This is precisely the problem with prayer, for too many of us the prayer text is Chinese. We don't understand a word of what we're saying. It should therefore not surprise us that it has become a tedious exercise that we would much prefer avoiding – or at least getting through as quickly as possible.

Therefore, the first step we must take in reshaping our attitude toward prayer is to study the words and get a basic sense of what the text means. Once we understand the words, prayer will become a much more rewarding and meaningful experience, one which we look forward to all day long.

In this book we will focus mainly on the simple, straightforward meaning of the *Amidah* text, but this by no means captures the full essence of the words of the *Amidah*. Quite to the contrary, our discussion here will barely scratch the surface of the vast treasury of profundity underlying our liturgy. The text of the *Amidah* was composed by the *Ansheh Kenesset Hagedola*, or "Men of the Great Assembly" – the 120 scholars that constituted the Rabbinic leadership toward the beginning of the Second Temple era. This group of towering figures included a number of prophets, as well. Each word of the *Amidah* is a bottomless wellspring of depth and spiritual meaning, and the masters of Kabbalah have unearthed many layers of profound, mystical insights latent within every word. For example, the opening *beracha* of the *Amidah* begins with the letter *bet*, which has the numerical value of two, and concludes with the letter *mem* ("*Magen Abraham*"), which has the numerical value of forty. Together, they equal 42, alluding to the "*Shem Mem-Bet*", the sacred 42-letter Name of the Almighty. This is but one of countless examples of the profundity underlying every word, and even every letter, of the *Amidah* prayer.

For us, though, it would be a significant accomplishment to gain a simple understanding of the meaning of the words, and this will be the primary point of focus in this volume.

L'iluy Nishmat

Yaakov ben Chana Chava
Aron ben Leah

Laurie and Isaac Mavorah

Standing Before the King

Rav Haim of Brisk (1853-1918) famously distinguished between two different types of *kavana* (intent) that one must have as he prays. He noted that the Rambam in one context (*Hilchot Tefila*, chapter 4) requires one to concentrate throughout the entirety of the *Amidah* prayer, whereas elsewhere (ibid, chapter 10) he rules that concentration is required only during the recitation of the first beracha. Rav Haim explained that in the latter passage, the Rambam refers to concentrating on the meaning of the words. When it comes to this type of *kavana*, although one should preferably concentrate on the meaning of the words throughout the entire *Amidah*, he nevertheless fulfills the obligation of prayer as long as he concentrates during the first *beracha*. There is, however, a different kind of *kavana*, which Rav Haim defines as "standing before the King". When a person prays, he needs to think in his mind that he stands before God and speaks to Him. Reading words from a book, or from memory, without being cognizant of the fact that one stands before God, does not qualify as prayer. The Biblical source of the obligation to pray is ולעבדו בכל לבבכם – the command to serve God with one's heart. Clearly, one does not serve with his heart by reading words. There has to be an emotional investment, and this is done by contemplating God's presence and connecting with Him. Thus by definition, Rav Haim explains, one must see himself as standing before God in order to be considered praying. Otherwise, he is just reading words. Hence, this awareness must be present throughout the entirety of the *Amidah* prayer. It is only the second *kavana*, concentration on the meaning of the words, which is not indispensable beyond the first *beracha*.

This concept, of viewing ourselves as standing before God, affects a number of other *halachot* relevant to the *Amidah* recitation, as well. For example, we begin the *Amidah* by stepping forward three paces, as though entering the King's presence, and after the *Amidah* we retreat three steps, taking leave of the Divine Presence. The Gemara (Yoma 53b) establishes that if one does not take three steps back after the *Amidah*, it would have been preferable for him not to have prayed to begin with. Similarly, Rav Alexander Ziskind comments that if one does not recite the concluding prayer of עושה שלום במרומיו at the conclusion of his *Amidah*, all the *berachot* he recited are retroactively considered to have been recited in vain. The likely reason is that if one does not respectfully step back as he would after a private audience with a king, then this demonstrates that he did not see himself as standing before the Almighty when he prayed. If he had truly prayed with this awareness that he was standing before the King, he would not have ended this "meeting" so abruptly.

Likewise, *Halacha* forbids walking in front of a person praying the *Amidah*. While this *halacha* is commonly understood as intended to avoid disrupting the worshiper's concentration, the Hayeh Adam (Rabbi Abraham Danzig of Vilna, 1748-1820) explains that it is based on the premise that the *Shechina* (Divine Presence) is in front of the worshiper. One may not pass in front of somebody praying the *Amidah* because God is, quite literally, right opposite the worshiper, and it would be disrespectful to the Almighty to walk right in front of Him.

Once a person realizes that during the *Amidah* he speaks directly to God, his entire mindset and attitude toward the prayer changes. He will not let his eyes wander around the room, look up every time somebody enters the synagogue, or stand with his hands on his hips or in his pockets, and he will certainly not check his phone. If we see ourselves as standing in God's presence, we will stand with reverence and attention, as a humble servant speaks to his master.

The *sadikim* pray with such a keen awareness of God's presence before them during prayer that they have a striking appearance as they pray. The Torah (Bereshit 24:63-64) tells that when Ribka came to marry Yishak and saw him for the first time, he was praying (ויצא יצחק לשוח בשדה). Upon beholding the sight of the great *sadik* praying, Ribka was so overwhelmed that she fell from the camel she was riding. The Nesiv (Rav Naftali Svi Yehuda Berlin of Volozhin, (1816-1893) commented that the sight left a lasting impression upon Ribka that affected the way she perceived him throughout her life. For this reason, the Nesiv explained, Ribka never demanded that Yishak banish Esav just as Sara demanded that Abraham banish Yishmael; she had such reverence for her husband as a result of that initial encounter that she was unable to approach him to tell him what to do.

It is told that during the time of the great Hassidic leader Rav Leibele Eiger, the Jewish reformers produced shows mocking religious Jews in order to promote their reformist agenda. Once, the people involved in producing such a show sent somebody to Rav Leibele's home to observe him so they could contemptuously imitate him on stage. The man went to the *sadik's* house and peered inside. He saw the rabbi praying and was struck by the awesome sight. He returned to the producers and urged them not to poke fun at the Rabbi. Seeing the *sadik* speaking directly with the Almighty affected him and filled him with awe and inspiration.

Another story is told of the grandfather (or perhaps great-grandfather) of Rav Moshe Feinstein, who had a job working for a certain non-Jewish man, and it was agreed that he could take some time from work in the afternoon to pray Minhah. Rav Feinstein prayed the *Amidah* slowly and with intense concentration, and the employer suspected that he was taking a long time simply out of laziness, to avoid having to work. One day, he tested the Rabbi by shooting a bullet just over his head as he prayed the *Amidah*. The Rabbi did not budge. He was so cognizant of God's presence in front of him that he did not even notice a bullet whizzing by his head. The employer realized he was sincere, and allowed him to take all the time he needed to pray.

It might be difficult for us to concentrate on the words throughout the *Amidah*, but we must, at very least, recognize the fact that at those moments we are speaking directly to the King of kings. This awareness will have a profound impact on the experience and upon our entire attitude towards *tefila,* and help us avoid distractions and concentrate more fully on the lofty act in which we are engaged.

Invoking the Merits of the Patriarchs

The *Magen Abraham* (Shulhan Aruch 98:1) commentary records a *segula* ("charm") which he heard can help a person keep foreign thoughts out of his mind during prayer. Before beginning the *tefila*, one should say, פִּי פִּי פִּי and then spit on the floor three times. The words פִּי פִּי פִּי refer to the three "mouths" mentioned in three successive *parashiyot* in the Book of Bamidbar. In Parashat Korah, we read of the פִּי הארץ, the "mouth" of the ground that opened to devour Korah's followers who rebelled against Moshe and Aharon. In the next *parasha*, Parashat Hukat, the Torah describes the פִּי הבאר, the "mouth" of the miraculous well of water which accompanied *Beneh*

Yisrael throughout their travels in the wilderness and provided them with water. Finally, the Torah in Parashat Balak tells the story of Bilam's donkey who spoke to Bilam to protest his violence. The verse says, ויפתח ה' את פי האתון ("God opened the mouth of the donkey" – Bamidbar 22:28). Reciting the word פי three times, alluding to these three miracles, helps to keep a person's mind focused during prayer and protected from distracting thoughts. The *Magen Abraham* comments that he does not know the reason for this *segula*.

The explanation might relate to the merit of our patriarchs which we invoke by reciting פִּי פִּי פִּי. The work *Or Lashamayim* comments that one who wants to keep his mind clear of improper thoughts should accustom himself to saying the names of the patriarchs – Abraham, Yishak and Yaakob. Just mentioning their names, it appears, helps us connect with their righteous souls, enabling us to keep our minds properly focused upon God. By reciting the words פִּי פִּי פִּי, we connect to the mouths of the three patriarchs, such that our prayers become pure like their prayers were pure. As mentioned earlier, these three instances of the word פי appear in the *parashiyot* Korah, Hukat and Balak. The names of these three *parashiyot* all contain the letter ק; it is the first letter of קורח, the second letter of חקת, and the third letter of בלק. These words allude to the three patriarchs, who, as the *Zohar* writes, are called קדושים ("sacred"). Thus, the letter ק in the names of these *parashiyot* allude to the three patriarchs, and when one says פִּי פִּי פִּי, he creates a link to the mouths of Abraham, Yishak and Yaakob which enables him to recite his prayer with a clear, pure mind.

Our Sages teach us that the forces of impurity intensify as the forces of sanctity intensify. When we create a link to the patriarchs, the כוחות הטומאה (forces of impurity) increase their efforts to oppose and destroy these connections we have made with Abraham, Yishak and Yaakob. This is why the *segula* requires spitting three times, to neutralize the forces of impurity so that they cannot sabotage our connection with the sacred *Abot*. We establish this connection by reciting פִּי פִּי פִּי and then ensure that this connection will not be undermined by the spiritually hostile forces that are abound.

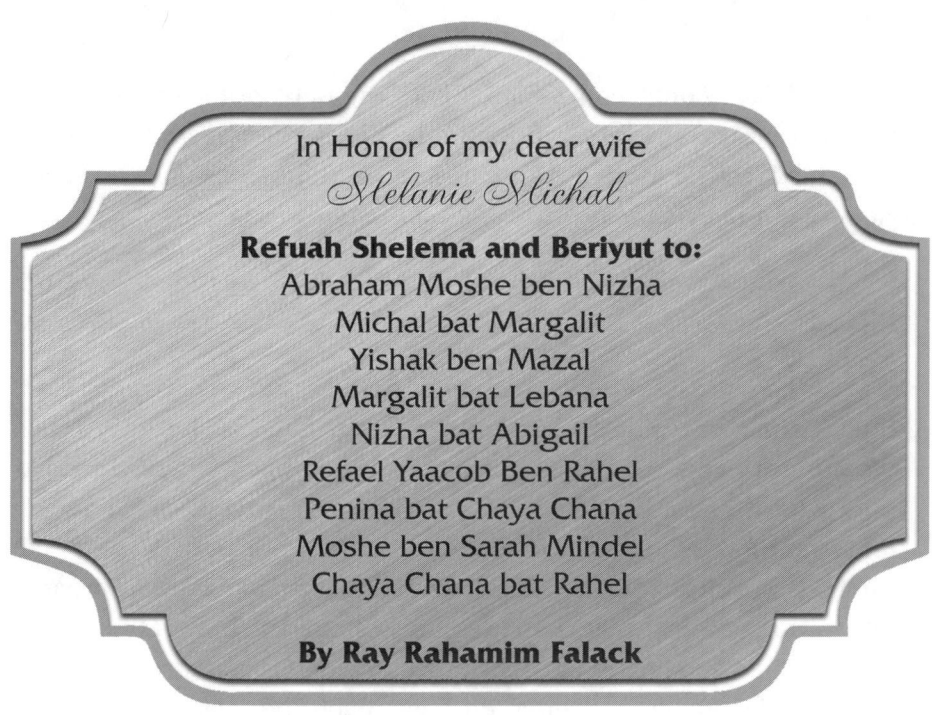

Prayer and Digging Wells

The Torah does not tell us much about Yishak Abinu, but it elaborates in great detail on the subject of Yishak's wells. In Parashat Toledot (Bereshit 26), we read of the wells that Yishak dug, and which the local Pelishtim later stuffed with dirt. We may assume that if the Torah chose to emphasize this aspect of Yishak's life, then it must convey an important message for us to internalize.

Yishak Abinu rose to the spiritual level at which he was able to find sanctity in, and recognize the Godliness of, everything on earth. We can appreciate the spiritual value of holy articles, such as *tefillin*, a *Sefer Torah* and the like, but we do not see the *kedusha* in ordinary objects, even though everything was created by God.

A *hasid* once came excitedly to the Rebbe of Kotzk and told him that he had just visited the Rebbe of Chernobyl, where he saw the table of the Ba'al Shem Tob. The Kotzker Rebbe was unimpressed. He brought his visitor outside and pointed upward.

"You see this sky?" the Rebbe asked. "It was made by God Himself".

The great *sadikim* can find holiness in everything, and thus Yishak was able to serve his Creator even as he dug wells. We are not expected to reach this level of connectedness to God, but, nevertheless, the image of Yishak's digging wells provides an important model for us to follow in our service of God. Serving the Almighty requires "digging", hard work and exertion. If we approach prayer as a relaxing experience, it will never be gratifying or meaningful. We have to dig, dig some more, and then more, and then continue digging even deeper, until we reach the "water" – genuine feelings of connection to God. There is no greater source of joy and satisfaction than the *debekut* (connectedness) that one can achieve through prayer.

The Torah relates that after Yishak dug the wells, ויסתמום פלשתים – the Pelishtim stuffed them with earth (Bereshit 26:18). On a deeper level of interpretation, the word ויסתמום relates to the word סתם, which means "plain" or "ordinary". Often, when a person begins investing greater effort and concentration into prayer or other forms of religious observance, the cynics start coming after him. They assail him with disparaging remarks, such as, "Look who's so religious all of a sudden" or "Who do you think you are?" Unable to come to terms with the fact that somebody is beginning to achieve more than they have, and is making his life more meaningful than theirs, they look to transform his *kedusha* into סתם, into something empty and devoid of meaning. Rather than humbly acknowledge and respect their peer's newfound religious commitment, they mock and jeer, insisting that he's not really doing anything significant.

The Pelishtim saw Yishak's towering spiritual heights, and ויסתמום – they laughed at it, they dismissed it as meaningless, as סתם. They represent the cynics who resent those who seek to grow spiritually, and try to knock them down with their mockery and sarcasm.

Especially when it comes to *tefila*, we must continue to "dig" without paying attention to the Pelishtim, the scoffers. When a person decides to approach prayer more seriously, he arrives on time, spends a few extra minutes on the *Amidah*, doesn't talk to his friends during the service, looks carefully at the words and occasionally closes his eyes to concentrate his thoughts and feelings on his relationship with God – it can be expected that he'll start receiving some snide remarks from his fellow congregants. He cannot take these comments seriously; he must continue digging, working to find meaning in his prayer, without being dissuaded by his detractors.

The Talmud lists prayer among the דברים העומדים ברומו של עולם ובני אדם מזלזלים בהם – "things that are positioned in the greatest heights, but people treat lightly". If we understood the value and importance of *tefila*, we would not treat it lightly. We would happily invest the hard work and effort to pray with intensity and concentration, and we would ignore those who poke fun at us for praying seriously. A close relationship with God is far too valuable a commodity to forfeit for the sake of appeasing the cynics. We must steadfastly persist in our efforts to reach greater heights of prayer, whereby we enhance our relationship with our Creator and bring it to an entirely new level.

Dedicated for
the Hatzlacha of my family

Steven Israel

It's Not All or Nothing

Many people mistakenly approach *tefila* as an "all or nothing" enterprise. When they realize somewhere in the middle of the *Amidah* that they had been daydreaming since the beginning, they despair altogether and get through the rest of the prayer without concentration. The Hafetz Haim (Rabbi Yisrael Meir Kagan of Radin, 1839-1933) emphasized that one should endeavor to salvage whatever he can from his prayer. If a person "wakes up" at *"Sim Shalom"* (the final blessing of the *Amidah*) and realizes he hadn't concentrated at all during the *Amidah*, his prayer is not lost. He should see the final *beracha* that remains as his final opportunity to pray meaningfully, and concentrate to the very best of his ability during that blessing.

The Hafetz Haim drew an analogy to a woman who carries a fruit basket when a dog comes along and suddenly knocks over the basket and grabs some fruit with its mouth. After the dog runs off, the woman obviously does not just leave everything and continue home. She rather gets down on her knees and collects whatever fruits still remain.

There is similarly no reason to forgo on the remaining blessings of the *Amidah*. Each word of the *Amidah* achieves a profound spiritual effect, and thus each word presents us with a new opportunity that must not be squandered. Regardless of how well or poorly one concentrated during the earlier part of the *Amidah*, it is not too late to direct one's attention back to his prayer and make the most of the *berachot* that remain.

Prayer in Our Time

The Arizal foresaw that during the period of עקבתא דמשיחא, the era preceding Mashiah's arrival – the era that the Torah sages have identified as our generation – our primary religious task will be in the area of prayer. While prayer is always a crucially important aspect of religious life, it assumes particular importance in our time.

The difference between the Hebrew word גולה (exile) and the word גאולה (redemption) is the letter א. If we add this letter to גולה, we achieve גאולה. We transform exile into redemption through the letter א, which symbolizes the *Shechina*, the divine presence. We bring the divine presence through prayer; תפילה is the mechanism by which we bring the letter א, the divine presence, into our lives, thus transforming the exile into redemption.

We find in the Torah (Vayikra 19:26) the prohibition of לא תאכלו על הדם, which literally means that one may not eat animal meat which contains blood. The Gemara, however, in Masechet Berachot, interprets this phrase to mean that one may not eat before praying in the morning, before he asks the Almighty for his "blood", for his life and sustenance. Before praying, we are mere דם, just ordinary flesh and blood. But through prayer, by connecting with the Almighty, we become אדם, human beings, special creatures whose significance transcends the blood that runs through our veins. By establishing a relationship with our Creator, we bring the א, the *Shechina*, into our lives, transforming ourselves from דם to אדם, from physical beings to spiritual beings.[3] The Torah forbids us from eating על הדם, when we are just דם, before elevating ourselves to the stature of אדם through our prayers.

The numerical value of אדם is forty-five – the same numerical value as that of the word גאולה. We bring redemption by becoming אדם, by transforming ourselves from דם to אדם. As we have seen, this is accomplished through prayer. Therefore, as the Arizal taught, the arrival of Mashiah must be preceded by a generation that excels and invests special effort in the area of prayer. It is through prayer that we bring the א into our lives and become אדם, and this א is what we need to transform גולה into גאולה.

Therefore, in our generation, more than in any other, we must focus our attention on our *tefilot*, ensuring to pray properly, sincerely, intently, and meaningfully. During this period of עקבתא דמשיחא, improving the quality of our prayers must receive a prominent place on our communal agenda. Individually and collectively, we must give special attention to the *misva* of prayer and ensure that our *tefilot* succeed in bringing the *Shechina* to the world, through which we will brought out of exile and into the Messianic Era.

---

3. Marriage, too, has the effect of completing a person, bringing the divine presence into one's life, transforming him from דם to אדם. This is why we recite the *beracha* at a wedding ceremony, האדם יוצר, celebrating the fact that the bride and groom have now been "completed" and thus risen from mere אדם to דם.

Are We Worthy of Having Our Prayers Answered?

A reader might understandably wonder, even after reading this book and expending great efforts to improve the quality of our prayers, will our *tefilot* really be worthy of a favorable response? Are we truly capable of praying on a standard where they are deserving of being answered? Our Sages teach that in ancient generations, every prayer was "sifted" through thirteen "filters" in the heavens, and if a single "particle" of impurity was found, even one foreign thought or the slightest lack of concentration, the prayer was discarded. Our prayers can hardly compare to even the deficient prayers of our predecessors in earlier generations. On what basis can we expect to have our prayers answered?

The Hafetz Haim answered this question through an analogy to a man who employed a servant of limited intelligence. The man once asked the servant to bring him a drink of water, and the servant quickly returned with a cup of cloudy, murky water.

"This is not how you serve water", the man said. "You first have to run the water through a filter to remove all the impurities. Only then is the water suitable for drinking!"

The servant proved to be a fast learner, and from that moment on, whenever he was asked to bring a drink of water, he ensured to first filter the water and serve a sparkling clear drink.

Sometime later, a fire broke out in one of the room's in the man's house, and the entire house burned to the ground. The man angrily berated the servant for failing to extinguish the flames.

"Why you didn't you pour water over the fire when it first started?" he bellowed.

"I was going to", the servant explained, "but by the time I finished filtering the water, the fire had gotten out of control".

"You fool!" the man shouted. "Water doesn't need to be filtered to put out a fire! When there is a fire, any kind of water is good enough!"

Under normal circumstances, the Hafetz Haim explained, God demands "filtered" prayers, that the Jewish people recite perfect, pristine *tefilot* with the proper concentration and feeling. But when the "fire" of the *yeser hara* is raging, when we face overwhelming spiritual challenges and pressures, our prayers need not be perfect. God lovingly accepts whatever we can offer. In a generation such as ours, any "water" we have to pour onto the "fire" of sin and impurity is an invaluable spiritual asset.

So the answer is that yes, indeed, our *tefilot* can be accepted. Though they may not be perfect, and they are a far cry from the heartfelt, soulful supplications of our ancestors, they are beloved by the Almighty. If He sees how we invest time and effort into improving the quality of our prayers, then He will certainly look kindly upon them and accept them with graciousness and love.

Recognizing the Limits of Prayer

There once lived a certain *saddik* in Jerusalem, who was so poor that he could not afford a pair of shoes. He offered a heartfelt plea to the Almighty: "Please, Hashem, I beg You to provide me with shoes for my feet, and if, in Your infinite wisdom, You determine that I should not have shoes at this time, then I beg You to give me the faith and wisdom to accept it and not be troubled by the fact that I have no shoes".

This story underscores a crucial – but often overlooked – aspect of the Jewish outlook on prayer. Although we absolutely believe in the power prayer, we also believe in the limits of prayer, that we don't always get what we ask for. The reason prayer is limited is because our understanding of our needs is limited. Parents must often deny their children's requests for the children's own benefit, despite the children's strident objections. A child is convinced that he wants the item in question, but the parent, who knows better, realizes that it would be to the child's long-term detriment. In relation to God, we are like young toddlers. We often pray, beg and even protest and complain, because we are certain that we need or want the thing for which we pray. But the Almighty knows better. He might decide, for reasons we cannot possibly comprehend, that a certain couple should not have children until after many years of frustration and difficult treatments. He occasionally determines that certain families must endure financial stress, or that other families should have especially difficult children. He knows far better than us what is in our best interests, and His decisions are always made to serve those interests.

At a certain point – though, in all honesty, I cannot specify precisely what that point is – a person should stop praying and accept the situation. If one prays and prays but his prayers are not answered, at some point he must say to himself, "God has declined my request – it must be in my best interests not to have this request granted".

Nobody loves us more than God. He cares for us and provides our needs 24/7, around the clock, non-stop. We have to trust and have faith in His decisions. Sometimes, we have to take "no" for an answer.

A powerful story is told of a college student from a fabulously wealthy family, who, before graduation, asked his parents for a luxury car as his graduation present. When graduation day arrived, his father hugged him, congratulated him, and presented him with a gift-wrapped box.

The graduate eagerly opened the box, and saw…a Bible!

The young man was furious. He knew his parents could easily afford the car he asked for, and yet, all they bought for him in honor of this momentous occasion was a Bible, a book. He threw the box down on the table, stormed out of the house, and resented his father for the rest of his life.

Many years passed, without any reconciliation. The father grew old, and finally, while lying on his deathbed, he called his son to inform him of his imminent death.

The son, realizing that this was his last and only chance for reconciliation, rushed to the car and drove to his see his father. Unfortunately, he was too late.

As the man was going through his father's belongings, he came across the box with the Bible. It was on the same table where it had been left some thirty years earlier. He nostalgically picked up the book and started flipping through the pages, reminiscing about that fateful day which he allowed to forever ruin his relationship with his father. Suddenly, he heard a clank, and noticed that something had fallen to the floor. The man looked down and saw a set of keys – car keys. He looked back at the Bible, and saw a slip of paper in the back of the book, with the words, "Dear son, Paid for in full".

All these years, he was mistaken. His father *had* bought him a car – but he wanted the son to discover the gift only after going through the Bible.

This is precisely our problem. We have in our minds very specific ideas about how our "gifts" will be wrapped. We paint images of precisely how our children should be, what kind of income we will have and exactly how it will be earned, and so on. We ask for gifts assuming they will come in a particular kind of "package". But this is not how it works. God is constantly showering us with blessings, but not necessarily in the "package" that we envisioned. We need faith and a healthy dose of flexibility to recognize, appreciate and feel content with the myriad of blessings we have been given.

Prayer is not like placing an order with a waiter at a restaurant, where we receive precisely what we request exactly the way we want it. The waiter does not know the customer, and this is precisely why he simply brings the customer what he asked for. But God is so much more than a waiter. He knows us and knows what's good for us – better than we do. He loves us and cares for us far too much to "fill our order" if He realizes that this is not in our ultimate best interests.

When we see a doctor to treat an illness, do we tell him what medication to prescribe, or do we trust his diagnosis and prescription? If we need to consult a therapist for guidance in dealing with a crisis in our life, do we decide which direction to take in therapy, or do we trust the therapist's decision? So why should it be any different with our relationship with God? Who knows better what we need – we, or the Almighty?

This is why we must not feel resentful when our prayers go unanswered. Just as the physician's diagnosis may not be to our liking, but we willingly undergo the treatment – difficult and painful as it may be – because we know it is to our benefit, similarly, we must accept God's "prescription". He is the expert, not us. He knows how to help us far better than we know how to help ourselves. If He decides to answer "no", then we must be confident that this is the correct decision.

One might reasonably wonder, then, what purpose is there to prayer at all? Once we accept the premise that only God knows what's best for us, then why do we even bother making requests? Why should we ask for something if we cannot even be certain that it serves our best interests? Using the example mentioned above, why should we pray for shoes if we do not know whether this is the best thing for us? True, as discussed earlier, prayer serves the vital purpose of allowing us to connect with God. But why should we connect to God by making requests if we cannot know for certain that these requests serve our best interests?

The Mishna in Masechet Ta'anit (15a) says that when communities would observe public fast days in times of drought or other crises, the *hazan* would recite special prayers, including מי שענה לאברהם אבינו בהר המוריה הוא יענה אתכם... ("He who answered Abraham Abinu at Mount Moriah – He shall answer you..."). Apparently, though this is not mentioned explicitly in the Torah, Abraham Abinu prayed and pleaded to God at the time of *akedat Yishak*, when he was commanded to offer his son as a sacrifice. Although he obediently fulfilled the command, and wanted nothing else than to obey God, he also prayed that his son should be saved. Abraham wanted to obey God, but he also wanted Yishak to live. This is no contradiction. We are entitled to beseech God that His decisions will be pleasant for us. While we acknowledge that only He knows what is best for us, and must accept whatever He decides, we are also allowed, and encouraged, to ask that He somehow, in His infinite wisdom, arrange that our best interests are served without anxiety, pain, misfortune or sorrow. We must be prepared to accept the possibility that it does not serve our interests to have shoes, but we may nevertheless pray that we receive shoes and that our best interests are still served. Abraham would have remained steadfast in his faith even if God had not told him to withdraw the knife – but he was certainly entitled to pray for Yishak to survive.

The proper approach to prayer is thus a complex one. On the one hand, we pray and beg for what we want, but on the other hand, we must go into prayer ready to take "no" for an answer.

In the thirteenth *beracha* of the *Amidah*, the *beracha* of על הצדיקים, we declare, כי בך בטחנו ("for in You we have placed our trust"). This is not simply a declaration; it is a prayer. Like the shoeless *saddik* in Jerusalem, we beseech the Almighty to give us the faith we need to accept the rejection of our prayers. Even as we pray the *Amidah*, we are reminded of the possibility that our heartfelt pleas might be denied, in which case we must gird ourselves with faith and confidence in God's unlimited benevolence, even when the answer is "no".

In Honor of

Mosie & Rosie Cabasso

An Exercise in Faith

The Sages describe *tefila* as עבודה שבלב, "service of the heart". The term עבודה connotes hard work and effort. According to the conventional, mistaken approach to prayer, it can hardly be described as עבודה, as something which entails effort. If prayer is about asking for what we want, then *tefila* is no more difficult than making a shopping list, or placing an order with a waiter at a restaurant, where the hardest part is deciding what we want. This clearly does not qualify as עבודה.

Jewish prayer is called עבודה because it is something much, much deeper and far more difficult than placing an order. In essence, *tefila* is about relinquishing control. It means placing our very lives, our entire existence, in the Almighty' hands. *Tefila* is hard work, because it is an exercise in faith – faith that everything that happens is, at all times, in God's hands. This is likely another reason why, as mentioned earlier, the Talmud speaks of prayer as something העומד ברומו של עולם, a lofty ideal that demands effort. We naturally feel in control over most areas of our lives. Until illness strikes, Heaven forbid, we feel confident in our general state of well-being. Until a person loses his job or his business collapses, he feels financially secure. *Tefila* is "lofty" because it requires a fundamental change of perspective. It is an עבודה because it is done properly only once a person has overcome this innate sense of self-sufficiency. In order to fulfill the obligation of עבודה שבלב, we must divest ourselves of our self-confidence, and place ourselves entirely in God's hands. *Tefila* is not a vending machine, where we recite the right words to get exactly what we want. Rather, prayer means standing helpless before God, acknowledging that we are dependent solely on His mercy and grace.

As such, our introduction to prayer is incomplete without addressing, at least briefly, the topic of *emuna*, faith and trust in God's control over every aspect of our lives. This belief is a fundamental prerequisite to proper *tefila*, and must therefore be included in any discussion of the significance and nature of prayer.

The story is told of Rabbi Meir of Parmishlan, who was once traveling in a carriage with his Rabbi. When they reached a steep incline, R' Meir was frightened that the horses would not make it safely up the hill, and that the carriage would roll down and crash. He expressed his fear to his Rabbi, who assured him that the carriage would climb the incline without any problem. Sure enough, the horses climbed the steep hill without incident.

As soon as the carriage was once again traveling on flat ground, R' Meir breathed a sigh of relief and said, "*Baruch Hashem*", while leaning back comfortably in his seat. A moment later, the carriage's wheels hit a rock in the road, and the carriage toppled over. The two Rabbis were thrown from the carriage and found themselves lying in a mound of snow.

"You see", R' Meir's Rabbi said to him, "when the carriage was climbing uphill, you were scared and placed your trust in Hashem. Once the danger passed, you relaxed and felt that you no longer needed the Almighty's help. At that moment, Hashem reminded you that we are always, under all circumstances, dependent upon His protection".

Hashem helps us when we recognize that we need His help; but when we feel self-sufficient, that we can manage perfectly fine independently, He comes to remind us that we in fact need Him.

Studies have shown that the majority of automobile accidents occur on local streets, and not on highways, despite the fact that people generally drive much faster on the open roads. Different theories have been espoused to explain these surprising statistics. But it is likely that they result from drivers' different attitudes toward their driving in these different settings. When a young, teenage driver tells his parents that he is driving upstate for the day, the parents feel nervous. They warn the son to drive carefully, they remind him or her to recite *tefilat ha'derech* and bring the cell phone, and, even so, remain anxious until they receive the phone call that the youngster arrived safely. But when a teenager tells his parents he's hopping over to the local pizza shop, they don't think twice about it. A long trip arouses anxiety, and people naturally feel dependent on Hashem for His assistance, whereas while driving the local streets, people feel comfortable and secure might not appeal to God for assistance. This may perhaps account for the higher accident rate on local streets. When people feel too confident and independent, God must come to remind them of their dependence on Him.

A Rabbi once called his students into his office and showed them a large fish lying on his desk. He cut open the fish, and they saw dozens of small fish inside the large fish's belly. The Rabbi noted to the students that all the small fish were facing the tail of the large fish. All the fish devoured by the large fish swam headfirst into the large fish's mouth; not a single fish was swallowed from behind. The Rabbi used this curious phenomenon as a compelling analogy to the concept of *emuna*. The small fish are aware of the dangers lurking under the sea, but feel confident in their ability to avert the dangers that lie in front of them. Their only fear is what happens behind them, where they cannot see; they fear being swallowed from behind, not from the front. Meanwhile, the big fish spends its time chasing small fish, but it never reaches them. Instead, it is fed by the small fish that carelessly swim right into its mouth.

This model so accurately depicts the mistake that we all make. Like the small fish, we ask God to help us only with the areas of life over which we feel helpless, such as sudden illness and the stock market. When it comes to everything else, that which we can "see", the areas of life where we feel confident and secure, we don't bother appealing for divine assistance. This is precisely where we are at risk of getting "swallowed". When we feel too secure, God comes along and shows us how desperately we depend on Him.

And, like the large fish, we spend our time pursuing a livelihood in a certain direction, but our sustenance actually comes from somewhere else. We think we have the knowledge and capabilities needed to "catch the fish", to obtain our needs, but then God, in His infinite kindness, comes and provides our livelihood from an entirely different source, from an investment we never counted on, or from a job offer we never dreamed of. So often in life, we are hurt in areas where we had always felt secure, and are helped in ways we had never imagined. This is God's way of showing us that our fate is dependent upon Him, and not upon our own efforts.

We read in Megilat Ester that upon hearing of Haman's plan to annihilate the Jews, Ester instructed the Jews to observe a three-day fast, and then invited Ahashverosh and Haman to a feast – seemingly, for the purpose of notifying the king that Haman was planning to exterminate her nation. But at the feast, all she did was eat, drink, and invite Haman and Ahashverosh to another feast the following day. It was only at the second feast that she "unmasked" Haman's plan and saved the Jewish people. Rather than appeal to the king immediately, at the first party, Ester waited until the following day.

The reason, it would seem, is that she wanted to remind the Jews that their salvation would come from God, and not from her. The Jews likely felt confident in the knowledge that they had one of their own in the palace, and that she would intervene on their behalf to rescue them from Haman's edict. Ester therefore intentionally delayed her petition to Ahashverosh and when nothing happened at the first party, the Jews despaired. They had hung their hopes on Ester, and she failed them. At that point, they had nowhere to turn except to the Almighty, and then, once they pinned their hopes on God, rather than on Ester, she intervened. At the second party, after the people recognized their dependence on the Almighty's grace, Ester spoke to Ahashverosh and the Jews were saved.

This theme of the Purim miracle is alluded to in the famous *halacha* requiring one to drink on this holiday until the point where עד דלא ידע בין ארור המן לברוך מרדכי – he cannot distinguish between "cursed be Haman" and "blessed be Mordechai". The Purim miracle demonstrates the fact that God exerts control over all events, both the ברוך מרדכי – the joyous, overtly "blessed" aspects of life, as well as the ארור המן – the troubles and misfortune that we must confront. The story of Purim reminds us that ultimately, there is no difference between the two. We need His assistance in both the comfortable and difficult areas of life. This is why the Sages say that on Purim, כל הפושט יד נותנים לו ("Whoever outstretches his hand – we give him"). Literally, this means that on Purim we do not make inquiries about people who request charity. But on a deeper level, it means that on this day, when we recognize our absolute dependence on God's kindness, whoever "outstretches his hand" in prayer receives God's blessing.

The key to prayer is acknowledging our dependence on the Almighty. We cannot stand before God to pray if we feel that we are the ones with the answers and the solutions. It is through the עבודה of relinquishing control and recognizing how limited we are that we become worthy of praying to the Almighty, and of having our prayers answered through His benevolence and grace.

To our dearest children

Devorah, Yeshaya, Esther Tova & Atarah

May the Gates of Heaven always
be open for your prayers

Love, Mom and Dad

"God – open my lips so that my mouth can speak Your praise"

אדני, שפתי תפתח, ופי יגיד תהלתך

This introductory verse, with which we begin the *Amidah* prayer, is likely the most important passage in the entire *Amidah* service, as it expresses the aura of awe and dread that one must sense as he comes before God. When a person approaches a renowned, distinguished figure, he might feel so nervous and anxious that he cannot even speak properly. Certainly, as one comes before the King of the universe who exerts unlimited control over our very lives, we must experience a sense of dread. We therefore introduce our prayer by beseeching, "God – open my lips so that my mouth can speak Your praise". We proclaim that if not for God's help, we would be unable to even mouth the words of our prayer.

The first word of this introduction is "Ado-nai", one of the Names of the Almighty. The privilege of being able to articulate God's Name must not be taken lightly. The *Shulhan Aruch* records a custom to rinse one's mouth upon awaking in the morning, in order to prepare it for uttering God's Name. Just as a synagogue must be kept clean, as befitting a place of holiness, one's mouth, too, must be cleaned before it can serve as a vehicle for the pronouncement of the Divine Name. By uttering God's Name, we transform our mouths into a sanctuary, endowing our vocal faculties with a status of *kedusha*.

The Divine Name chosen as the first word of the *Amidah* prayer is the Name of *Adnut* – אדני. Kabbalistic teaching finds great significance in the selection of this Name specifically, which is comprised of the four letters *alef*, *dalet*, *nun* and *yod*. The numerical value of *alef* is 111, *dalet* equals 434, *nun* has a value of 106, and the word *yod* equals 20.[4] Altogether, these sums add up to 671, the numerical value of the Aramaic word *tar'a* (תרעא), which means "gate". The Arizal (Rav Yishak Luria, 1534-1572) explained that the Name of *Adnut* serves as the gateway for our prayers, the door through which our prayers enter and from where they will ascend to the heavens. This Divine Name refers to the manifestation of God on our level here on earth, and it is here, on this lowly, earthly level, where the prayers must be uttered and from where they make their way toward the Divine Throne. Furthermore, the scholars of Kabbalah teach

---

4. Every word has two numerical values. The first is simply the sum of the numerical values of all the word's letters. The second, known as milui, is computed by spelling out the names of all the word's letters, and then combining the numerical values of all the names. Thus, to determine the milui value of אדני, we spell out the names of the four letters – אלף, דלת, נון, יוד – and then combine the numerical values of these four names.

that the Name of *Adnut* has the capacity to eliminate the harmful spiritual forces that threaten to prevent our prayers from ascending to the heavens. As we begin praying, we must do a "mine sweep", clearing the way for our prayers to reach their desired destination. We therefore introduce the *Amidah* with the Name "*Ado-nai*", which eliminates the forces that seek to sabotage our prayers. This word is thus the "gate" through which we must begin our prayers in order for them to succeed.

Dedicated in Honor of

Mr. Ken and Lillian Cayre

for their unlimited generosity and
dedication to our amazing community

May Hashem bless you and your
family for generations to come

The First Three Berachot:
Awakening the Abot

The rabbis teach us that one of the ways of ensuring the acceptance of our prayers is connecting with the *sadikim*. The prayers of the *sadikim*, it seems, are given an "E-Z Pass" allowing them to proceed straight through the gates of the heavens. While our prayers, independently, cannot be guaranteed to reach God, we can help ensure that this happens by praying together with the righteous members of *Kelal Yisrael*, both past and present.

The Sages have taught us the concept of שפתותיו דובבות בקבר

– "His lips murmur in the grave". This means that when we study a page of Gemara and learn a statement made by R' Meir, for example, our learning awakens the soul of R' Meir, and he studies the passage together with us. When we learn the Torah of Hillel and Shammai, Abayeh and Raba, R' Yohanan and Resh Lakish, Rav and Shemuel, R' Eliezer and R' Akiba, we "activate" their souls, and they come to sit by our side. We connect with the souls of these righteous sages, and they then join us in our process of Torah study.

The same is true of prayer. If we can somehow connect with the soul of a *sadik*, then that righteous person joins us in our prayer, helping it gain acceptance from God. Thus, for example, there is a custom recorded in a number of works to light a candle in memory of a *sadik* on his *yahrtzeit* before each prayer service. One thereby connects with the *sadik*'s soul, such that the soul will join in the prayer and help it pass through the heavenly gates.

In the first three *berachot* of the *Amidah*, we endeavor to awaken the souls of the greatest *sadikim* of all – Abraham, Yishak and Yaakob. Each of these blessings corresponds to one of the patriarchs, and serves to bring him to our side as we stand before the Almighty and beg for His kindness and compassion.

The first *beracha* concludes, "Blessed are You, Hashem, Shield of Abraham". It thus clearly corresponds to Abraham, the first of our patriarchs. The second *beracha*, the blessing of *geburot*, discusses the Almighty's unparalleled strength and power. The concept of *gebura* (power) very closely relates to the divine attribute of *din*, strict justice, a quality which is commonly associated with Yishak (as opposed to Abraham, who was characterized by *hesed* – boundless kindness). This *beracha* concludes with מחיה המתים, the theme of God's power of resurrection, which is also closely associated with

Yishak. A number of sources mention that when Abraham placed Yishak upon the altar at the *akeda*, Yishak actually died. In order that Abraham could fulfill the command to sacrifice his son, God took Yishak's soul and transferred it to the ram which Abraham later offered as a sacrifice. He then implanted a new soul within Yishak. Yishak thus experienced *tehiyat hametim* (resurrection), and this *beracha*, which highlights this particular manifestation of God's power, corresponds specifically to Yishak. Significantly, this *beracha* also makes reference to the dew which God sends upon the earth (מוריד הטל), which alludes to the טל תחייה, the "dew of rebirth", with which God will resurrect the dead in the Messianic Era.

The third *beracha* of the *Amidah* focuses on the theme of *kedusha*, God's singular stature of holiness. The prophet Yeshayahu (29:23) refers to God as "the sacred One of Yaakob" (והקדישו את קדוש יעקב). Yaakob is thus associated with the quality of *kedusha*, such that the third blessing of the *Amidah* corresponds to Yaakob.

When we begin the *Amidah*, we first take a trip to Hebron, to *Me'arat Hamachpela* (Tomb of the Patriarchs), and start knocking on the doors of the graves. We ask the immortal souls of Abraham, Yishak and Yaakob to stand at our side and serve as our advocates as we present our requests before God. Their involvement is critical in our efforts to ensure that our prayers penetrate the heavens and come before the Divine Throne.

David HaMelech writes in the Book of Tehillim (55:18), ערב ובוקר וצהריים אשיחה ואהמה (literally, "In the evening, morning and afternoon I pray and moan"). The second letter of the name "Abraham" is ב, which represents the word בוקר ("morning"); the second letter of "Yishak" is צ, corresponding to צהריים ("afternoon"); and the second letter of "Yaakov", ע, alludes to ערב ("evening").

David HaMelech speaks here of the three daily prayers which were established by the three patriarchs: Abraham instituted the morning *shaharit* service, Yishak introduced the afternoon *minha* prayers, and it was Yaakob who first prayed the evening *arbit* service. David HaMelech concludes this clause with the word ואהמה, which has the numerical value of 57 – three times the number 19, thus alluding to the three daily *Amidah* prayers, each of which contains 19 *berachot*. We call out to the Almighty through the recitation of the three prayers instituted by our sacred patriarchs, invoking their merit in our efforts to assure our prayers' acceptance before God.

The First Beracha: Abot

ברוך
"Blessed"

At this point in the *Amidah*, as one recites the word "*Baruch*",
he lowers his spine while keeping his head straight. While reciting
the word "*Ata*", one bends his head down. Then, during the recitation
of "*Hashem*", one rises back into his original position, lifting his
head last. (This is contrast to the practice of the Ashkenazim, who
bend their knees while reciting the word "*Baruch*"; Sepharadim bow
without bending the knees.)

What does the word "*Baruch*" mean? The literal meaning
of the word is "blessed". But if God is "blessed", then, seemingly,

He requires someone's blessing, which is, of course, inconceivable. What, then, do we mean when we describe the Almighty as "*Baruch*"?

This word is related to the Hebrew word *berecha*, or "pool". A pool is a receptacle that contains water. When we speak of God as "*Baruch*", we refer to the fact that He contains all blessings; He is the source of all blessings in the universe. In effect, the recitation of this word reminds us why we are turning to God with our requests. All blessings are under His control; it is He who has the exclusive ability to dispense blessing and kindness. Hence, it is only to Him that we must pray for the many different blessings that we wish for.

אתה
"You"

"*Ata*" might very well be the most remarkable word in the entire *Amidah*. When we speak with distinguished Rabbis, we refer to them in third person: "Would the Rabbi like something to drink?" or "Does the Rabbi need a ride?" It is deemed disrespectful and irreverent to address a prominent Rabbi directly, with the word "you", which suggests a kind of resemblance or equation between the speaker and the Rabbi. We employ the third person form to demonstrate that we see ourselves as occupying a fundamentally lower plane than the Rabbi.

Yet, when it comes to the Almighty, we are allowed – and in fact required – to address Him in second person form, with the word "*Ata*". The reason is that despite the obvious, infinite gulf that separates between us and God, He nevertheless invites us to speak with Him as a child speaks to his father. Despite our unworthiness, God specifically wants us to address Him directly, personally, like a son. This is why we lower our heads while reciting the word "*Ata*". We feel ashamed and embarrassed to address God so personally, and we therefore hide our faces in shame.

The Mishna in Pirkeh Abot (3:1) advises, "דע מאין באת ולאן אתה הולך"–"Realize from where you came, and where you are going".

The word "*ata*" ("you") in this Mishna may allude to our recitation of the word "*ata*" in the *Amidah* prayer. The Mishna urges us to contemplate our lowliness before we approach the Almighty to speak to Him. We must bring to mind our humble beginnings, a putrid seed, and think "לאן אתה הולך" – to where our recitation of "*ata*" is going. We, who are so small, are standing before the King of kings, the Master of the universe. These are the frightening thoughts that must fill our minds as we begin to pray.

At the same time, however, reciting this word also gives us reassurance. The fact that we are allowed and even obligated to address God directly demonstrates that regardless of our stature, God loves us, cherishes our relationship with Him, and very much desires to hear our prayers. Thus, while the concept of "*Ata*" is certainly frightening and intimidating, it is also a great source of encouragement and reassurance.

Furthermore, addressing God in the second person form of "*Ata*" expresses the certainty with which we acknowledge His existence. Although we do not see God, we speak to Him directly – "*Ata*" – as though He stands right in front of us. The Sages teach that our ancestors at Mount Sinai heard the first two of the Ten Commandments – "I am the Lord your God" and "You shall have no other Gods besides me" – directly from God Himself. Most of the Torah – 611 of the 613 commandments – was spoken to Moshe, who then conveyed the information to the rest of the nation. These two commands, however, the fundamental belief in a Creator and the prohibition against worshiping anything else, were spoken by God in the presence of the entire nation.

This is what enables us to speak directly to God. We do not simply *believe* that He exists; we *know* that He exists, because our ancestors heard Him speak to them. As such, we recognize His presence just as we recognize the people standing next to us, whom we can see with our own eyes. By saying, "*Ata*", we express our firm, confident knowledge in His existence.

ה'
"Hashem"

What is the meaning of the Divine Name of *Havaya*: י-ה-ו-ה?

Whenever one recites this Name, he must have two fundamental concepts in mind. The first is that of "*adon kol*", the notion that God is the unchallenged Master over all creatures on earth. Secondly, one must think of the precept of היה הווה ויהיה – that God is eternal, He transcends time, and has always been and will always be in existence, and because He is eternal, He can place all our requests in perspective. Only He, who is above time, knows what is in our long term benefit and can determine whether our requests should be granted.

אלהינו
"our God"

We have now come to a third Name of God – "*Elokim*". The Shulhan Aruch explains that this term refers to God's omnipotence, His unlimited control over all the natural forces. Wind, rain, thunder, lightning, tsunamis, earthquakes – all of nature is controlled directly and exclusively by the Almighty, who, as the term suggests, is "all mighty" – the most powerful force in the universe. This is the reason why we turn to Him – and only Him – in prayer, as He has the capacity to fulfill all our requests.

We speak of God here not as simply "*Elokim*", but rather as "*Elokenu*" – "our God", emphasizing God's personal involvement in our lives. He is not just "God"; He is "our God". A person who builds a building can then leave and have nothing else to do with the structure. The occupants can live and use the building without depending upon the builder any further. But this is not the case at all with the world. God created the universe, and continues to sustain it and all its inhabitants at every moment. He controls, oversees and governs every aspect of the earth, everything that transpires in our lives, down to the most minute detail.

The phrase "*Hashem Elokenu*" thus conveys a critically important message. The Name of "*Havaya*", as discussed, signifies God's eternity and transcendence. When we refer to Him as "*Hashem Elokenu*", we declare that despite His transcendence, He is also "*Elokenu*" – our "personal" God who is intimately involved in every detail of our lives. God transcends time, yet He is well aware of the electric bill I need to pay, or that I need a new job or have a sick relative. He is not just God – He is "our God". (See also below, in our discussion of the term g*adol*.)

Most *berachot* begin with the phrase, "*Baruch Ata Hashem Elokenu Melech ha'olam*". The phrase "*Melech ha'olam*" ("King of the world") refers to God's control over the world's major events – wars, epidemics, natural disasters, drought, upheavals, and so on. As opposed to "*Elokenu*", which describes God's personal care of and supervision over each individual, "*Melech ha'olam*" refers to His involvement in the larger-scale events that transpire on earth. The *Zohar* comments that the main *shefa* (abundance of divine blessing) that one earns is received through the recitation of "*Melech ha'olam*". When a person proclaims divine kingship, subjugating himself to the rule and authority of God, he is granted abundant blessing from the King, who wishes to bestow kindness upon all His loyal subjects.

Curiously, however, the Men of the Great Assembly did not include the phrase "*Melech ha'olam*" in the *Amidah* prayer. Although this phrase constitutes an integral part of *berachot* generally, and, as mentioned, is even the primary medium through which we earn God's blessing, it is omitted from the *Amidah*.

Tosafot (Masechet Berachot 40b) raise this question, and explain that it is not necessary to recite "*Melech ha'olam*" in the *Amidah*, since we recite "*Elokeh Abraham*" – "God of Abraham" (see next section). It was Abraham who introduced the belief in God's kingship to a world overrun by pagan beliefs. Thus, when we speak of God as "*Elokeh Abraham*", the God which Abraham taught mankind, we are in effect proclaiming His kingship over the universe – for this was precisely the belief that Abraham worked to disseminate. As such, we have no need to recite the phrase "*Melech Ha'olam*" in the *Amidah* since we recite "*Elokeh Abraham*" which conveys the same message.

Tosafot's answer may shed light on the blessing God conveyed to Abraham when He appeared to him for the first time and commanded him to relocate in Canaan: "I shall make you into a great nation, and I shall bless you, and I shall make your name exalted, and you shall be a blessing" (Bereshit 12:2). Rashi, in his Torah commentary, explains this verse as a reference to the *Amidah* prayer. The promise of "I shall make you into a great nation" alludes to the fact that Abraham's descendants will refer to the Almighty in the *Amidah* as "God of Abraham". The next promise, "I shall bless you", refers to the phase "*Elokeh Yishak*", in which we speak of God as the God of Abraham's son, Yishak. "I shall make your name exalted", the third promise in this verse, refers to "*Elokeh Yaakob*", our description of God as the God of Abraham's grandson Yaakob.

But what does God mean when he concludes, "and you shall be a blessing"?

Rashi explains this promise to mean that although we refer to the Almighty as the God of all three patriarchs, we conclude the first *beracha* of the *Amidah* by describing God as "*Magen Abraham*" – "Shield of Abraham". The promise of "you shall be a blessing" means that the blessing concludes with special mention of Abraham specifically. In light of *Tosafot*'s comments, however, another possible explanation emerges. It is because of Abraham that this *beracha* in the *Amidah* is considered a *beracha*. His efforts to spread monotheism enable us to recite "*Elokeh Abraham*" in place of "*Melech ha'olam*", as *Tosafot* explained. The promise of "You shall be a blessing" thus might allude to the fact that it was Abraham who transformed the first *beracha* of the *Amidah* into a formal "blessing", as the missing phrase "*Melech ha'olam*" is replaced by the reference to God as "*Elokeh Abraham*".

ואלהי אבותינו
"and God of our forefathers"

Our belief in God comes to us through the chain of tradition, which has been passed from father to son since the time of our patriarchs. Our recognition of the Almighty as the source of blessing, then, is due to the belief and efforts of our righteous patriarchs, Abraham, Yishak and Yaakob. In a pagan world, they were the trailblazers of monotheism, bringing the belief in the One true God to the forefront of religious belief. As we recognize God's exclusive power and dominion, we note as well the source of this belief – the tradition that dates back to our patriarchs.

אלהי אברהם, אלהי יצחק, ואלהי יעקב
"God of Abraham, God of Yishak and God of Yaakob"

Rather than describing the Almighty as "God of Abraham, Yishak and Yaakov", we instead refer to him as the personal God of each patriarch: "God of Abraham, God of Yishak and God of Yaakov". Each of the patriarchs related to the Almighty in his own way. Abraham embodied the quality of *hesed*–kindness, emphasizing the need to recognize the kindness God dispenses to His creatures, and the obligation to follow His example of compassion and loving kindness. Yishak represented the attribute of *gebura* – justice. He stressed that although the Almighty is a God of kindness, there is a system of strict justice in the world that holds us accountable for our conduct. Finally, Yaakob embodied the attribute of *emet*, absolute truth.

We mention the names of our patriarchs as we begin the *Amidah* in order to invoke their merit, in the hope that they will come before the Almighty to plead to Him on our behalf. Furthermore, this phrase has a total of 26 letters, the numerical value of the Divine Name of *Havaya*.

האל הגדול הגבור והנורא

"The God who is great, mighty and awesome"

האל The Divine Name of *El*–אל refers specifically to the divine attribute of kindness, God's quality of dispensing kindness to His creatures. This is the most critical of all the divine attributes in the context of prayer, for it is only because of this quality of האל that we have the ability to pray. We are invited to approach God in prayer because He is kind, because He wants to deal kindly with His creations. The centrality of this attribute with regard to prayer emerges from the verse, "*tefila l'el hayai*" – "a prayer to the *El*–אל of my life" (Tehillim 42:9). Prayer is offered to *El*, to the aspect of God that relates to the attribute of kindness, as it is only due to divine kindness that we are able to pray to the Almighty.

הגדול The term *Gadol* "great", as the Vilna Gaon (Rabbi Eliyahu of Vilna, 1720-1797) explained, describes something that begins on the ground and extends to the heavens. This is in contrast to other Hebrew words for "big" or "high", which refer to something that is entirely in the heavens, and does not extend from the ground. According to this understanding of *gadol*, our use of this term in reference to the Almighty assumes great significance. Other faiths believed that God is too lofty and exalted to take interest in what takes place here, on our lowly earth, in the realm of human beings. We, however, believe that God is *gadol* – He is situated here on earth, together with us, but His stature obviously extends well beyond our world. This is precisely the reason why we pray, and why our prayers can be answered – because the Almighty is right here with us and intimately involved in what occurs in our lives.

A verse in Tehillim (99:2) states, "ה' בציון גדול ורם הוא על כל העמים" – "Hashem is great in Zion, and high upon all the nations". In Zion, among the Jewish people, the Almighty is *gadol* – He is situated both here on earth as well as in the heavens. But "above all the nations", in the mindset of the gentile peoples, He is "*ram*" רם – only in the heavens, and not involved in human affairs. We avow our belief in God as *gadol*, as a divine being whose unlimited greatness does not preclude the possibility of His direct involvement and interest in what happens here on earth.

Another meaning of the term *gadol* is offered by the *Sefer Ha'Tanya* (Rabbi Sheneur Zalman of Liadi, 1745-1813), in the *Sha'ar Ha'yihud* section. There, *gadol* is defined as referring to God's infusing life into every creature on earth. Every organism receives its existence directly from the Almighty at every moment, and it is in this sense that we refer to God as *gadol*.

הגבור The word *gibor* ("might") refers to the kind of might and power which the Mishna describes in *Pirkeh Abot* (4:1): "Who is mighty? He who restrains his inclination". God, too, is "strong", in that He restrains His anger. Rabbi Moshe Cordovero (1522-1570) suggested an analogy to an angry citizen who pelts the royal chariot with stones. Rather than apprehending or punishing the criminal, the king continues to supply him with stones to enable him to continue his violence. Similarly, God continues sustaining the lives of sinners, thereby facilitating their acts of betrayal against Him. In His infinite "*gebura*", strength and power, He restrains His anger, as it were, and allows even the wicked to continue living.

Why does God run the world with such "might"? Why does He withhold His vengeance, and not immediately punish those who disobey Him?

God delays punishment in the hope that the sinner will repent. *Teshuba* is always available, and God restrains His anger to allow transgressors the opportunity to avoid punishment through repentance.

Additionally, God must restrain His anger in order to ensure the human being's *behira hofshit* – free will. If God were to deliver immediate retribution upon every sinner, we would have no free will; we would never even contemplate wrongdoing, realizing the immediate consequences of sin. God therefore restrains His anger and delays punishment to allow people the opportunity to choose evil – for without the opportunity to choose evil we could not earn reward for choosing righteousness.

Finally, God restrains His anger in order to allow His supporters the opportunity to defend His honor. God has been compared in this regard to an accomplished but humble king, whose administration made the kingdom phenomenally successful, but he refused to take credit for his achievements. An imposter in the kingdom, seeking to seize the throne, began persuading the citizens that he is to thank for all the government's achievements. The imposter gradually attracted a significant following, yet the king took no action against him, and made no efforts to refute the challenger's false claims.

With time, it became clear why the king chose the route of inaction. The king's supporters, recognizing the threat posed by the brewing rebellion, eventually mobilized in full force to defend the king and inform the citizenry of his tireless efforts on the country's behalf. By remaining silent and passive, the king allowed his supporters the opportunity to rise in his defense, and he took great pleasure in seeing how many subjects vocally expressed their fervent support and worked to spread awareness of his achievements.

Similarly, God remains silent in the face of evil, tyranny and heresy in order to give His "supporters" the opportunity to rise in His defense. He specifically wants us, those who recognize His unlimited power and might, to stand up and announce to the world that there is an omnipotent Creator who sustains the entire universe. God therefore exercises the quality of *gebura*, restraint, in order to allow us the opportunity to defend Him against the "imposters" who deny His existence or everlasting power.

והנורא The term *nora* ("awesome") refers to the combination of *gadol* and *gibor*, the merging of these two qualities of close involvement in our world and the restraint of anger.

Additionally, *nora* denotes God's tendency to bring punishment for the purpose of preparing a person to receive blessing. Our matriarch Sara, for example, was denied children for ninety years, during which time she prayed and repented in the hope of earning the blessing of a child. When she finally conceived and bore a child, it became clear why God had kept her barren all those years. In the merit of her years of prayer and *teshuba*, she was blessed with a righteous son Yishak, the greatest child with whom a parent could possibly be blessed.

God is *nora* in the sense that He will sometimes frighten a person by denying his request, so that the individual will develop himself spiritually until he becomes deserving of great *beracha*. The denying of the request is like the frightening thunderclap that precedes the rainfall. Before we can receive the "rain", the blessing from the heavens, we need to be frightened and intimidated, inspired to repent, grow and turn to God. In that merit, we will then be deserving of God's unlimited blessing.

אל עליון
"The Supreme God"

The word "*elyon*" literally means "high". The notion of God being "high" refers to more than just the geographic distance between us and the highest point beyond the heavens where God 's throne resides. It means that God is unfathomable, that the human mind cannot possibly begin to understand God's essence, or grasp the extent of His greatness.

To put this into perspective, it is impossible for people like us to relate to a mind like that of Hacham Ovadia Yosef *zt"l*. We are awed by a single human with a brain that can contain and process such an enormously large corpus of intricate knowledge. All the more so, we can hardly comprehend the intellect of sage like Rashi, who composed commentaries to the entire Tanach and Talmud, or like the Rambam, who codified all of *Halacha* in a monumental fourteen-volume work. God's knowledge, of course, extends so far beyond that of these sages, and is, in fact, on a fundamentally different plane. No human mind can even begin to grasp the infinite wisdom of the Almighty.

For this reason, it is senseless to question God's governance of the world. Questions on God's actions are simply ludicrous, because our minds are inherently incapable of grasping His wisdom and perfection.

A person once said to his Rabbi, "I don't understand what God is doing to me!"

The Rabbi replied, "Do you want a God whom you could understand?"

God is, by definition, "(אל עליון) *El Elyon*", unfathomable and beyond human comprehension. It should therefore come as no surprise that we often find ourselves unable to understand how He runs the world in even the simplest matters.

גומל חסדים טובים
"Who performs good kindnesses"

Despite being "*Elyon*", well beyond the limited realm of human beings, He nevertheless "performs good kindnesses" and shows interest in us. As the Sages commented, "Wherever you find the greatness of the Almighty, you find there His humility". In several instances in the Tanach, a description of God's power and authority is immediately followed by a description of His benevolence and concern for people, particularly for the poor and underprivileged. Generally, people who rise to prominent statures of wealth and prestige show little interest in members of lower socio-economic classes. God, however, the greatest Being, seeks a relationship with us, His creatures. He does not remain distant and remote; He plays a direct, active role in every aspect of our lives.

This notion is alluded to in the numerical value of the Divine Name of *Havaya*, which is 26. Adding the digits of this number (2+6) yields eight. If we multiply the Name by two, we arrive at 52, and the digits (5+2) add up to a smaller number, seven. Multiplying the Name by three yields 78, and if we add the digits (7+8=15; 1+5=6) we reach six. This trend continues with the multiple of four, 104, which results in the number five. This alludes to the fact that the more we contemplate God, the more humble He appears – and the more we recognize how He lowers Himself to care for the individual needs of all creatures. As the verses state in Tehillim (113:5-6), "Who is like Hashem our God, who dwells on high – yet lowers Himself to see heaven and earth!"

What is meant by the expression, חסדים טובים – "good kindnesses"? Aren't all kindnesses "good"? Is there such a thing as a "bad" kindness?

Everything God does is a *hesed*, a kindness, even if it appears differently. When a surgeon takes a scalpel and cuts open a patient's flesh, an observer who does not understand the context would consider the incision an act of cruelty. Similarly, God must occasionally perform "surgery" that causes us a degree of pain and discomfort, but is ultimately for our well-being and in our best interests. A person might be destined to die, Heaven forbid, but God will mercifully take some of his money in place of his life. The financial loss will appear as an act of cruelty, but is, in reality, an expression of love and kindness.

We therefore emphasize in the *Amidah* that God performs "good kindnesses", that all His kindnesses are "good". Even if sometimes it may appear that He wrongs us, in truth, everything He does is a *hesed*.

קונה הכל
"and creates everything"

We do not say that God "created", but rather that He "creates", in the present. A manufacturer usually has nothing at all to do with his product once he creates it and sells it. God, however, continues to sustain the universe which He created, at every moment. If He would stop "creating" for even a fraction of a millisecond, the universe would cease to exist.

This phrase refers to an additional aspect of creation, as well. Rav Haim Vital taught that there are 72 forms of kindness that God bestows upon the earth, as alluded to by the word *hesed*, which has the numerical value of 72. However, God was forced to withhold seventeen of these forms of *hesed* due to people's unworthiness, and He will restore them only in the time of the Messianic Era. We therefore describe God in the *Amidah* as גומל חסדים טובים – "Who performs good kindnesses". The numerical value of *tob* ("good") is 17, corresponding to the seventeen withheld manifestations of God's kindness. We emphasize in our prayer that although we currently experience only 55 of the 72 expressions of kindness, we acknowledge God's ability to bestow the additional 17 kinds of *hesed*, which we hope to experience with the coming of *Mashiah*. We then add, קונה הכל, that God currently creates הכל, which has the numerical value of 55 – referring to the 55 types of kindness which He continues to bestow despite our unworthiness.

Finally, it should be noted that the word קונה actually means "owns", rather than "creates". We acknowledge that God is the true owner over all existence, even that which happens to be under our possession. It is customary to write inside books the words, לה' הארץ ומלואה ("The earth and all it contains belong to Hashem" – Tehillim 24:1), to express our recognition that although we appear to be the owners over our possessions, in truth, everything belongs to the Almighty.

וזוכר חסדי אבות
"and remembers the kindnesses of the patriarchs"

This refers either to the kindness God performed for the patriarchs, by promising that a great and eternal nation will emerge from their offspring, or to the kindness of the patriarchs themselves, who lived their lives in faithful devotion to God. Either way, the special relationship that God had with our patriarchs is what guarantees our redemption.

ומביא גואל לבני בניהם
"and He brings redemption to their progeny"

Even though the final redemption has not yet arrived, we say that God "brings" the redemption, in the present tense. Each moment brings us closer to redemption. Everything that transpires, even if seems to lead in the opposite direction, is part of God's plan and the process of our national redemption. We must therefore never despair, regardless of how difficult the circumstances, because we know that God "brings" the redemption already at the present time, bringing us closer to our final salvation at each moment.

The word מביא ("brings") also serves as an acronym, representing the words מצרים, בבל, יון, אדום – the four nations that have exiled the Jewish people (Egypt, Babylonia, Greece and Rome). The redemptions that our nation has experienced from the first three exiles gives us hope and assurance that we will similarly be redeemed from this fourth and final exile. Just as God freed us from Egyptian bondage, brought us back to *Eretz Yisrael* from Babylonia, and helped us overthrow the Greeks, He will likewise deliver us from the current exile, which began with the Second Temple's destruction at the hands of Edom (Rome).

למען שמו באהבה
"for His Name's sake, with love"

The Gemara (Shabbat 55a) cites two views as to whether or not the merit of our patriarchs has been exhausted ("*tama zechut abot*"). According to one view, we can no longer access the merits of Abraham, Yishak and Yaakob, because those merits have already been used to protect previous generations of Jews. We thus declare here in the *Amidah* that even if our forefathers' merit does not suffice to earn us redemption, God will nevertheless bring us redemption "for His Name's sake", despite the fact that we don't have the merits to deserve it.

Even if this happens, God redeems us "with love". We might draw an analogy to a father who purchases tickets to a ball game for himself and his son. The day before the ball game, the child misbehaves, and clearly does not deserve the special treat. Nevertheless, his father tells him, "You really don't deserve to go, but since I bought the tickets already, I'll take you anyway". Neither the father nor the son can properly enjoy the experience; the outing will undoubtedly be marred by the tension between them and the knowledge that the father really did not want to bring the son.

However when this situation happens between us and God, He none the less redeems us "with love". Even if we are unworthy, and He is compelled to redeem us "for His Name's sake", He does so with love, because His love for *Am Yisrael* is unconditional. No matter what the circumstances, God still loves His nation.

Of course, this love must be reciprocal. As we recite these words in the *Amidah*, we should contemplate God's immense love for us, and how we owe Him the same degree of unconditional commitment. For this reason, a number of works mention that before one recites the words למען שמו באהבה he should accept upon himself the four forms of court execution (stoning, burning, decapitation and strangulation). As we speak of God's boundless love for *Am Yisrael*, we should feel within ourselves unconditional love for Him, to the extent that we are even prepared to give our lives for His sake.

This phrase may also be explained differently, according to the view that we still benefit from the merit of our patriarchs. The names "Abraham", "Yishak" and "Yaakob" contain a total of 13 letters, the numerical value of the word "*ahaba*". Their piety and devotion to God has ensured the Almighty's continued, ongoing love for their descendants, upon which we rely as we appeal to Him for mercy and salvation. We therefore proclaim that God redeems us "with *ahaba*", through the righteousness of our patriarchs.

The word באהבה ("with love") may also be read to mean ב' אהבה, or "twice *ahaba*". The names of the four matriarchs – Sara, Ribka, Rahel and Leah – also contain a combined thirteen letters, and they, too, are a source of merit for us as we pray for redemption. God thus brings redemption to us "twice *ahaba*", through the combined merit of our righteous patriarchs and matriarchs. As we begin the *Amidah* prayer, we look to invoke the boundless merit of these seven righteous ancestors – Abraham, Yishak, Yaakob, Sara, Ribka, Rahel and Leah – to help ensure that our prayers are accepted by God.

מלך עוזר ומושיע ומגן
"The King who assists, brings salvation, and protects"

What is the difference between these three terms – ,עוזר מושיע, מגן ("helps", "brings salvation" and "protects")? There are no synonyms in the Hebrew language; each term bears its own nuance and subtleties. What different qualities of God are expressed by these three descriptions?

Let us first address the difference between עוזר and מושיע. The word עוזר means "helps", and refers to helping a person help himself. "Help" implies that the beneficiary already works toward obtaining his needs, while the "helper" participates to make the process easier and more successful. As the famous proverb says, "God helps those who help themselves". When we say that God "helps", we mean that when we do our share and make a sincere effort to improve our plight, God steps in to ensure the success of our efforts. מושיע, by contrast, means that God helps a person who cannot help himself. "Salvation" is necessary when a person is in a situation from which he cannot extricate himself independently, with his own capabilities. We mention עוזר first, before מושיע, because the normal state of affairs is God "helping" us when we help ourselves. It is only when we've reached our limits, when we've come to the point where our strengths are insufficient, that God steps in to grant "salvation".

We cannot sit back idly and expect God to provide our needs and solve our problems. God first waits for us to do all we can to help ourselves, and then He steps in to do the rest, to complete the part of the job which we cannot complete ourselves.

The Torah tells in the Book of Bamidbar (Chapter 3) of the census taken of the Levite tribe. Unlike the rest of the nation, of whom only the adults were counted, the *Leviyim* were counted from the age of thirty days. Rashi (Bamidbar 3:16), citing the Midrash, relates that Moshe asked God how he would conduct this census. After all, it would be improper for him to walk into every tent to inquire about the number of infants and small children. God answered him, "You do yours, and then I'll do Mine". Moshe was to stand outside each Levite tent, and God would inform him the number of people in each household.

The obvious question arises, if it was necessary in any event for God to prophetically convey the information to Moshe, then why did Moshe have to go to each tent? For that matter, why did he have to conduct a census at all? Why couldn't God simply speak to him and tell him the number of *Leviyim*?

The answer lies in God's comment to Moshe: "You do yours, and then I'll do mine". God comes onto the scene to fulfill His role only after we have done ours. God would not allow Moshe to stay at home and just hear the number through prophecy. Rather, He commanded Moshe to do whatever he could through natural means, to go up to the doorstep of every tent, and then, when he could go no further, God would arrive to complete the process.

Earlier in the Torah, in the Book of Bereshit (15:5), we read that God instructed Abraham Abinu to count the stars, and added, "so shall your offspring be". This is commonly understood to mean that

Abraham's descendants, the Jewish people, would be as numerous as the stars in the heavens. As we know, however, this is far from being the case. Our nation has many remarkable strengths, but large numbers isn't one of them; in fact, we rank among the smallest nations on earth. Rav Meir Shapiro of Lublin therefore suggested an entirely different interpretation of God's promise. God instructed Abraham to count all the stars in the heavens – clearly an impossible task for even the most gifted mathematician. The Midrash relates that God lifted Abraham above the heavens, from where he was able to see all the stars and count them accurately. Once Abraham counted all he could, God intervened to enable him to complete the job.

This, Rav Shapiro suggested, is the promise of "so shall your offspring be". God promised Abraham that He will forever grant "salvation" to his descendants after they have exerted themselves to the furthest extent. Just as He helped Abraham perform an impossible task once he had done all that was possible, similarly, Abraham's offspring, *Am Yisrael*, will always be given special divine assistance to perform the impossible once we've done all we can.

Nobody knew this better than Rav Meir Shapiro, who introduced the idea of *Daf Yomi*, the daily program of Talmud study through which people from all backgrounds and in all professions learn a page of Gemara each day. For most, this program initially seems like an impossible task. An entire page of Gemara, seven days a week, 365 days a year without any exceptions made – on business trips, on vacation, on Tisha B'Av, on Yom Kippur, on Purim. We might wonder, who in their right mind could make such a commitment? Who would have imagined that they could keep up with this kind of program? But Rav Shapiro insisted it could be done. Wherever he went throughout the Jewish world, he told people they could do it, no matter how incredulous they were. Sure enough, many decades later, thousands upon thousands of Jews of all ages and from all backgrounds follow this program without missing a single page.

Once a person invests maximum effort, God will step in to take care of the rest. "You do yours, and then I will do Mine". This is the mantra of the Jewish people, the motto by which we have lived and through which we have survived and prospered throughout the generations.

There is, however, an additional explanation for the words עוזר and מושיע. The *Beneh Yissaschar* (Rav Zvi Elimelech Shapiro of Dinov, 1783-1841) suggests that עוזר means to help somebody before he requests help, whereas מושיע refers to assistance granted in response to a request. There are times when God comes to a person's aid even before he prays, as mentioned in the famous verse, והיה טרם יקראו ואני אענה ("It shall be that even before they call out, I shall answer" – Yeshayahu 65:24). This is the meaning of עוזר – helping before being asked. The Torah describes Hava, the first woman, as Adam's "helpmate" – עזר כנגדו. A wife is an עוזר, caring for her husband and providing his needs before he even asks. A husband does not need to ask for dinner at night; his wife prepares it for him without his asking. She does not wait for him to make requests; she fulfills his wishes even before they are expressed.

The word מושיע, by contrast, means responding to a call for a help. Describing the case of an assault upon a betrothed girl, the Torah writes (Debarim 22:27), צעקה הנערה המארסה ואין מושיע לה ("the betrothed girl cried out – but there was no one to rescue her"). The term מושיע is used in reference to answering a call to help, and thus here in the *Amidah*, too, we use this term to describe God's responding to our prayers in situations of crisis.

On this basis, the *Beneh Yissaschar* explains the verse in Tehillim (20:3), ישלח עזרך מקדש ("He sends your help from the sacred domain"). The most sacred component of a person's being is his soul, which is situated in his mind. David HaMelech here prays that God should send עזרה, "help", from the "sacred domain", when the request is still in the individual's mind and has yet to be articulated.

Before the *Amidah* of the *shaharit* service, we say, עזרת אבותינו אתה הוא מעולם, מגן ומושיע להם ולבניהם אחריהם בכל דור ודור ("You were forever a source of help for our forefathers, a shield and savior in every generation"). We first describe God as a "helper" (עזרת), and then speak of Him as a "shield and savior" (מגן ומושיע). Our forefathers were more meritorious than we, and God therefore assisted them even before they prayed. In reference to our ancestors, we describe God with the word עזרת. But "in every generation", including our own, where we are not deserving of being helped even without prayer, God is מושיע, coming to our side when we call to Him in situations of hardship.

The Gemara in Masechet Rosh Hashanah (10b-11a) records a debate between two great Sages – R' Eliezer and R' Yehoshua – as to in which month during the year was the world was created. R' Eliezer claimed that the world came into being in the month of Tishri, Month 1, whereas R' Yehoshua held that creation occurred in Nissan, Month 7. Tosafot clarifies that these two positions are actually not in disagreement with one another. Rather, according to both views, it was in Tishri when God conceived of the idea to create a world, but the creation actually took place in Nissan.

בדבר ה' שמים נעשו – The process of creation occurred through the utterances of God, as it says in Tehillim (33:6), "Heavens were made through the word of God". Therefore, R' Yehoshua, whose name relates to the concept of ישועה, salvation in response to prayer, focuses on the speech, the time when God spoke to create the world, which occurred in Nissan. R' Eliezer's name, however, is derived from the word עזר. Accordingly, he focuses his attention on the thought process, the point at which God conceived of the world in His mind, which took place in Tishri.

This definition of עזר also explains why Abraham assigned his servant Eliezer the task of selecting a wife for Yishak. Recall that when Eliezer reached the city of Aram Naharayim, he decided that he would select a girl for Yishak by requesting water from the well and seeing if the girl he requests offers to give water to both him and his camels. In other words, he wanted to see if the girl had this quality of עזר, of assisting people without waiting to hear their request. Eliezer, whose name stems from the word עזר, was uniquely suited for this role, for finding a girl who possessed this special quality.

The concept of עזר also helps explain the verse in Tehillim (145:18), קרוב ה' לכל קראיו לכל אשר יקראהו באמת ("Hashem is close to all who call to Him, to all who call to Him in truth"). This verse seems self-contradictory: it first describes God as close to "all who call to Him", without exception, but then limits this closeness to only "all who call to Him in truth". The explanation lies in the fact that the second half of the verse employs the future tense (יקראהו), and thus refers to those who "will call out in truth", but haven't yet done so. God comes to the assistance of the righteous *sadikim*, whose prayers are always recited "in truth", with sincerity and devotion, even before they pray. Everyone else, however, must pray before receiving a response. Hence, "Hashem is close to all who call to Him", but helps the *sadikim*, who serve Him with special devotion, even before they pray.

Interestingly, in the first *beracha* of the *Amidah*, we mention God's quality of עזר, helping even before He is asked, before the quality of מושיע – offering salvation in response to prayer. However, later in the *Amidah*, in the *modim* section, we reverse the sequence, describing the Almighty as האל ישועתנו ועזרתנו ("The God who is our salvation and our source of help"). The reason for this discrepancy lies in the difference between two concepts: *shebah* (praise for God) and *hoda'a* (expressing gratitude to God). When we praise God, we extol His great qualities. His quality of עוזר, of helping before He is asked, is certainly a greater quality than מושיע, and we therefore mention עוזר first in this context. In *modim*, however, we offer thanksgiving for the kindnesses that God performs. As a practical matter, God is מושיע far more often than He is עוזר; since very few people are worthy of being assisted even before they request it, God answers prayer much more commonly than helping without prayer. When we express our gratitude for God's kindness, then, we first mention the more common phenomenon of ישועתנו before the far less frequent phenomenon of עזרתנו.

The third quality with which we describe God in this passage is מגן which means "protects", or, perhaps more accurately, "shields". A warrior uses a shield to protect himself from harm; the shield deflects the weapon so that the body is unscathed. When we speak of God as a "shield", we refer to the countless times when He prevents crisis from occurring in the first place. Whereas עוזר and מושיע refer to God's intervention in situations of crisis, מגן describes God's preventative intervention, the way He steps in to keep us safe from harm. We cannot even begin to guess the number of illnesses from which we have been spared thanks to God's protection, or the number of accidents and other mishaps that have been avoided without us even knowing. Whether we realize it or not, we live our lives surrounded by God's protective "shield" that keeps us safe from all kinds of problems. He not only intervenes to extricate us from crisis, but so frequently intervenes to prevent crises from unfolding in the first place.

ברוך אתה ה' מגן אברהם
"Blessed are You, Hashem, the Shield of Abraham"

God protected our patriarch Abraham on numerous occasions, shielding him from the fires of the furnace in Ur Kasdim, and helping him and his tiny army defeat four powerful kingdoms in battle. We therefore conclude this *beracha*, which speaks of God's kindness to us and our ancestors, by describing Him as "Shield of Abraham".

The Sages (Pesahim 117b) teach that God made a special promise to Abraham that this *beracha* would conclude exclusively with his name. Although this *beracha* earlier makes mention of all three patriarchs (אלהי אברהם, אלהי יצחק, ואלהי יעקב), God promised

Abraham that לא יהיו חותמין אלא בך – "they will conclude [the *beracha*] only with you". The conclusion of the *beracha* thus mentions only God's relationship to Abraham, and not with the other patriarchs.

What deeper message might underlie this promise to Abraham, that his descendants would "conclude" specifically with his name?

Rav Eliyahu Bakshi-Doron, former Sephardic Chief Rabbi of the State of Israel, explained that the implications of this promise extend far beyond the narrow context of the *Amidah* prayer, and relate to Abraham's extraordinary commitment to *hesed*, kindness. Each of the three patriarchs embodied a certain aspect of religious life. Abraham was the bastion of *hesed*, dispensing loving-kindness to all people. Yishak specialized in the area of prayer, while Yaakob excelled in the particular area of Torah learning.

If we honestly examine the current state of *Am Yisrael*, we will immediately notice an alarming decline in the quality of our nation's prayer and Torah study. In previous generations, the prayer books in the synagogues were worn from the rivers of tears that flowed from the congregants' eyes during the prayer services. The Mishna in Masechet Berachot speaks of some especially pious Jews who would spend an hour in intensive meditation before and after each prayer service. Prayer used to be an intense, emotional experience of sincere supplication. Today, unfortunately, prayer in many synagogues has turned into a verbal car race, and the only tears being shed come from the eyes of those suffering through the 45-minute "ordeal" of *tefila*. For many, the prayer service is simply a social event, a place to chat with friends about sports, business and community news. Sadly, heartfelt prayer is becoming a lost art, a rare relic from a bygone era.

At first glance, those of us who are concerned and troubled about the sorry state of affairs may wish to take comfort in the blossoming of Torah study in our times. The number of young men spending their days in study halls devoted to full-time learning far exceeds that of previous generations, as does the number of Torah material that is published. However, while we certainly take pride in our dedicated yeshiva and kollel students and those who generously support them, we are nevertheless witnessing a sharp decline even in this area. Among the tens of thousands of yeshiva and kollel students and staff around the world, is there even one scholar on the level of the Hafetz Haim? Is there anyone alive today who has come anywhere near the league of the Ben Ish Hai? We man boast about quantity, but we lag far behind when it comes to quality.

It is only natural for concerned Jews to begin thinking, how can *Mashiah* come? How can *Am Yisrael* earn redemption if we have declined so dramatically in our commitment to prayer and learning? If *Mashiah* didn't come in the generation of the Hafetz Haim and Ben Ish Hai, why would he come in our generation?

The answer, Rav Bakshi-Doron said, lies in the third quality, the quality embodied by Abraham Abinu – *hesed*. Our generation pales in comparison to our predecessors in the areas of Torah and *tefila*, but we have far exceeded them in the area of *hesed*. Up until recently, kindness was dispensed on a one-on-one basis. A generous person would prepare a meal for somebody in need, or give him some money. Just one generation ago, Jews did not have the means to perform *hesed* on such a mass scale. Over the last generation, however, the amount of *hesed* dispensed by Jews has increased exponentially. We have organizations today that prepare literally hundreds of meals each day for people in need. We have organizations to provide virtually any need, whether it's clothing, furniture, appliances, visits to ill patients, drug and alcohol rehabilitation, or anything else a person might desperately need. There is even an organization that raises money to allow cancer patients to purchase a new insurance policy so they can afford the highest quality medical care. This is how specialized and extensive *hesed* has become in our generation. True to our calling as the heirs of Abraham Abinu, we have succeeded in bringing *hesed* to an entirely new level, building a whole industry dedicated to lending assistance to people who need it.

"They will conclude only with you". God informed Abraham that his descendants will "conclude" their exile and suffering by following his example of loving kindness. The quality through which we will be redeemed is the quality of *hesed*. We must certainly not neglect our Torah and prayers; we must work as hard as we can to improve our *tefila* and raise our standards of Torah scholarship. But the redemption will come in the merit of the vast amounts of *hesed* that is being performed on a mass scale at every moment. "Zion shall be redeemed through justice, and those who return to it, through charity" (Yeshayahu 1:27). It is through the charity we extend to one another that Jerusalem will be rebuilt and our nation will return to its previous state of glory.

This is the deeper meaning behind the conclusion of this first *beracha*. We conclude with Abraham because our nation's exile will conclude with Abraham, in the merit of the quality which he so vigorously championed and exemplified.

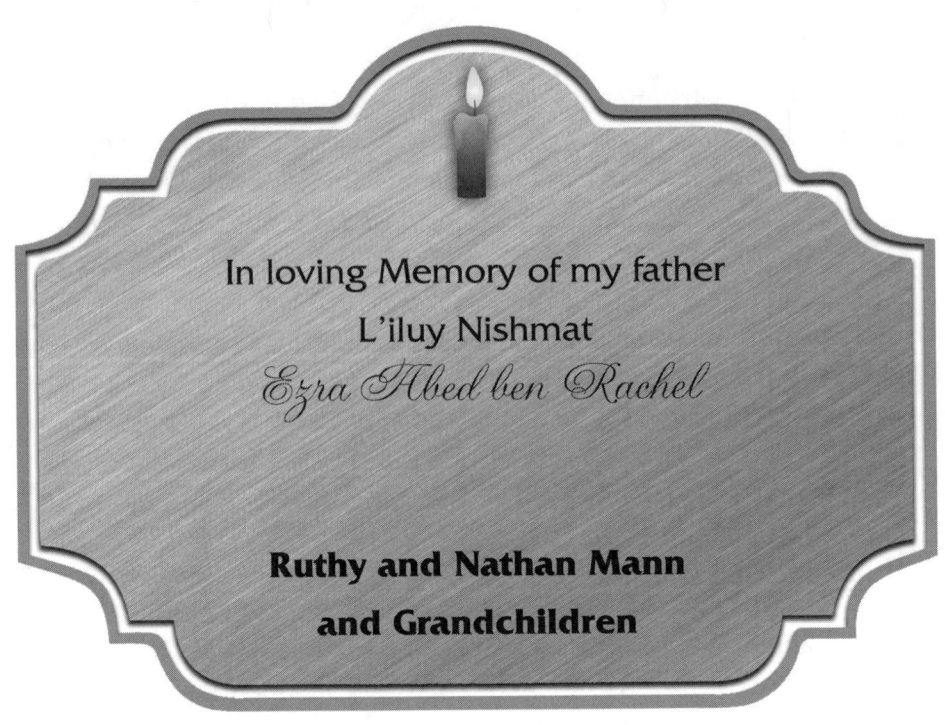

In loving Memory of my father

L'iluy Nishmat

Ezra Abed ben Rachel

Ruthy and Nathan Mann
and Grandchildren

The Second Beracha:
Geburot

Tehiyat Hametim – the Resurrection

The second *beracha* of the *Amidah*, which focuses of the unparalleled might and power of God, mentions on three occasions God's quality of "*mehayeh metim*" – His power to resurrect the dead. Why is this theme repeated three times?

The Abudarham (Rav David Abudarham of Seville, Spain, 14th century) explained that in this *beracha* we acknowledge three different manifestations of "resurrection". The first occurs each morning, when our souls are restored to us when we awaken. Sleep is a form of death, as our souls temporary leave us, and God mercifully "resurrects" us in the morning and restores our consciousness. The second manifestation of *tehiyat hametim* alluded to in this *beracha* is the "resurrection" of vegetation. When a seed is planted, it dissolves and decomposes underground. It is a miracle of nature that the seed then "comes to life" in the form of healthy, edible produce. We therefore describe God in this blessing as מכלכל חיים בחסד מחיה מתים ברחמים רבים – "He sustains life with kindness, resurrecting the dead with abundant compassion". God "sustains life" through the process of "resurrection" by allowing for the growth of vegetation, through which we are nourished. The final mention of resurrection, of course, refers to the actual resurrection of the dead that will occur during the Messianic Era.

The eventuality of resurrection constitutes one of the thirteen *ikareh emuna* – the fundamental principles of Jewish faith outlined by the Rambam. One who rejects this belief, or who does not believe that it is alluded to in the Torah has no share in the world to come. As the blessing of *geburot* places particular emphasis on God's power of *tehiyat hametim*, it is appropriate during the recitation of this *beracha* to reaffirm one's belief in this tenet.

What exactly is *tehiyat hametim*, and how will this process unfold?

The event of *tehiyat hametim* is described in great detail by Rav Shimon Aharon Agasi, one of the great rabbis of Bavel (Iraq) in his work *Yesodeh Ha'Torah*. He emphasizes that resurrection does not mean the creation of new beings. The resurrected souls will not be placed within new bodies, but rather in the exact same bodies they had occupied originally. Even if the body had decomposed and turned to earth, God will bring all the pieces of earth together and form the body anew. This applies to the bones, as well. If the bones happened to have been scattered (such as if a gravesite was plowed over), God will collect all the pieces of bone at the time of the resurrection. Even if the particles of earth or bone were scattered by the wind to different corners of the earth, or into the sea, or if they were consumed by animals or birds, this will not prevent God from rebuilding the body from the original elements from which it had been composed. Moreover, Rav Agasi writes, God will form each part of the body from the original particles that constituted the given part. The eyes, for example, will be formed from the precise same elements as they had been originally, regardless of to where those elements had been scattered.

Rav Agasi further writes that all resurrected people will arise from their graves clothed. Indeed, this is the reason why bodies are clothed in shrouds before burial. At the time of the resurrection, untold numbers of people will suddenly come to life, and there will obviously not be enough clothing available in the world for all the earth's new inhabitants. The shrouds will function as the temporary clothing for the resurrected masses until new clothing can be prepared.

The resurrection will take place only in the Land of Israel, and for this reason Rav Agasi writes that every Jew should endeavor to at least live the end of his life in the Land of Israel, so he could be buried there and experience *tehiyat hametim*. Otherwise, the body will be forced to roll in underground tunnels to the Land of Israel in order to be rejoined with its soul. However, the righteous *sadikim* buried outside Israel will experience a partial resurrection in their graves, and will be able to walk upright through underground tunnels to *Eretz Yisrael*.

The "Four Keys"

The Gemara teaches that there are four phenomena which are controlled exclusively by God. The Sages referred to these phenomena as the four "keys" which are entrusted into God's hands, and not into the hands of human beings, and the Gemara found verses from Tanach that verify God's exclusive dominion over these areas. The first of these "keys" is rainfall. Human beings cannot make it rain, or predict accurately or with certainty when and how much rain will fall. The Gemara infers this precept from the verse in Debarim (28:12), "Hashem shall open for you His good warehouse, the heavens, to provide the rain of your land in its time..."

The second "key" is that of sustenance. As we can all attest to from personal experience, God alone controls how much a person earns and possesses. The famous verse in Tehillim (145:16) states, "You open Your hand and satiate every living creature to contentment" (פותח את ידך ומשביע לכל חי רצון), explicitly establishing God as the sole provider of our livelihood.

The key to childbirth is also entrusted solely in the hands of God, as indicated in the verse, "God remembered Rachel; God listened to her and opened her womb" (Bereshit 30:22). Nobody except God can determine when a woman will go into labor and deliver her child, and thus the "key" of childbirth, too, lies in God's exclusive domain.

The fourth and final "key" listed by the Gemara is resurrection, which quite obviously belongs only to God. Our generation has been blessed with countless medical wonders that can save and improve lives, but no drug or procedure has been found to resurrect the dead. The Gemara cites as the source of this "key" the verse in Yehezkel (37:13), "You shall know that I am Hashem when I open your graves and when I bring you from your graves, My nation".

The *Tur* (Rav Yaakob ben Asher, 1275-1349), in his discussion of the *Amidah* (Orah Haim 114), noted that these four verses cited by the Gemara as the sources for these four "keys" have a combined total of 51 words. Significantly, the *Tur* writes, this is also the number of words that comprise the second *beracha* of the *Amidah*, the blessing of *geburot*, which speaks of God's singular power. This blessing was composed with a subtle allusion to the "four keys", the clearest manifestations of God's unlimited and unparalleled might.

אתה, גבור לעולם אדני
"You are powerful, for eternity, Hashem"

As mentioned, this *beracha* speaks of the divine attribute of *gebura*, power, which closely relates to the attribute of *din*, judgment. This is why we refer to God in this blessing with the Name אדני, which relates to the word דין and thus signifies judgment, as opposed to the name of *Havaya* which refers to God's attribute of compassion.

However, the *Shela Ha'kadosh* (Rav Yeshayahu Horowitz, 1565-1630) notes that the "judgment" spoken of in this *beracha* differs from ordinary divine judgment. The judgment in this *beracha* is what the *Shela* calls גבורה מתוקה, or "sweet judgment". This means that the judgment is directed not against us, but rather against the Angel of Death. Indeed, as discussed at length above, this blessing places particular emphasis on the resurrection of the dead. God's "power" is most prominently manifest and displayed in the ultimate elimination of death, as prophesied by Yeshayahu (25:8), "בלע המות לנצח ומחה אדני ה' דמעה מעל כל פנים" ("He shall permanently devour death; and the Lord God shall eliminate tears from every face"). This *beracha* thus naturally focuses on God's power of *tehiyat hametim*, His final "triumph", as it were, over the Angel of Death, and this is the "judgment" alluded to by the Divine Name of אדני.

There is a grammatical irregularity in this clause which might, at first glance seem like nothing more than a trivial curiosity, but in truth sheds light upon the deeper meaning and significance of this passage. A basic rule in Hebrew grammar establishes that the letters ב,ג,ד,כ,פ,ת receive a *dagesh*, a dot, when they appear in the beginning of a word, except when the previous word ends with one of the following letters – א,ה,ו,י. The second word of the *beracha* of *geburot* is *gibor*, which, of course, begins with the letter ג. The previous word, אתה, ends with the letter ה, and we would therefore expect for the ג of *gibor* to appear without a *dagesh*, in light of the aforementioned rule. However, the Sages who composed the *Amidah* nevertheless chose, for some reason, to add a *dagesh* in the ג of *gibor*.

The *dagesh* has direct ramifications regarding the proper pronunciation of this letter. Sephardic custom distinguishes between the pronunciation of a ג that has a *dagesh* and that of a ג without a *dagesh*. When a ג has a *dagesh*, we pronounce like the letter "g" in

English (as in "give"). Without a *dagesh*, however, the ג is pronounced as a guttural sound, similar to the modern Israeli pronunciation of the letter ר.

The obvious question arises, why did the authors of the *Amidah* deviate from standard grammatical procedure, and include a *dagesh* in the ג of *gibor*?

The answer stems from a corollary to the aforementioned rule of ב,ג,ד,כ,פ,ת. Namely, if there is a period, comma, or other kind of pause between the word beginning with one of these letters and the previous word, then the letter receives a *dagesh* regardless of the previous word's final letter. Since the word appears after a pause, we ignore the previous word in determining the status of the first letter of the word. Evidently, the authors of the *Amidah* intended to make a pause in between the words אתה and גבור, and this accounts for the *dagesh* in the ג of *gibor*.

In other words, we must read this phrase as follows: "*Ata – gibor le'olam*" ("You – are mighty forever"). We emphasize that only God possesses eternal might. Human beings may be powerful for a certain period of time, but eventually they age and their strength diminishes. God, however, is *gibor le'olam*; His power is everlasting and does not wane with time.

There is also another reason why the ג in *gibor* appears with a *dagesh*. The first letters of this clause – אתה גבור לעולם אדני – spell א.ג.ל.א, which is one of the Names of God. This Name relates to the word אגאל, which means "I shall redeem", and thus refers specifically to God's capacity to bring redemption. This Name is embedded within the first clause of this section of the *Amidah* because this *beracha* emphasizes God's power of resurrection, which will be manifest at the time of the final redemption. The Biblical source of this Divine Name is a series of four verses in the Book of Bereshit (49:8-11), in the context of Yaakob Abinu's blessing to his fourth son, Yehuda. The first letters of the first four verses of Yehuda's blessing spell this Divine Name:

1) אתה יודוך אחיך (This verse begins with the name "Yehuda", as Yaakov called to his son before beginning the blessing, but the actual text of the *beracha* begins with the word אתה.)

2) גור אריה יהודה

3) לא יסור שבט מיהודה

4) אוסרי לגפן עירה

The Davidic dynasty, from which the Messianic King will descend, emerged from the tribe of Yehuda, and therefore the Torah alludes to the Divine Name of א.ג.ל.א, which refers to attribute of redemption, in the context of the blessings to Yehuda.

This easily explains why the letter ג in the word *gibor* receives a *dagesh*. This letter represents the letter ג in the Divine Name of א.ג.ל.א, and thus corresponds to the letter ג at the beginning of the verse גור אריה יהודה. Since this letter refers to the first letter of a verse, it receives a *dagesh* as though there were no words preceding it. The letter ג in *gibor* does not merely begin this word, but also signifies the verse גור אריה יהודה, and it therefore is given a *dagesh* in accordance with the rule requiring a *dagesh* anytime a ג begins a new sentence.

משיב הרוח ומוריד הגשם
"He blows the wind and brings down the rain"

During the winter months, the primary season of rainfall, we insert this passage to give praise to God for providing us with rain. We give praise as well for the winds, because wind is indispensable for rainfall. The ocean waters evaporate and then condense in the skies over the sea, forming clouds. Once the clouds are filled with water, the water falls down to the ground. If not for the winds that blow the clouds over land, the rain would simply fall back into the ocean, and thus provide no benefit for people. The winds are critical for bringing the clouds to the inhabited regions, where the rain is needed. The Gemara in Masechet Ta'anit (3b) therefore comments, "Just as the world cannot exist without Israel, similarly, the world cannot exist without winds". Winds are also necessary to clear the air from impurities, and to spread pollen among the plants, thereby ensuring the ongoing process of vegetation.

But this phrase – משיב הרוח ומוריד הגשם – perhaps refers not only to God's providing rainfall, but also His providing Torah. Our Sages (Debarim Rabbah 7:3) often compare Torah with water, as both are indispensable for human life on earth. God blows the "ru'ah", He infuses the world with spirituality, which enables us to then receive the "rain", the Torah from the heavens.

Indeed, there exists a close connection exists between rain and Torah, two special gifts bestowed upon us from the heavens.

The Gemara in Masechet Hulin (139b) raises the question of where in the Torah we may find an allusion to Moshe Rabbenu, and it responds that such an allusion appears in Parashat Bereshit. When God saw that mankind had become evil during the generation of the flood, He bemoaned their state of sinfulness, and observed, "בשגם הוא בשר" ("insofar as they are mere flesh" – Bereshit 6:3). The word בשגם in this verse has the same numerical value as the name "Moshe" (345), and this verse thus alludes to Moshe Rabbenu.

Why does the Gemara search for an allusion to Moshe – who is, of course, mentioned many times throughout the Torah – and why does it point specifically to this verse?

A number of scholars explained that Moshe Rabbenu's soul originates from the time of the flood, and in fact, Noah himself had the potential to be Moshe. The association between Noah and Moshe is expressed in the fact that both had experiences in a *teba*. Noah lived in a *teba* (ark) during the flood, and Moshe was placed in a small *teba* as an infant when his mother tried to hide him from the Egyptian authorities. Noah, whose soul was connected to that of Moshe, could have been the one to bring the Torah down from the heavens to the earth. However, as he and his generation were unworthy of the Torah, the descent of the Torah was replaced by the descent of floodwaters. Instead of a forty-day period of the Torah's transmission from God to man, the world experienced instead a forty-day period of floodwaters falling from the heaven to the earth. The "flood" of spirituality that was intended to overrun the earth was transformed into a "flood" of physical matter – rain.

For this reason, the Midrash relates that at the time of *Matan Torah*, as God prepared to give the Torah to *Beneh Yisrael*, the nations of the world frantically approached their prophet, Bilam, asking if God was going to flood the earth. Bilam clarified that God was not bringing a flood, but was rather transmitting the Torah to *Beneh Yisrael*. The gentile nations were correct in sensing the onset of a flood. But God transformed the physical waters into the spiritual waters. Instead of sending an actual deluge, God "flooded" the earth with spirituality – משיב הרוח ומוריד הגשם. He blew the "winds" of *kedusha* into the world and brought down the spiritual "rain", filling the earth with holiness.

In this second *beracha* of the *Amidah*, we express our gratitude not only for rainfall itself, but also for the Torah, which guarantees the world's spiritual sustenance, much like rain guarantees the world's physical sustenance.

מכלכל חיים בחסד
"He sustains life with kindness"

The verb כלכל refers to the provision of a person's basic, elementary needs. For example, in the Book of Bereshit, the Torah uses this verb in reference to Yosef's supporting his brothers during the drought years (ויכלכל יוסף את־אביו ואת־אחיו – Bereshit 47:12). Clearly, under the conditions of that time, he could not provide them with luxuries, but he rather ensured the provision of their basic needs. Sometimes, God grants a person only what he and his family need to live, but not enough for comfort and luxury. We must understand that even this is done בחסד, as an act of kindness. God does not wish for us to receive our full reward in this world, and so He at times chooses to deny us wealth, providing only our basic necessities, so that we will receive our full reward in the next world.

This phrase may also be understood to mean that God "sustains life" through the kindness that people perform. The Hafetz Haim writes that if a person is involved in גמילות חסדים, in performing acts of kindness for other people, then God accepts his prayers and grants him success and prosperity. Thus, God "sustains life through kindness" – in the merit of the acts of kindness which people perform.

מחיה מתים ברחמים רבים
"He resurrects the dead with abundant mercy"

The resurrection that will occur in the times of *Mashiah* can take place only with "abundant mercy". According to the standard of God's strict judgment, most people will be undeserving of having their life restored. But God will judge the deceased mercifully so that they merit the great miracle of *tehiyat hametim*.

Furthermore, tradition teaches us that even as the deceased body decomposes, the shrouds worn by the deceased remain intact throughout the years, so that they will be usable at the time of resurrection. After *tehiyat hametim*, people will need their shrouds as clothing until sufficient clothing is produced for all the newly resurrected people. It is therefore an expression of divine compassion that God maintains the shrouds throughout the years after death.

סומך נופלים
"He supports those who fall"

Though we rarely notice it, let alone contemplate it, God implanted a mechanism in the ear to help us maintain our sense of equilibrium, so that we don't feel dizzy and we can regain our balance when we trip. This gift, which we usually take for granted, is the way we are "supported" when we fall, enabling us to easily regain our balance if we stumble.

Additionally, this phrase may also refer to the support God provides to those who continually "fall" in the spiritual sense. People sometimes find themselves caught in the agonizing cycle of sin, repentance, and sin; though they make a sincere commitment to improve and avoid the mistakes of the past, they fall back into sin soon after repenting. These situations could easily lead a person to despair and depression. We must remember that God is סומך נופלים, He supports those who continually fall. As many times as a person falls, God will always catch him so that he does not fall completely. Just as a parent will pick up a toddler each time he falls, no matter how many times this occurs, so will the Almighty help to lift us back up each time we fall. He always affords us the opportunity of *teshuba*, no matter how many times we have stumbled. God never gives up on us – so we may never give up on ourselves.

ורופא חולים
"and heals the sick"

While reciting the words ורופא חולים in this *beracha*, one should have in mind the ill patients whom he knows. The *Beneh Yissaschar* writes that often, when a person submits a request to God, the *mekatregim* – the prosecuting angels – begin raising valid questions about the petitioner, or about the person for whom the petition is submitted. They examine the conduct of the supplicant, noting that he is likely unworthy of having his prayers answered. Or, if somebody prays on behalf of his friend, the angels might object, questioning the friend's merits. This allows them to hijack the prayers before their reach the heavens, so they cannot have the desired effect.

This cannot happen when a person speaks only words of praise. If a person simply praises God for His power of healing, without articulating a specific request, then the prosecuting angels cannot interfere. Therefore, here in the second blessing of the *Amidah*, when we praise God who "heals the sick", it is advisable to think in one's mind ill patients in need of God's mercy.

ומתיר אסורים
"and released the imprisoned"

This phrase can refer to several different types of "imprisonment". Firstly, it refers literally to Jews who are held in captivity. Just as God miraculously ensured Yosef's release from an Egyptian dungeon when there seemed to be little hope for his freedom, similarly, He is capable of freeing all prisoners from captivity regardless of the circumstances. Secondly, מתיר אסורים perhaps refers to the specific "imprisonment" of every fetus in the mother's womb. A fetus is, in a very real sense, trapped in the confines of the womb, and if a child remains in the womb for even an instant after it needs to exit, he will perish. One of the great and most frequent miracles of nature is the release of an infant from the mother's womb when the time comes for him to enter the world. According to some opinions, this is reason why the verse, הודו לה' כי טוב כי לעולם חסדו ("Give thanks to Hashem, for He is good, for His kindness is everlasting") is recited at a *berit mila*. A person who is freed from prison is required to recite the *birkat ha'gomel* blessing to thank God for his salvation. Since a newborn is unable to recite this blessing, the father recites the verse of הודו לה' כי טוב to thank God on his behalf.

Furthermore, God releases us from the "chains" of the evil inclination that bind each and every person. The *yeser hara* holds us all in its "prison", preventing us from serving God as we should. It is only through the Almighty's merciful assistance that we are able to free ourselves, overcoming our sinful impulses and instincts, so that we can observe the Torah.

Finally, this phrase praises God for, quite simply, granting us the ability to leave our beds in the morning. During sleep, we are immobile, as though "trapped" in our beds. The blessing of being able to awaken allows us to move, to leave the confines of our beds, and for this, too, we must give praise and express gratitude to Hashem.

ומקים אמונתו לישני עפר
"and fulfills His commitment to those who lie in the dust"

According to one interpretation, this clause refers to God's commitment to the patriarchs, who are now deceased. He promised them that He would redeem their ancestors, and we express here our firm belief that God will fulfill that promise and bring *Am Yisrael* complete salvation.

Alternatively, however, we perhaps speak here of God's promise of *tehiyat ha'metim*, His commitment to all who "lie in the dust" that they will ultimately be resurrected. Why are the deceased referred to with such an unusual term – "those who lie in the dust"? This phrase is likely based upon a similar phrase used by the prophet Yeshayahu (26:19), who foresaw the resurrection of שוכני עפר (literally, "dwellers of dust"). The Sages commented that this phrase should be read as מי שנעשה שכן לעפר בחייו – "one who became a neighbor of dust during his lifetime". The miracle of resurrection is reserved for those who spend their lives "in the dust", conducting themselves with humility. People who act with arrogance and condescension, looking down at their peers and asserting their authority, will not be worthy of having their lives restored at the time of *tehiyat ha'metim*. We thus describe God as fulfilling His commitment "to those who lie in the dust" – referring to those who act humbly and unassumingly, as though they live "in the dust".

מי כמוך בעל גבורות
"Who is like You, Master of Powers"

The term בעל גבורות is perhaps more accurately translated as "administrator of powers", or "controller of powers". God not only contains power; He exercises full control over that power. Imagine a strong, powerful man who can hurl a spear further than anybody else. Once the spear leaves his hand, he no longer exerts control over it. As strong as he is, he becomes helpless and powerless once the spear is flying through the air. Even a boxer loses control over his fist at a certain point in his thrust. God, however, exerts full control over His power at all times. He can issue a decree and then revoke it; He can begin administering punishment, and then bring it to an immediate halt. Only He is בעל גבורות, the "controller" of all powers.

ומי דומה לך מלך ממית ומחיה
"and who resembles You, the King who brings death and resurrects"

There are stories in the *Tanach* of prophets who restored life to the dead. However, although certain righteous *sadikim* are capable of resurrecting the dead, their resurrection is only temporary; any people they are able to resurrect will eventually die again, like all people. Only God has the power of everlasting resurrection, of restoring life permanently to the dead. We therefore exclaim as we conclude this blessing, "Who resembles You, the King who brings death and resurrects!"

ומצמיח ישועה
"and who brings forth salvation"

The process of salvation is described here with the verb צמח, which means "grow", and is used mainly in reference to the growth of vegetation. (צמח is the Hebrew word for "plant".) Salvation unfolds gradually, much like a plant extends slowly and unnoticeably from the ground. Just as the growth of a plant cannot be discerned from one moment to the next, or even from one day to the next, similarly, we are not necessarily able to see how each day brings us closer to our complete national salvation. But we firmly believe that our redemption is already in process, and is already "growing" and developing, one small step at a time.

ונאמן אתה להחיות מתים
"And You are trusted to resurrect the dead"

The work *Yesod Veshoresh Ha'aboda* writes that a person should recite this concluding passage with immense joy and fervor, rejoicing over the knowledge that God will, one day, resurrect all the deceased people who had ever lived and perished. One should feel intense love of God at this moment, and rejoice in this special emotional bond with his Creator.

ברוך אתה ה' מחיה המתים
"Blessed are You, Hashem, who resurrects the dead"

We speak of God as the One who "resurrects the dead", in the present sense, because He restores life to our bodies each morning when we wake up. This daily phenomenon of "resurrection" reassures us that He will also eventually resurrect those who have actually died.

נקדישך
נקדישך ונעריצך. כנועם שיח סוד שרפי קדש המשלשים לך קדושה. וכן כתוב על יד נביאך. וקרא זה אל זה ואמר:

"We shall proclaim Your sanctity and exalt You like the pleasant, secret words of the sacred *serafim*, who declare Your sanctity three times, as it is written by Your prophet: They each call to one another and say…"

The *Ben Ish Hai* (Rabbenu Yosef Haim of Baghdad, 1833-1909) writes that before a person recites נקדישך, he should think in his mind that he now fulfills the Torah command to glorify God – ונקדשתי בתוך בני ישראל ("I shall be sanctified among the Israelites" – Vayikra 22:32). The public declaration of קדוש קדוש קדוש ה' צבאות fulfills this *misva*, and one should therefore have this intention in mind as he prepares to recite נקדישך.

Besides the fulfillment of this important *misva*, there is something else that we should keep in mind when we reach this section of the prayer service:

There is perhaps no institution in Jewish practice that demonstrates God's love for *Am Yisrael* more powerfully than the recitation of נקדישך. This part of the prayer service, which we conduct at least twice each day, has become so routine that we rarely stop to think about what it says about us, about our innate potential for greatness, and about our unique relationship with the Almighty.

We know that this recitation is important. We must stand silently, with our feet together, and not make any interruptions during the recitation of נקדישך. But what exactly are we saying in this prayer?

The introductory sentence of נקדישך makes it perfectly clear what this section is all about: "We shall proclaim Your sanctity and exalt You like the pleasant, secret words of the sacred *serafim*, who declare Your sanctity three times…" Meaning, God invites us to praise Him in the same format in which He is praised by the *serafim*, one of the groups of heavenly angels. We are earthly beings – and yet, God wants to hear us praise Him the same way the angels praise Him.

Rav Levi Yitzchak of Berditchev (Poland, 1740-1810) noted how the very concept of נקדישך reflects the extent of God's love for us – and, perhaps even more importantly, His regard for us. Who are these *serafim* whom we are to join in praising the Almighty twice each day? What kind of beings are we supposed to try to resemble every time we recite נקדישך? We read about them every morning, in the *beracha* of יוצר אור which we recite before the morning *shema* prayer:

כלם אהובים, כלם ברורים, כלם גבורים, כלם קדושים, כלם עושים באימה וביראה רצון קוניהם. וכלם פותחים את פיהם בקדושה ובטהרה בשירה ובזמרה...וכלם מקבלים עליהם על מלכות שמים זה מזה. ונותנים רשות זה לזה להקדיש ליוצרם בנחת רוח, בשפה ברורה ובנעימה, קדושה כלם כאחד עונים באימה ואומרים ביראה: קדוש | קדוש קדוש ה' צבאות...

"There are all beloved [by God], they are all clear [of any wrongdoing], they are all powerful [in serving God], they are all sacred – and they all perform with awe and fear the will of their Maker. And they all open their mouths with sanctity and purity, with song and praise... And they all accept from one another the yoke of Divine Kingship, and grant permission to one another to sanctify their Maker with calmness of spirit, with clear language and with pleasantness – in unison they all declare with awe and say with fear: "Holy, holy, holy is the Lord of Hosts..."

The prayer text emphasizes the angels' credentials, as pure, loyal, beloved servants of the Almighty who unfailingly obey His will "with awe and fear". They inspire one another each day to "accept... the yoke of Divine Kingship", and together, in perfect unison, proclaim the sanctity of God at sunrise each day. How holy are these beings? The *Zohar* writes that every angel must immerse in the fiery river of Dinor 365 times before singing praise to God, and we, mere flesh and blood, are allowed, and in fact required, to join these holy beings in praising the Almighty!

What's more, it is only the highest angels that praise God with this declaration of "*Kadosh, kadosh, kadosh*" ("Holy, holy, holy"). The Gemara in Masechet Hulin (91b) writes that there are three different groups of angels, who reside on three different levels. The first group resides on the lowest level, the realm of עשיה, and they praise God by simply declaring, "*Kadosh*". The second group, which is positioned in the realm of יצירה, recite the double expression of "*Kadosh kadosh*". It is only the highest group of angels, which exist in the realm of בריאה, that praise God with the triple expression of "*kadosh, kadosh, kadosh*". It is this final and most distinguished group of angels that we join in reciting *kedusha* and giving praise to the Almighty! We are assigned the role of praising God together with the angels – and specifically with the highest and most exalted class of angels!

Would God assign us this job if He didn't think we were

worthy? If He didn't regard us as exceptional creatures?

Many of us suffer from low religious self-esteem. We find it difficult to "get into" religion because we think lowly of ourselves and our abilities. Too many people mistakenly consign themselves to lifelong mediocrity, presuming that they are unworthy or incapable of living as God's servant. God Himself thinks otherwise! He wants us to serve Him just as the ministering angels serve Him in the heavens. Can there be any greater indication of our potential, of how great we can be?

There is another critical lesson conveyed by our invitation to recite *kedusha* together with the angels. Quite simply, we cannot be "angels" in the synagogue and then "devils" outside the synagogue. If we join with the heavenly *serafim* in singing God's praises, then we must conduct ourselves at all times as holy beings, and act in a dignified manner. We must, like the angels, "accept...the yoke of Divine Kingship" by committing ourselves to strict Torah observance. God sees us as capable of rising to the stature of the angels – but we must do our part by conducting ourselves in accordance with the Divine will.

Finally, if we are to recite God's praises like the angels, then we must do so "with calmness of spirit, with clear language and with pleasantness", as they do. We must recite the words clearly, sincerely, passionately, and in a pleasant chant. This section, especially, must be chanted slowly and with intense concentration. We recite this section of the service not as human beings, but rather as the heavenly angels, and we must therefore recite it in the same fashion as the angels do.

קדוש | קדוש קדוש קדוש ה' צבאות מלא כל-הארץ כבודו
"Holy, holy, holy is the Lord of Hosts; His glory fills the entire earth"

This verse is taken from the Book of Yeshayahu (6:3), where

the prophet describes his vision of the angels – the *serafim* – giving praise to God with these words.

What does "holy" really mean? It's a word that we throw around very often, but what exactly does it mean to be קדוש, "holy"?

Rashi in the Book of Vayikra (19:2) explains that קדושה denotes "separation", separating oneself from his natural or previous state of being. For example, when a man betroths his bride, he declares that she is מקודשת to him (הרי את מקודשת לי), effectively "separating" her from all other men in the world. Every unmarried woman has a de facto state of eligibility for all men; the act of betrothal separates her from this condition, designating her specifically for the groom.

When applied to human beings, the term קדושה means separating from the physical activities with which people are normally preoccupied in order to devote oneself to spiritual pursuits. The holy person is the one who, rather than indulging in physical delights and pursuing material excess, "separates" from this natural tendency and aspires to achieve spiritual excellence.

With regard to God, the concept of קדושה assumes the precise opposite meaning: drawing away from the spiritual, heavenly realm. God, of course, is entirely spiritual, and has no physical properties. When we say that God is "holy", we mean that in His infinite humility, He "separates" from the spiritual realm to care for us here in the earthly realm. We separate from the physical domain to relate to the spiritual domain; the Almighty separates from the spiritual domain to relate to the physical domain.

This is why the verse concludes, מלא כל הארץ כבודו – "His glory fills the earth". We emphasize that God, a purely spiritual Being, fills the "earth", the physical world, separating Himself, as it were, from his natural condition of pure spirituality.

This definition of קדושה helps explain the practice to lift oneself with his feet when reciting קדוש קדוש קדוש. Just as God leaves

His heavenly realm to "fill the earth", conversely, we attempt to leave our earthly realm to attach ourselves to God. We lift ourselves up to demonstrate our desire and effort to rise above our physical qualities and become spiritual beings.

Another reason for this custom is that we seek to resemble the fiery *serafim*. A flame does not stand still; it constantly flickers. In our effort to resemble the angels, we move ourselves up and down as though we "flicker" like the fiery *serafim*.

(See below, in our discussion of the fourth *beracha*, where we present an additional meaning of the term קדוש.)

לעמתם משבחים ואומרים: ברוך כבוד ה' ממקומו

"Opposite them, [other angels] give praise and declare: Blessed is the Glory of God from His place!"

Another assembly of *serafim* stand opposite the first group, and respond to the declaration of קדוש קדוש קדוש by exclaiming, "Blessed is the Glory of God from His place". Meaning, God is the source of all blessing. These angels proclaim that God is the source of blessing "from His place", emphasizing the fact that "His place" is unknown. Nobody – not even the angels – can identify a specific location where God is located. His existence is above the confines of geometric space, and therefore even the angels are unable to speak of God as being in any particular place.

ובדברי קדשך כתוב לאמר: ימלך ה' לעולם אלהיך ציון לדר ודר הללויה

"And in the Holy Scriptures it is written: God shall reign for ever – your God, O Zion – for all generations, Halleluyah!"
(Tehillim 146:10)

Just as the angels give praise to the Almighty each morning of every day for all eternity – because God's reign is eternal – similarly, we hope to have the privilege of joining in giving praise to Hashem each and every day, forever.

Hatzlacha of

Yenon Argy and Family

The Third Beracha

אתה קדוש

אתה קדוש

"You are holy"

Earlier, in our discussion of נקדישך, we defined the term "*kedusha*" to mean separating oneself. In reference to God, as we saw, this meant that He leaves the spiritual domain of the heavens to relate to physical human beings living in the physical earth.

But God is "separate" in a different sense, as well. Namely, He is completely different and unlike anything else. God has no physical properties at all, and it is forbidden to ascribe to Him any physical properties. As we say in the *Yigdal* hymn, אין לו דמות הגוף ואינו גוף – "He does not have the image of a body, and He is not a body". The Almighty is a completely incorporeal Being.

At this stage in the *Amidah*, it is important for us to be reminded that God is "holy", separate and apart from this world. In the first two *berachot* of the *Amidah*, we speak about the kindness that God performs, how He "supports those who fall, heals those who are sick", and so on. His direct involvement in the world and in the lives of its inhabitants may give the mistaken impression that He is similar to us, that He is a physical being and this is what enables Him to relate to us and to care for our needs. We therefore proclaim at this point in the *Amidah* that God is holy, that He is fundamentally separate and distinct.

ושמך קדוש
"and Your Name is holy"

"Your Name" refers to the Torah. The Ramban writes that the entire Torah is a series of different configurations of God's Names. This is why we recite in the morning *birkat ha'Torah* blessing, ונהיה אנחנו...יודעי שמך ולומדי תורתך לשמה ("We...shall all be people who know Your Name and study Your Torah for its sake"). We pray that we should know God's Name through the study of His Torah, which encompasses the different Names of the Almighty. We thus declare that both God and His Name – the Torah – are holy. Just as God is entirely separate and distinct from all other beings, similarly, the Torah is fundamentally different and distinct from all other disciplines.

The theme of the Torah's sanctity is relevant to this *beracha* which corresponds to Yaakob Abinu, who embodied the ideal of diligence in Torah study. The Torah describes Yaakob as a יושב אהלים ("dweller of tents" – Bereshit 25:27), referring to the "tents" of Torah. Therefore, in the *beracha* corresponding to Yaakob, we make mention of the sanctity of the Torah which we study.

וקדושים בכל יום יהללוך

"and the sacred ones praise You each day"

Who are the קדושים ("holy ones") who praise God each day?

On one level, this refers to the heavenly angels, who, as we discussed earlier, praise the Almighty each day with the declaration of קדוש קדוש קדוש. They are called קדושים because they are separate and distinct from human beings, in that they have no physical properties. The fact that these holy creatures give praise to God testifies to His unique "sanctity" and distinctness. It demonstrates that He is above and separate from even the angels; there is but one Deity who is entirely different from all creatures in existence, including the angels.

Additionally, however, this refers to us, the Jewish people, who are commanded קדושים תהיו ("You shall be holy" – Vayikra 19:2). Just as God is separate and distinct from everything else in existence, and the angels are separate and distinct from all other creatures, *Am Yisrael* is separate and distinct from all other people. In a certain sense, our sanctity exceeds that of the angels. The angels' sanctity is automatic, by virtue of their inherent nature. Our sanctity, however, entails difficult struggles and hard work. It is a challenge to be a holy person; there is no challenge to be an angel. For this reason, the Sages teach that the angels do not recite *kedusha* in the heavens until the Jewish people recite *kedusha* here on earth.

Every Jew is Sacred

This description of the Jewish people's recitation of *kedusha* – וקדושים בכל יום יהללוך סלה – conveys a very powerful lesson regarding the inherently sacred quality of each and every Jew. Nowhere is it written that a non-observant Jew does not recite *kedusha*. We do not find any *siddur* that makes a note before *kedusha* stating that this section is restricted for Torah observant Jews. Even though *kedusha* must be recited by קדושים, by "holy ones", all Jews who attend a *minyan*, regardless of their level of observance, are invited and encouraged to participate in this service.

The inescapable conclusion that emerges is that all Jews are קדושים, irrespective of their current spiritual standing. There is a spark of holiness, a sacred soul that is a piece of the Almighty Himself, as it were, within each and every Jew. Just as stoves have a tiny pilot light that can be turned into a large flame, similarly, even the sinners of our nation have a small "pilot light", a tiny spark that waits to be ignited. The sanctity of *Am Yisrael* parallels the sanctity of the Almighty. His holiness is unconditional; nothing can ever make God "unholy". By extension, then, the status of קדושת ישראל is unconditional. A Jew is inherently sacred even if he sins and is far from religious observance. As the Sages famously comment (Sanhedrin 44a), ישראל אף על פי שחטא ישראל הוא ("A Jew – even though he has sinned, he is still a Jew").

This is why we must not give up on any Jew, no matter how far he is from Torah observance. When we see a Jew who does not act or dress in a way even remotely resembling a religious lifestyle, we must nevertheless see the holy spark, the spiritual potential lying beneath the surface. It so often happens that a Jew attends a Torah class or experiences a Shabbat and suddenly that spark is ignited. That single experience can inspire a person to embrace Torah observance, because the "pilot light" was burning within him all along, just waiting for someone or something to turn it into a raging flame of religious devotion.

David HaMelech says in Tehillim (37:10), ועוד מעט ואין רשע והתבוננת על מקומו ואיננו ("another little bit – and there is no wicked man; you will closely examine his place – and he's gone"). Even the sinners of our nation have a "little" place inside them where "there is no wicked man", where there is purity and sanctity. If we carefully examine their characters, we will find a place where the sinfulness is "gone", and as a result we will unearth an area of holiness. This is precisely why the Torah famously commands us to love all Jews as we love ourselves – ואהבת לרעך כמוך (Vayikra 19:18). We like ourselves despite our many mistakes and failings, because we focus our attention on our many fine qualities. Even though we occasionally err and do the wrong thing, we are justified in defining ourselves based upon the many *misvot* we perform and the admirable qualities that we possess. The Torah commands us to love our fellow Jews the same way we love ourselves – meaning, to love them because of their fine qualities despite their failings. והתבוננת על מקומו ואיננו – if we look carefully enough, we will find what to respect and admire about each and every Jew. We will identify that place of purity, that spark waiting to be ignited, and that should lead us to genuinely love and care for all Jews, regardless of their religious standing.

The Mishna in Pirke Abot (4:3) exhorts, אל תהי בז לכל אדם... שאין לך אדם שאין לו שעה... ("Do not dismiss any person...because there is no person that does not have his moment..."). On the simplest level of interpretation, this means that we should show respect to all people even if they seem lowly and unimportant, because all people have their moment when they rise to prominence. We never know how fortunes will change, and one day in the near or distant future we might need the help of somebody who today is lowly and unimpressive. Additionally, however, this Mishna teaches us never to give up on any Jew, because everyone has his "moment", his opportunity for his inner spark to be ignited. We cannot give up on non-observant Jews, because they, too, are קדושים, they are holy and have the potential to rise to spiritual greatness.

God declares through the prophet Yeshayahu (59:21): ואני זאת בריתי אותם אמר ה': רוחי אשר עליך ודברי אשר שמתי בפיך לא ימושו מפיך ומפי זרעך ומפי זרע זרעך אמר ה' מעתה ועד עולם – "And as for Me – this shall be My covenant with them", says God: "My spirit which is upon you and My words which I have placed in your mouth, shall not depart from your mouth, nor from the mouth of your children, nor from the mouths of your children's children," says God, "from now and forever". The Sages interpret this to mean that if Torah is studied in a family for three generations, then it is guaranteed to remain in that family among its descendants forever. Here, God promises that if the Torah does not depart "from your mouth, from the mouth of your offspring, or from the mouth of your offspring's offspring", then it will remain among that family's descendants "from now and forever". Tosafot clarify that this promise applies only when all three generations lived and studied Torah at the same time. But if the grandson did not learn Torah until after the grandfather's death, then the family is not guaranteed to have Torah in the family forever.

Abraham lived for fifteen years after the birth of his grandson, Yaakob. The *Sefer Hahasidim* writes that during this period, Abraham and Yaakob studied Torah 24 hours a day; even in their sleep, they somehow remained attached to Torah study. These fifteen years ensured that the Torah will forever remain among their descendants. Any descendant of Abraham, Yishak and Yaakob can acquire the Torah, provided that he takes the first step, that he shows an interest in receiving it. Every Jew has the potential for Torah greatness; it is simply a matter of igniting the spark within him.

Tradition teaches that every Jew corresponds to a letter in the Torah. This concept is alluded to in the word ישראל, which may be read as an acrostic for יש ששים רבוא אותיות לתורה ("The Torah has 600,000 letters"). The word ישראל alludes to the 600,000 letters in the Torah because each Jew corresponds to a letter. Similarly, the word ישרן, which is another name for the Jewish people, stands for יש ששים רבוא נשמות ("There are 600,000 souls"). If every Jew is represented by a letter in the Torah, then we can perhaps learn about the nature of a Jew from the halachot that apply to a Torah scroll. The Shulhan Aruch (Orah Haim 32:27) rules that if a letter from the Torah is erased, the Torah scroll is nevertheless valid, if רישומו ניכר – meaning, its form is still visible. This halacha characterizes the way we should relate to non-observant Jews. If they are still here among us, if we can still see them, then they are very much part of the Sefer Torah, part of the Jewish people, and deserving of our unconditional love and concern. They, too, are letters of the Torah, and must be treated as קדושים, holy beings.

It is told that the Hafetz Haim was once lodging at an inn and saw there a non-observant Jew. This man was dressed in messy, unbecoming clothing, wore an angry look on his face, and ate in a rude, unrefined and gluttonous manner. The Hafetz Haim approached the man and began speaking with him. Discovering that this Jew had been conscripted and served in the Russian army, the Rabbi asked him whether he still believes in God.

"Sure", the man said, "I believe in God". "Incredible!" the Hafetz Haim exclaimed. "I wish I could have your share in the next world!"

"My share in the next world?!" the man asked, puzzled. "I am not even religious. Why would a distinguished Rabbi want my share in the next world?"

"You must be very special to have served in the Russian army, spending many years in that kind of environment, and still have your faith in God intact. They took away everything from you – except your faith. I can't imagine that I would still be a believing Jew if I had gone through such an experience".

Upon hearing the sage's words, the man began weeping. Eventually, he repented and returned to religious observance.

The Hafetz Haim found that small spot of sanctity within that man. Everyone else saw a crass, unrefined person who had no connection to Torah. But the Hafetz Haim dug deep enough to see the spark of holiness which could not be extinguished even over the course of many years in the Russian army. Once that spark was identified and ignited, it was just a matter of time before this man became a righteous Jew.

When we recite the words וקדושים בכל יום יהללוך סלה, we should be reminded of this critical message, of the *kedusha* latent within each and every Jew, and of never allowing ourselves to despair from a single member of our great nation.

סלה
"forever"

We praise God in this world and will continue doing so in the next world. This phrase in the *Amidah* is taken from the famous verse in Tehillim (84:5), אשרי יושבי ביתך עוד יהללוך סלה ("Fortunate are those who dwell in Your home; they will continue praising You, forever!").

The word סלה literally means "forever", but what precisely does it denote, and how is it different from the other, more common Hebrew words for "forever"? Such as לעולם ועד?

God relates to this world both with the Name of הוי"ה, which signifies the divine attribute of kindness, and with the Name אדני, which refers to His attribute of strict justice. We cannot survive in the world if we are exposed to God's strict justice, and we must therefore ensure to combine the attribute of הוי"ה with the attribute of אדני in order to "sweeten" God's judgment. The numerical value of הוי"ה is 26, and the numerical value of אדני is 65. When we combine the two names יאהדונהי for the sake of "sweetening" the judgment, we arrive at a total of 91. This must be our intention during Berachot whenever we answer אמן – which has the numerical value of 91. We answer אמן in order to bring the attribute of הוי"ה, of kindness, into the strict justice signified by אדני.

However, the Rabbis teach that in the future, after the world's redemption, God's Name of הוי"ה will be changed to יהיה (as indicated in the famous verse, ביום ההוא יהיה ה' אחד). The letter י, which has the numerical value of ten, will come in place of the letter ו, which has the numerical value of six. The value of the combination of this name with אדני is 95 – the numerical value of סלה. Thus, when we say that we will praise God סלה, we refer to the Messianic Era, when the divine attribute of הוי"ה will be supplanted by the attribute of יהיה.

ברוך אתה ה' האל הקדוש
"Blessed are You, Hashem, the God who is holy"

The word אל signifies God's attribute of *hesed*, kindness. Normally, sanctity and kindness are at odds with one another. Holiness, as discussed, denotes separateness, whereas kindness means being concerned about and involved in somebody else's needs. God is both אל and קדוש. Despite being totally and fundamentally separate and distinct from physicality and physical beings, He nevertheless deals kindly with them and provides them with all their needs.

The expression האל הקדוש also means that God's kindness is "holy", fundamentally separate and distinct from any other form of kindness. Any kindness which we perform is necessarily limited, given the inherent limitations of human beings. We must care for our own needs, thus limiting the extent to which we can provide others with what they need. For example, all people need to sleep, and therefore nobody can dispense kindness without stop, 24 hours a day. God, however, performs kindness on a fundamentally different level. He cares for and sustains the entire universe at every moment, without ever stopping. His *hesed* is far removed from the *hesed* that even the kindest and most selfless people perform. Thus, just as God Himself is קדוש, similarly, אל, God's kindness, is also קדוש, fundamentally different from any other form of *hesed*.

In Honor of my Wife
Victoria

Steve Jemal

The Fourth Beracha
אַתָּה חוֹנֵן

The fourth *beracha* begins the middle section of the *Amidah* service, the section of בקשות, requests. After giving praise to God in the first three blessings, we now begin submitting our requests. The Sages established that the first request we submit to God in the *Amidah* is for דעת, wisdom.

Why was specifically this *beracha* chosen as the opening request of the בקשות section?

One reason for this selection of אתה חונן relates to the insert of אתה חוננתנו which we add to this *beracha* on *Mosa'eh Shabbat*. The Sages (Berachot 33a) determined that we should recite *habdala* after Shabbat not only over a cup of wine, but also during the *arbit* prayer on *Mosa'eh Shabbat*. The most appropriate place in the *Amidah* for inserting this *beracha*, the Gemara states, is the *beracha* of אתה חונן, in which we pray for wisdom. The real "*habdala*" ("distinction") is made not with our mouths, but with our minds. It is the intellect which enables us to distinguish between the sacred and the mundane, between that which is holy and that which is ordinary. Indeed, the Ben Ish Hai noted that the sequence of *habdala* follows the arrangement of a person's face, from the bottom upward: we first recite the *beracha* over wine, which we drink with our mouths, followed by the *besamim*, which we smell with our noses, and then the fire, which we see with our eyes. The last stage of the *habdala* service is the *beracha* of המבדיל, which speaks of the theme of distinction, which we do with our brains.

For this reason, אתה חונן had to be the first *beracha* of the בקשות section. *Halacha* forbids making specific weekday requests to God on Shabbat. Therefore, before we can begin submitting our requests on *Mosa'eh Shabbat*, we must first recite *habdala*. The Sages thus designated אתה חונן as the first *beracha* of the בקשות section, so that we recite *habdala* before we begin submitting our requests during the first weekday prayer after Shabbat.

Additionally, however, we begin with a request for wisdom because this is the most vital asset of all. As the Sages (Vayikrah Rabba 1:6) teach us, דעת קנית, מה חסרת? חסרת דעת, מה קנית? ("If you've acquired wisdom, what are you lacking? If you are lacking wisdom, what have you acquired?"). Wisdom and intelligence hold the keys for acquiring everything else, and without them, we can't even know what to pray for. When God informed Shelomo Hamelech that He would grant him whichever request he made, Shelomo Hamelech requested wisdom. He understood that wisdom is the key to all other blessings, that it is the most vital and valuable possession that a person could have. For good reason, then, the very first request we submit to the Almighty is a request for wisdom.

There are four areas in which we aspire – or should aspire – to reach the level of שלמה, completion and perfection. They are: אמונה שלמה (perfect faith in God), תשובה שלמה (complete repentance), גאולה שלמה (the complete redemption of the Jewish people), and רפואה שלמה (perfect health). In the first *berachot* of this middle section of the *Amidah*, we ask God to grant us these four requests. In the *beracha* of אתה חונן we ask for the wisdom we need to arrive at perfect faith, to believe in God and His Torah with complete confidence and without any doubts or ambivalence. In the two subsequent *berachot* we ask for the ability to achieve תשובה שלמה, complete repentance, the thorough cleansing of our souls and change of heart, through which we obtain complete forgiveness. We then beseech God to bring us גאולה שלמה – the complete redemption. Although God frequently intervenes to save us from our troubles, we must continue to pray and long for the day when our nation finally achieves its complete, eternal redemption. Finally, we pray for רפואה שלמה – perfect health. We ask God not only to keep us alive, but to ensure that our bodies work flawlessly, without any pain or discomfort.

The first letters of these four words (אמונה, תשובה, רפואה, גאולה) spell the word אתרג. This is why it is customary among righteous *sadikim* to use a perfect, unblemished *etrog* for the *misva* of *arba minim* on Sukkot. The *etrog* is symbolic of these four areas of life, in which we must aspire for absolute perfection. Therefore, the *etrog* itself should be perfect, such that it reflects our hopes and dreams for perfection in faith, repentance, health and our national redemption.

אתה חונן לאדם דעת
"You graciously grant knowledge to a person"

Shelomo Hamelech teaches in Mishleh (2:6), ה' יתן חכמה מפיו דעת ותבונה ("God grants wisdom; knowledge and understanding come from His mouth"). All the wisdom that we possess is a gift from the

Almighty. Every idea that comes to our minds is from God. Every Torah insight that we are able to understand is a gift from God. All our children's success in school is a gift from God, and our ability to make prudent decisions, to distinguish right from wrong and plan our course of action accordingly, is a gift from God.

Our concentration during this prayer, to a large extent, determines our level of wisdom and knowledge, our ability to succeed in our learning, our ability to make the right decisions, and our children's academic achievement. It is told of a certain Rabbi that whenever he would have difficulty understanding a comment of Tosafot, he would put the question aside until after the next prayer service. During that prayer, he would concentrate with special intensity while reciting the *beracha* of אתה חונן. Without fail, he would be able to properly understand the Tosafot when he returned to it after the prayer.

In the ברכת התורה blessing which we recite each morning, we describe God as המלמד תורה לעמו ישראל ("He who teaches Torah to His nation, Israel"). God is our teacher; it is He who infuses us with the intellectual capacity to understand, absorb, and retain the profound wisdom of the Torah (obviously, on the condition that we apply ourselves diligently to studying Torah). Likewise, all our wisdom and intelligence is granted to us by God, and we therefore petition Him three times each day to give us the wisdom we need to make the right choices and to succeed in all our endeavors.

The word חונן ("grant") refers to an undeserved gift. We must realize that God owes us nothing, certainly not wisdom. Our intelligence is a special gift which we do not deserve and have not necessarily earned, and we must recognize it as such if we want to continue receiving this precious blessing of wisdom.

ומלמד לאנוש בינה
"and teach the human being understanding"

In this clause, in contrast to the opening clause of this

beracha, we refer to people as אנוש instead of אדם, and we speak of God granting בינה ("understanding") as opposed to דעת ("knowledge"). What is the difference between God granting דעת to אדם and His granting בינה to אנוש?

One explanation is that these two clauses refer to two different types of people. The term אדם refers specifically to the *sadikim*, who are endowed with *ru'ah hakodesh* – prophetic insight. The word אנוש, by contrast, refers to ordinary people, who are not worthy of receiving דעת, but whom the Almighty nevertheless blesses with בינה, basic wisdom and intelligence.

Alternatively, the term אדם refers specifically to a person's state before he sins, whereas אנוש is used to describe the human being's condition after he transgresses. Before sin, a human being is like Adam Harishon, and is endowed with the special level of דעת. One loses this exalted stature as a result of his wrongdoing, and drops to the level of אנוש, but God mercifully grants him בינה, the intelligence to repent and work toward regaining his prior status of perfection.

Yet a third explanation is that אדם refers specifically to *Am Yisrael*. The Talmud (Yebamot 61a) cites R' Shimon bar Yohai's comment, אתם קרויים אדם ואין אומות העולם קרויים אדם – "You are called *adam*, but the nations of the world are not called *adam*". In this *beracha* we acknowledge that God has given *Am Yisrael* דעת, unique wisdom which enables us to study, understand and practice the Torah.

וחננו מאתך חכמה בינה ודעת
"Graciously grant us from yourself wisdom, understanding and knowledge"

The word חכמה ("wisdom") refers to the material one learns, the information that a person absorbs when he listens to a *shiur* or reads. After praying for חכמה, we then ask for בינה, the ability to use the knowledge we have absorbed to understand other concepts. The Sages referred to this ability as להבין דבר מתוך דבר ("understanding one thing based on another thing"). The information we have helps us reach conclusions and learn about other matters, but this requires intellectual skill, to which we refer in this *beracha* with the term בינה. Finally, we petition God for דעת, the knowledge to properly apply and implement the information in daily life. We ask for the ability to not only acquire knowledge, but also to put that knowledge to practical use each day, as we try to live our lives according to God's will.

In Memory of their Poppy

Samuel Cooper a"h

Josh and Selena Malka

The Fifth Beracha

הֲשִׁיבֵנוּ

After praying for wisdom, we proceed to the fifth *beracha* of the *Amidah*, in which we ask for the Almighty's assistance in our attempt to perform *teshuba*, to repent for our misdeeds.

The *Tur* explains the reason why the request for assistance in *teshuba* follows the prayer for wisdom. When a person acquires wisdom and insight, he begins thinking seriously about himself and his future. He takes an honest look into himself and recognizes that he will eventually depart this world and stand in judgment before God. These thoughts naturally lead one to aspire towards *teshuba*, to try to erase the mistakes of his past, and to correct his deviant behavior, so that he will earn a favorable judgment. The *Tur* cites in this context a verse from the Book of Yeshayahu (6:10) which describes how wisdom, insight, and understanding lead a person to repentance: פן יראה בעיניו ובאזניו ישמע ולבבו יבין ושב ורפא לו ("...lest he see with his eyes, listen with his ears and understand with his heart, and repent and then be cured"). When a person thinks intelligently and with sound reason, he naturally begins to contemplate his conduct and he looks to perform *teshuba*.

Teshuba Reaches the Heavens

The *Tur* also notes that this *beracha* contains fifteen words. The connection between this number and repentance stems from the Talmud's statement (Yoma 86a), גדולה תשובה שמגעת עד כסא הכבוד ("Repentance is great, for it reaches until the Heavenly Throne"). The impact of our repentance extends far beyond this world, to the Almighty's Throne, which is situated above the seven heavens. The Sages (Hagiga 13a) teach that the length of each of the seven heavens is the distance covered by 500 years of walking, and this is also the distance in between each of the seven heavens. *Teshuba* is so powerful that its impact extends fifteen times this distance – the distance of each of the seven heavens (7+), the distance between each of the heavens (7+), and the distance from the highest heaven to the Throne (1) – (7+7+1=15). The *beracha* of השיבנו contains fifteen words to allude to the remarkable power of repentance, its ability to extend fifteen realms beyond our world, directly to God's Throne.

What exactly does it mean that our *teshuba* reaches to the Heavenly Throne?

The human soul originates from underneath God's Throne. It is there where all the souls are stored, and from there is where each soul is sent down to the earth. But when the soul is sent to the earth, part of it remains there, in the heavens, underneath the Throne, and a "rope" connects the soul on earth with its half up in the heavens.

Anytime a person develops his soul, it affects the part of his soul underneath the Throne. When a person pulls one end of a rope, the person holding the other end feels a tug. Similarly, whenever a person's soul is developed and refined, it has an impact in the heavens.

When a person sins, he severs that connection between his soul and its origin; he tears the "rope" that links him to God's Throne. *Teshuba* has the effect of restoring this connection, of repairing the link between him and the heavens, enabling him to once again have impact upon the highest levels of the universe.

Teshuba and the Letter: Opening the Door

In his discussion of this *beracha*, the *Tur* also observes that it begins and ends with the letter 'ה (בתשובה, השיבנו). He explains that the numerical value of this letter is five, and thus the two instances of the letter 'ה allude to the number ten, referring to the *Aseret Yemeh Teshuba*, the ten days from Rosh Hashanah through Yom Kippur that are especially earmarked for repentance, and especially conducive for change and self-improvement.

There is, however, an additional connection between *teshuba* and the letter 'ה. The Arizal taught that this letter symbolizes repentance, because it is formed with an "opening" at the side (in the upper left). The image of the letter 'ה – a box with an opening at the side – accurately illustrates the concept of repentance. Sin has the effect of spiritually banishing a person from this world, from his presence before God. Repentance means returning and finding one's way back into God's presence. In His infinite mercy, the Almighty "opens a door" for a person, allowing him the opportunity to restore his relationship with his Creator through sincere repentance.

The Hebrew word for "repentance" is therefore תשובה, which may be read as תשוב ה' – restoring the letter 'ה. This letter is symbolic of man's relationship with God; of God opening the door to invite the individual to stand before Him, and *teshuba* means restoring this relationship through repentance.

This concept of *teshuba* is also alluded to in the verse in the Book of Vayikra (5:16), ואת אשר חטא מן הקודש ישלם ואת חמישיתו יוסף עליו ("He shall repay that which he misappropriated from the Temple treasury, and add onto it a fifth"). Beyond the plain meaning of the verse, which refers to the fine imposed on a person who misuses the property of the Temple treasury, this verse also alludes to the process of *teshuba*. Sins have a harmful effect upon the letter 'ה in God's Name. One must therefore "repay", or repair, "that which he misappropriated from the *kodesh*" – the letter of the Holy Name which He has ruined. This is done by "adding onto it a fifth" – adding the fifth letter of the alphabet, the letter 'ה, through the process of repentance.

The Arizal further noted that the letter 'ה can be written in two ways. It can be formed as a 'ד with a 'י, in which case there is a large "door" on the side, or as a 'ד with a 'ו, such that there is only a small "window" into the area of the letter. These two formations, the Arizal explained, allude to the two stages of repentance. In the first stage, the sinner must "squeeze" his way back in through a narrow "window". God opens a small opening for him, and he must work to get in, to return. Eventually, however, the penitent sinner develops and refines himself until he reaches the point where he had been prior to his wrongdoing. This second stage is symbolized by the 'ה written with a 'י, which has a large opening, indicating that God lovingly welcomes the sinner back and embraces him as He had prior to the sin.

The Ben Ish Hai insightfully noted that this process is alluded to in the famous phrase, אני לדודי ודודי לי (Shir Hashirim 6:3 - "I am for my beloved, and my beloved is for me"), the first letters of which spell the word אלול. The word דודי contains two pairs of letters: דו – which together form the first kind of 'ה – and די – which form the second type of 'ה. During Elul, the month of *teshuba*, our job is to first achieve דו, by working to "squeeze" back into our relationship with

God through the small opening He provides, and then to continue working until we reach the point of די, where we have fully regained our previous standing before the Almighty.

The divine Name of *Havaya* (י-ה-ו-ה) contains two ה's, the first of which appears after the letter י, and the other appears following the letter ו. These two ה's symbolize the two stages of *teshuba*. The first half of the divine Name (י-ה), which contains a ה together with a י, symbolizes the second level of repentance, where the "door" is wide open, so-to-speak, indicating a fully restored relationship with God. The second half of the Name (ו-ה) corresponds to the first level, the ה formed with the letter ו, alluding to a small opening through which a sinner must struggle to enter.

The Sages refer to these two stages of repentance with the terms תשובה מיראה – repentance performed out of fear of retribution – and תשובה מאהבה – repentance motivated by genuine love of God. The lower level of *teshuba*, תשובה מיראה, has only the minimal effect of achieving forgiveness, enabling the penitent sinner to avoid retribution. The higher, more exalted level of repentance, תשובה מאהבה, has the ability to actually transform a person's sins into *missvot*, into merits. When a sinner repents out of genuine love, not only is he not punished as a result of his misdeeds, but he will earn reward for them, as they are retroactively transformed into *missvot*.

The Ben Ish Hai commented that this is the reason why we commonly refer to a penitent sinner as a בעל תשובה, which literally means "the husband of repentance". If somebody "marries" *teshuba*, if he repents out of love and affection, like a groom marrying his beloved bride, then he and *teshuba* form a union capable of producing offspring – just like a husband and wife. This "offspring" is the additional merits that the individual accrues as a result of his performing תשובה מאהבה.

Protecting Oneself From the Forces of Strict Judgment

As we discussed in the "Introduction to Prayer" section, there are five letters in the Hebrew alphabet that appear differently at the end of a word – מ,נ,צ,פ,כ. (20–כ,80–פ,90–צ,50–נ,40–מ) Whenever one of these "final letters" (ם,ן,ץ,ף,ך) is written, nothing more can be added to the word. These letters thus symbolize the concept of restriction and confinement, and represent the divine attribute of justice, which follows a strict, rigid system, as opposed to the open and flexible system of divine mercy. The combined numerical value of these letters is 280, and this number thus alludes to the forces of דין, of strict, harsh justice.

Teshuba works as a shield to protect oneself from these forces of דין. It obstructs their path so that the individual can continue to enjoy the benefits of God's boundless kindness, without being subjected to strict justice.

The Ben Ish Hai noted that this quality of repentance is alluded to in the sequence of the Pesah *seder*. The first four stages of the *seder* are *kadesh, urhatz, karpas* and *yahatz*. The words *kadesh* and *urhatz* can be read as exhortations to "sanctify" and "cleanse" oneself of his wrongdoing. The word *karpas* can be divided into two parts: the middle two letters, רפ, and the outer two letters, סך. The letters רפ have the combined numerical value of 280, and the word סך means "sum" or "amount". The word *karpas* thus alludes to the sum of 280, the forces of דין that threaten a person who has committed a sin. The word *yahatz* relates to the word חציצה, "obstruction", and it alludes to the possibility of blocking the *karpas*, protecting oneself from the divine attribute of justice. Hence, the sequence of *kadesh, urhatz, karpas, yahatz* alludes to the extraordinary power of *teshuba*, the ability we have to shield ourselves from the threatening forces of justice by "sanctifying" and "cleansing" ourselves after we've acted wrongly.

השיבנו אבינו לתורתך
"Return us, our Father, to Your Torah"

Teshuba means "return", and we begin this *beracha* by asking God to "return" us to His service. Our original, natural state is one of loyalty to Torah. The Gemara comments in Masechet Nidda (30b) that every child is taught the entire Torah by an angel in the womb, and the Torah is then forgotten just before birth. This means we all begin life with a connection to Torah. Our goal and desire, for which we pray in this *beracha*, is to return to that original state of connectedness with God and the Torah.

We refer to God in this phrase as "our Father", rather than "our King", for several reasons. For one thing, we appeal to God's compassion, asking that He show us the kind of love and mercy that a parent shows to a child. Secondly, according to *halacha*, a father is able to waive the child's obligation to show him honor, whereas a king is not entitled to forego on the honor owed to him by his subjects. We remind the Almighty that as our Father, He is authorized to forego on His honor, and excuse the offenses committed against Him.

But there is also another reason why we refer to God here specifically as "our Father". We begin this *beracha* by asking God to "return us...to Your Torah". Our sins generally result from a lack of proficiency in Torah; if we knew, understood and internalized the Torah as we should, we would not violate it. We therefore ask God to teach us Torah, to help us acquire the knowledge we need to avoid mistakes in the future. For this reason, we refer to the Almighty as "our Father", because a father bears the responsibility to teach his children Torah. We turn to our "Father" and plead, "It is Your obligation to teach us, to guide us, to give us the Torah education we need! Please teach us, so that we will never sin again!"

וקרבנו מלכנו לעבודתך
"and draw us close, our King, to Your service"

Since the destruction of the *Beit Ha-mikdash*, we have been unable to achieve the level of Torah proficiency that was attainable when the Temple stood. As the verse famously states, כי מציון תצא

תורה ודבר ה' מירושלים ("For Torah shall come forth from Zion, and the word of God from Jerusalem"). The full dissemination of Torah can occur only when Jerusalem is properly built. When Jerusalem was destroyed, the level of Torah proficiency naturally declined. Today's sages do not have the ability to unearth the "seventy facets" of every word of Torah like the sages of yesteryear. We therefore beseech God to "draw us close…to Your service", to restore the service in the *Bet Hamikdash*, which will enable us to properly learn and understand the Torah at the highest level, and thereby avoid further wrongdoing.

והחזירנו בתשובה שלמה לפניך
"and bring us back before You with complete repentance"

Our goal must be to repent בתשובה שלמה, with complete repentance, out of love, rather than fear. "Complete repentance" also means that we reach the point where we would no longer succumb to temptation if we were placed in the same position in which we committed the sin originally. If a person does not repent until he is old and frail, such that he no longer experiences temptation, he is nevertheless considered as having performed *teshuba*, but this does not qualify as תשובה גמורה, the highest level of repentance for which we must aspire.

We express here our wish to repent "before You", an ambiguous phrase which lends itself to several interpretations. First, this phrase might mean that we want to perform *teshuba* before God forces it upon us through crisis and calamity. If we do not repent of our own accord, then God will compel us to repent by having troubles befall us, such that we have no choice but to turn to God. We ask God to help us perform *teshuba* "before You", before He must force it upon us.

Additionally, this means that we want our repentance to completely restore our relationship with God, to not simply achieve forgiveness, but to enable us to return to God's presence. We might draw an analogy to an ordinarily honest man who saw an apple in a fruit store, and, not having any money with him, quietly slipped it into his pocket. The shopkeeper saw what he did, and began shouting and threatening to call the police. The shoplifter immediately returned the apple and begged the store owner to forgive him, explaining that he is not a thief but succumbed in a moment of weakness. The storekeeper forgave the man and agreed not to call the police, but warned him never to step foot in his shop again.

As we stand before God in the *Amidah*, we seek to not only receive forgiveness for our wrongdoing, but also to regain the privilege of "before You", of standing and living in God's presence. We want Him to not simply forgive us, but to welcome us in His presence despite the wrongs that we have committed, as though we had never sinned.

ברוך אתה ה' הרוצה בתשובה
"Blessed are You, Hashem, who wants repentance"

This conclusion differs from the conclusions of most of the other *berachot* of the *Amidah*. In the other *berachot*, we conclude by describing God's actions, such as granting us wisdom (חונן הדעת), extending forgiveness (המרבה לסלוח), bringing redemption (גואל ישראל), healing the sick (רופא חולי עמו ישראל), and so on. Here, we speak only of what God *wants*, but not what He *does*. We describe God as desiring our repentance, but not as bringing us back through repentance.

The reason for this formulation is clear. God cannot bring us to *teshuba*; only we can do that. He can help us and provide us with sources of inspiration, but the rest is up to us. We do not ask God to give us *teshuba* the way we ask Him to give us wisdom, good health and a livelihood. Rather, we ask Him to help us in our efforts to achieve complete *teshuba*.

The story is told of a sardonic Jewish apostate who came before the Maggid of Dubna to ridicule Judaism.

"If God truly wants the Jews to repent", he said, sarcastically, "then why doesn't He make me repent!"

The Maggid responded to the challenge by telling a story of a merchant who, along the way home from a successful business trip, decided to buy his family gifts. One of the gifts he purchased was a bellows for his housekeeper, to help her light the furnace. The housekeeper was very excited about the new gadget, which she mistakenly thought was capable of igniting a flame independently. When the time came to light the fire, she took the bellows and blew it continuously in an attempt to start a fire. Of course, nothing happened, and she went to her boss to complain.

"Don't you realize", the man said, "that you first need a spark before the bellows can create a flame? The bellows cannot create a fire; all it can do it transform a spark into a large flame!"

The Maggid explained that God works the same way. He allows us the free will to decide whether or not to ignite a spark within our souls. Once we ignite the spark, if we take the first step in the direction of self-improvement, then He will then blow the spark into a raging flame of spirituality. He is, indeed, הרוצה בתשובה; He very much wants us to repent rather than languish in sin and guilt. But it is up to us to make the first step and work towards achieving teshuba, and He will then step in to help us complete the process and realize our goal of תשובה שלמה.

In Beloved Memory of
and L'iluy Nishmat

Nicole & Raymond Levy

The Sixth Beracha
סלח לנו

The *Tur* explains that after we've asked God in the fifth *beracha* to help us repent, we are then ready to ask Him for forgiveness. We are able to ask God to forgive us only after we have repented. Therefore, immediately after the *beracha* of השיבנו, when we ask for the ability to repent, we beseech God to pardon our wrongdoing.

While reciting this *beracha*, a person should think of whatever transgressions that he has committed of which he is aware. This is the point in the *Amidah* when a person should contemplate his wrongdoing and humbly beg the Almighty for forgiveness while committing himself to improve his conduct.

סלח לנו אבינו כי חטאנו
"Forgive us, our Father, for we have sinned"

The *beracha* of סלח לנו is unique in that besides presenting a request, it also describes the condition that necessitates the request. In the *beracha* of רפאנו, for example, in which we pray for health, we do not say, "Heal us, God, for we are sick". Likewise, in the *beracha* of ברך עלינו, in which we beseech God for our livelihood, we do not explain, "because we have families to feed". Here, however, as we pray for forgiveness, we specify, "כי חטאנו...כי פשענו", that we need forgiveness because we have sinned. Besides asking God for what we need, we explain why we have this need.

The reason for this is simple. In the beginning of his *Hilchot Teshuba* (2:2), the Rambam lists the specific requirements of repentance, one of which is וידוי, verbal confession. *Teshuba* requires us to verbally confess that we have transgressed, that we bear guilt. Therefore, it is not enough to simply ask God for forgiveness; we must honestly confess our guilt and explicitly acknowledge that we have acted wrongly.

מחל לנו מלכנו כי פשענו
"Pardon us, our King, for we have betrayed"

What is the precise difference between חטאנו ("we have sinned") and פשענו ("we have betrayed"), and why do we refer to God as "our Father" in the context of חטאנו, but as "our King" when we confess "פשענו"?

The term חטא denotes שגגות, inadvertent sins, whereas פשע refers specifically to intentional violations. A father normally tends to downplay his child's wrongdoing. Even if the child misbehaves intentionally, the father's natural affection and compassion for the child will lead him to view it as a חטא, as an unintentional act. He will attribute the mischief to some external factors that affected the child, such that the child cannot bear full responsibility. With respect to a king, however, the exact opposite is true. Even the slightest infraction on a king's honor, and even a minor, accidental mishap, is looked upon with severity. A king demands strict and meticulous compliance, and there is no margin of error.

God is both our Father and our King, and we therefore ask His forgiveness as both His children and His subjects. As His children, we refer to our wrongdoing as חטא, because He, as our Father, treats us compassionately and views even our intentional violations as mistakes. But as God's subjects, we must ask Him to forgive us כי פשענו, because we have grievously sinned. From the perspective of our status as God's subjects, even our minor, inadvertent mistakes are viewed as grave violations, and our confession must reflect this severity.

What is the difference between סלח ("forgive") and מחל ("pardon")? סליחה means the complete "erasure" of the sin from our accounts, whereas מחילה refers to the mere suspension of punishment. In the case of מחילה, the stain on the sinner's record remains, but practically, he escapes punishment. When it comes to our חטאים, our inadvertent sins, we have the right to ask for סליחה, that they be completely erased from our records. But we cannot make such a request with regard to our פשעים, our willful violations, for which we ask only for מחילה, that God spare us the harsh consequences of our wrongdoing.

כי אל טוב וסלח אתה
"For You are a benevolent, forgiving God"

The divine Name אל denotes God's attribute of kindness. It is only through this quality of God, His attribute of kindness, that we are able to approach Him to ask for forgiveness. Through the attribute of דין, strict justice, there is no possibility of earning a pardon for our wrongdoing. We therefore appeal specifically to the attribute of אל in our petition for atonement.

We also emphasize that God is טוב ("good" or "benevolent"). A benevolent king is one who wants his subjects to live peacefully and happily, who is not interested in executing every offender. God proclaims through the prophet Yehezkel (18:23), "החפץ אחפץ מות רשע...הלוא בשובו מדרכיו וחיה" – "Do I desire the death of a wicked man... Is it not [that I desire] his return from his ways, so that he lives?" Nobody wants us to repent and earn forgiveness more than the Almighty Himself. As we recite in the *ne'ila* prayer on Yom Kippur, אתה נותן יד לפושעים. God extends His hand to us, imploring us to take hold of it and return to Him in sincere repentance. He is טוב, a King who wants His subjects to live, and punishes them only as a last resort.

This is also why God makes repentance so accessible, well within the reach of every sinner. As Moshe Rabbenu famously exhorts in the Book of Devarim (30:11-14): לא נפלאת היא ממך ולא רחוקה היא. לא בשמים היא...ולא מעבר לים היא...כי קרוב אליך הדבר מאד בפיך ובלבבך לעשותו - "It is not beyond you, and it is not distant. It is not in the heavens...and it is not across the sea...For the matter is very close to you – in your mouth and in your heart, so that you can achieve it".

Because God wants us to repent rather than languish in sin, He ensured that *teshuba* would not be an overly demanding process. It is certainly a challenge, and oftentimes a daunting challenge, but it is always within our reach. One can never despair from repentance, because the Torah has guaranteed us that it is attainable.

ברוך אתה ה' חנון המרבה לסלוח
"Blessed are You, Hashem, the Gracious One, who offers abundant forgiveness"

The inclusion of this *beracha* in the daily *Amidah* prayer text reflects the extent of our confidence in the Almighty's compassion. There is a famous halachic rule of ספק ברכות להקל, which means that we may never recite a *beracha* if there is any question as to whether or not it is warranted. For example, in cases of a debate among the halachic authorities concerning the recitation of a *beracha* in a certain situation, we refrain from reciting the *beracha* in order to ensure that we do not recite a ברכה לבטלה (*beracha* recited in vain). Here, at the conclusion of the sixth *beracha* of the *Amidah*, we recite a *beracha* describing God's extending forgiveness. Apparently, there is no doubt in our minds whatsoever that God will forgive us in response to our sincere repentance. Were there any degree of uncertainty, we would be halachically barred from reciting such a *beracha*. The formulation of this *beracha* itself testifies to Hashem's guarantee to pardon our sins when we approach him with sincere remorse and beseech Him for forgiveness.

How are we to understand the description of God as המרבה לסלוח ("who offers abundant forgiveness")? What precisely does "abundant forgiveness" mean?

Firstly, it means that God is prepared to forgive regardless of how many times we stumble. Of course, He does not forgive sinners who repent insincerely, with the intention of repeating the sin, or those who say אחטא ואשוב ("I will sin and then repent"). However, if a person repents with sincerity and genuinely commits himself to improve, but then later regresses and repeats the sin, God will still welcome him back with open arms, so-to-speak. Even if this repeats itself countless times, Hashem is still המרבה לסלוח, and is prepared to accept sincere *teshuba*. Repentance is not a "three strikes, you're out" system. As long as an individual is sincere in his efforts to change and improve, God will not "call him out" no matter how many times he "swings and misses".

But God is מרבה לסלוח in a different sense, as well. Namely, He has provided us with many different means through which to achieve atonement. In the times of the *Bet Hamikdash*, a sinner would bring a sacrifice as part of his quest for expiation. But even in the absence of the Temple, we have many ways of earning forgiveness. Prayer, fasting and charity are all meaningful expressions of *teshuba* and effective means of arousing divine compassion. Additionally, as Rabbenu Yona discusses in *Shaareh Teshuba*, Torah study is a critical part of the process of repentance. Learning Torah purifies a person's soul the way fire purifies a non-kosher utensil. The Torah writes that utensils that had been used with non-kosher food are rendered permissible for use by exposing them to the same level of heat at which the non-kosher food was cooked. Thus, for example, as the Torah writes, כל דבר אשר יבא באש תעבירו באש וטהר ("Anything that came through fire – you shall pass through fire, and it becomes pure" – Bamidbar 31:23). A utensil that is used through direct exposure to fire must be exposed to fire for the non-kosher food particles to be expunged. By the same token, Rabbenu Yona comments, the *yeser hara*, the "fire" of sinful instinct that burns within a person, is expunged through direct exposure to the "fire" of Torah. Thus, in addition to prayer, charity, fasting and sacrifices, Torah learning is also a valuable and effective means of achieving God's forgiveness.

Since God wants us to repent, He provided us with several different opportunities for achieving this goal. There is never any excuse not to perform *teshuba*, to give up on oneself and despair from regaining God's favor. He eagerly anticipates our *teshuba*, and has ensured that each and every one of us is capable of repenting. We must all seize the opportunities He has given us, and take full advantage of His boundless compassion and standing invitation for us to return.

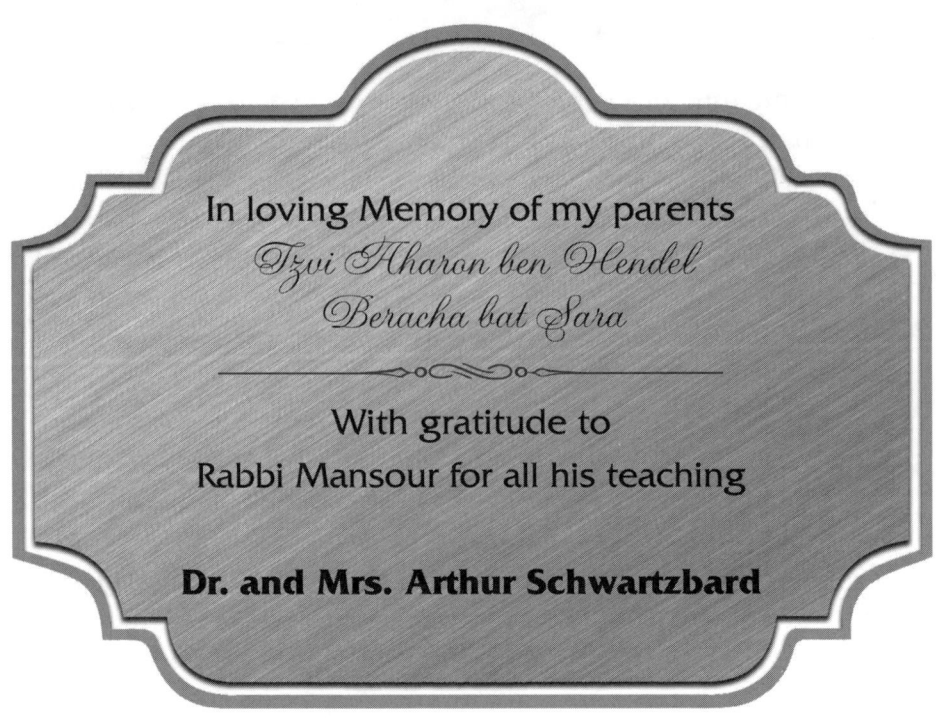

The Seventh Beracha

ראה נא בעינינו

ראה נא בעינינו וריבה ריבנו

"See, please, our suffering, and wage our battles"

Most commentators explain that this prayer, though it describes God as the "Redeemer" (כי אל גואל חזק אתה ברוך אתה ה' גואל ישראל), does not refer to the final redemption. Later in the *Amidah*, we find a number of *berachot* in which we pray for Mashiah, for the final redemption of the Jewish people. The redemption for which we pray in this seventh *beracha* of the *Amidah*, by contrast, is "redemption" from all other troubles and crises, both personal and national. We pray to God to assist us in all our struggles against adversity, in all its various forms. The opening phrase of this *beracha* – ראה נא בענינו – is based upon a verse in the Book of Debarim (26:7) that describes God's compassion for *Beneh Yisrael* during the period of Egyptian slavery: וירא את ענינו ("He saw our suffering"). We ask Hashem to take note of our hardships and alleviate our suffering, just as He alleviated the suffering of our ancestors in Egypt. When we pray that He "wage our battles" (וריבה רבנו), we refer to all our struggles, on all levels. This includes the constant struggle to secure a livelihood, our nation's ongoing struggle against anti-Semitism, and all difficulties that we confront as both a nation and as individuals

This is also the *beracha* in which we pray for the release of all Jewish captives. While reciting ראה נא בענינו, we should have in mind all Jews in captivity, such as Israeli soldiers being held by terrorists, and beseech God to free them and return them to their families.

It is interesting to note that the first letters of the first three words of this *beracha* – ראה נא בענינו – are רנ"ב (252), and it was in the 252nd year of this millennium (5252/1492) that the Jews were driven from Spain. The Sages who formulated the *Amidah* text foresaw the suffering of their descendants, and within this *beracha*, which prays for relief from our distress, they embedded a subtle allusion to one of the greatest calamities in Jewish history.

This phrase has also been understood as a specific prayer for children. Bearing children is one of the main aspirations of every Jewish man and woman, and one might have wondered why *Hazal* did not include a prayer for children in the *Amidah* prayer. Some commentators therefore claim that it is here, in the seventh *beracha*, where we offer a prayer to God to bless all Jewish couples with healthy children. The basis for this explanation is a comment in the *Haggada*, which interprets the aforementioned verse from Debarim (וירא את ענינו) as a reference to the forced separation between husbands and wives in Egypt, which precluded the possibility of procreation (זו פרישות דרך ארץ). Here, too, the prayer of ראה נא בענינו

may be understood as a prayer for fertility. Therefore, it is proper to have in mind during the recitation of this *beracha* that God should grant children to childless couples.

When we pray to God to alleviate our distress, we should also have in mind to ask that He grant us the strength and fortitude we need to withstand the troubles we face. Sometimes, for reasons which we cannot know, God determines that it is to our benefit to have to endure a certain kind of hardship. Therefore, we must pray that if it is necessary for us to confront a difficult situation, we should have the wherewithal to bear the hardship without breaking down. We pray not only to be protected from hardship, but also for the ability to retain our composure, joy and serenity when hard times come upon us.

It should be noted that the Arizal emphasized the importance of including the word נא in this phrase, as it bears profound Kabbalistic significance in this context. Although some *siddurim* omit נא from the beginning of this *beracha*, one should ensure to include it and recite ראה נא בעניינו.

ומהר לגאלנו גאלה שלמה
"and quickly grant us a complete redemption"

We acknowledge that God can bring redemption and resolve even the most difficult crises "quickly", and instantly. The Jews in the time of Mordechai and Ester were condemned to annihilation, and the next day Haman was hung on a tree and Mordechai assumed his position as viceroy. The mighty Soviet Empire crumbled practically overnight. God does not need a long time to figure out how to solve even the most difficult problems; He can have them solved instantaneously. We therefore pray that He grant us the assistance we need מהר, quickly. Similarly, we pray in the *Yamim Nora'im* prayer service, והרשעה כולה בעשן תכלה – "all wickedness shall, in its entirety, disappear like smoke". Just as a thick cloud of smoke can dissipate within minutes, our "thickest" problems can be swiftly resolved –

whether it's a problem in business, marriage, child-rearing, and so on – no matter how intractable they seem to be.

למען שמך
"for Your Name's sake"

We ask God to help us not for our own benefit, but primarily for His sake. When the Jewish people experience hardship, God's Name is disgraced; it gives the impression that He is incapable of caring for His people. The *beracha* of ראה נא בעינינו is a selfless prayer; we ask God to help us for His Name's sake, to avoid the חילול ה' (defamation of the divine Name) that results from our troubles.

If we spell the names of the letters that comprise God's Name in a format called *Miluy* – יוד, הא, ואו, הא – and add the numerical values of these words, we arrive at a total of 45. As the Arizal noted, this is the same numerical value as the word גאולה ("redemption"). When God brings redemption to the Jewish people, it allows for His Name to be established in the world. We pray for a גאולה שלמה ("complete redemption"), alluding to the "full" spelling of the word גאולה, with the letter ו (as opposed to the short spelling, גאלה), because only through this "complete" spelling do we reach the numerical of 45 which represents the manifestation of God's Name in the world.

כי אל גואל חזק אתה
"for You are a strong God who redeems"

We refer to the Almighty here as אל, the divine Name that signifies God's attribute of kindness, because it is only through this attribute that we are able to earn redemption.

God is "strong" (חזק) in the sense that He can break the rules that He himself established. For example, when *Beneh Yisrael* left Egypt and were trapped against the sea, the prosecuting angel lobbied against them before God, noting that they, like the Egyptians, had worshiped idols. Strictly speaking, then, *Beneh Yisrael* did not deserve to be miraculously saved from the Egyptians. But God nevertheless rescued *Beneh Yisrael.* Even though by His own rules they were undeserving, He, as a גואל חזק, redeemed them despite their unworthiness.

ברוך אתה ה' גואל ישראל
"Blessed are You, Hashem, who redeems Israel"

We describe God as one who "redeems" us, in the present, and not as one who will redeem us in the future. At every moment, God works to protect and save us from harm. More often than not, we are unaware of the threats to our existence, and how God shields us from danger. In this *beracha*, we acknowledge that God "redeems" us at every moment, ensuring our continued survival.

God is currently "redeeming" us in an additional sense, as well. Earlier, we noted that according to some commentators, this *beracha* is a prayer for children. The Sages (Niddah 13b) teach, אין בן דוד בא עד שתכלה כל הנשמות שבגוף ("The son of David, will not come until the *guf* is emptied of all the souls"). There is a chest in the heavens called *guf* which contains all the souls waiting to be born, and Mashiah will not arrive until all those souls have come into the earth. Thus, with every child that is born, we inch closer to the day of our final redemption. We therefore conclude this *beracha*, in which we pray for children, by noting that we move closer to our final redemption through every birth, and God should therefore bring redemption closer by granting children to childless couples.

The Eighth Beracha

רפאנו

The Gemara in Masechet Megilla (17b) comments that the Sages instituted רפאנו, the prayer for health, as the eighth *beracha* of the *Amidah* because circumcision occurs on the eighth day of a child's life. Since a child requires God's help to recover from the procedure of *berit mila*, the prayer for health was established as the eighth *beracha*, and it was instituted primarily as a prayer for the recovery of newly-circumcised children.

Why did the Sages establish the prayer for health primarily as a prayer for children who have underwent a *berit mila*? Do they need a recovery more urgently than other ill patients?

The Sages teach, אין יסורין בלא עוון – all suffering results from sin. Physical illness is the outward manifestation of an internal, spiritual illness. Millennia ago, in the times of prophecy, ill patients would consult with a prophet to determine where they needed spiritual improvement in order to restore their health. Even more recently, the Arizal was able to discern the underlying spiritual ailments that caused poor health. One story is told of a man who suffered from pain in his shoulder, and the Arizal correctly determined that the man had spoken in between the washing of *mayim aharonim* and the recitation of *birkat hamazon*, in violation of *Halacha*. The prohibition against speaking in between washing and *birkat hamazon* is formulated in halachic literature as תכף לנטילה ברכה, and the letters of the word תכף also spell the word כתף – shoulder. The Arizal thus determined that the man's shoulder injury was the result of his negligence with regard to this requirement.

Accordingly, the real "cure" for illness is *teshuba*. Once a person corrects the spiritual illness, he will naturally be cured of the resultant physical ailment. Seeking medical treatment without performing *teshuba* is akin to asking a mechanic to fix the flashing warning light in the car so it stops flashing. Stopping the flashing will not solve the problem; the mechanic must look inside the car to find the mechanical problem and then correct that problem. Similarly, illness can be cured only by searching through the "engine", the soul, to find what went wrong, and then fixing that problem. Tending only to the physical ailment is like fixing the flashing light without finding the mechanical flaw.

This is why the Sages instituted this *beracha* primarily in reference to *berit mila*. It would be inappropriate to formulate a prayer for a cure from standard illnesses, since that cure depends upon the patient's *teshuba*. In formulating the *beracha* for good health, therefore, the Sages focused on illnesses that result not from sin, but rather from a *misva*, specifically a child's condition after undergoing the painful procedure of *berit mila*.

רפאנו, ה', ונרפא

"Heal us, Hashem, so that we will be healed"

Rabbenu Bahya noted that whenever the verb ר.פ.א. ("heal") is used in reference to God, the letter פ is written in the רפויה form, meaning, without a dot (such that it is pronounced as an *f* sound). Here, for example, the words רפאנו and ונרפא, which are used in reference to God's healing, as pronounced "*refa'enu*" and "*venerafeh*". However, when this verb appears in the context of a human physician, the פ is written with a dot, as in the phrase ורפא ירפא (pronounced, "*verapo yerapeh*") used in the context of an injured person seeking medical attention (Shemot 21:19). The reason, Rabbenu Bahya explained, is that the word רפויה literally means "loose" or "easy". When God brings a cure, it is done easily and effortlessly. A human doctor, however, must exert considerable effort and hard work as he practices his trade. The different punctuations of the word thus allude to the fundamental difference between divine and human healing, as God can cure an ill patient an instant, without any effort or complex procedures.

Why do we emphasize in this prayer that once God heals us, "we will be healed"? Isn't this superfluous? Is it not obvious that once God cures us, we are cured?

The answer is that we ask God to cure us from our spiritual ills, and we will then be cured from our physical ailments. The request of רפאנו is a plea for help in healing our spiritual sickness, which will then yield the result of ונרפא – the healing of all physical maladies.

Rav Avraham, son of the Vilna Gaon, suggested a much different interpretation. In his view, the word ונרפא is part of the request, not a description of the desired result. We ask God to assist us in both stages of the healing process – רפאנו, and ונרפא. The first stage is enabling the physician to identify the illness and prescribe the proper treatment. But this must be followed by the second stage, namely, the willingness and wisdom on the part of the patient to follow the prescribed course of action. Often, a doctor gives the patient instructions for improving his health, but the patient is not able or willing to comply. We therefore pray that God helps ensure not only that we receive the proper medical guidance, but also ונרפא – that we are wise and disciplined enough to follow the sound guidance that we receive. (Later, we will see yet another explanation for this phrase, suggested by Rav Chaim of Volozhin.)

Why do we emphasize the divine Name of הוי"ה in this phrase (רפאנו ה' ונרפא)?

The Name הוי"ה, which literally means "being", signifies God's capacity to create, to bring into existence something which had not previously existed. A human physician can utilize existing medical knowledge and remedies to help his patient, but God can go even further and create new cures. We know we can turn to God even when the physicians despair. While they are limited to current medical science, God's healing powers are unlimited; He can cure any illness under any condition.

The story is told of a gravely ill patient who was told by physicians that there was no cure for his condition, and he had only three days to live. The man came to the Hazon Ish and told him the doctors' prognosis.

"Don't worry", the sage told him. "God created half the world in three days – He can certainly create a remedy in that same time span!" Sure enough, three days later the first shipment of penicillin arrived, and the man was cured.

We invoke the divine Name of הוי"ה in this prayer because it expresses our firm belief in God's power to rescue us from any illness – even when there is no current available cure.

הושיענו ונושעה
"save us, and we shall be saved"

The Hida explained this phrase as a reference to the prosecuting angel that a person creates each time he commits a sin, which threatens to cause him harm as a result of his wrongdoing. We pray that God saves us from the prosecuting angels that threaten us, and then, once we are protected from these harmful forces, we will be saved from calamity and distress.

כי תהלתנו אתה
"because our praises are to You"

Rav Chaim of Volozhin explained this phrase in light of the concept of עמו אנכי בצרה (literally, "I am with him in distress" – Tehillim 91:15), which means that God experiences suffering, as it were, when *Am Yisrael* is in distress. Just as a parent feels pain when the child suffers, similarly, in ways which we obviously cannot understand, it pains God when His children, the Jewish people, are suffering.

In our prayer for health, Rav Chaim explained, we ask God to end the suffering of ill patients for His sake, so that He, too, will stop suffering. Our primary intention is not for our own sake, and not even for the sake of the patients, but rather for the sake of the Almighty Himself, as it were. This is how Rav Chaim understood the phrase, רפאנו ה' ונרפא, which, as discussed above, appears superfluous. We plead with God to cure us, and then ונרפא – we, both ourselves and the Almighty, will be cured. The reason we make this request is כי תהלתנו אתה – our primary aspiration is to exalt God. Our main concern is not our own well-being, but rather the "well-being" of God, as it were.

Of course, this is not the intention that most of us should have while reciting this *beracha*. Rav Chaim of Volozhin achieved the spiritual stature where he prayed for "God's sake", for the purpose of alleviating the "suffering" of the Almighty. For people on our level, it suffices to have in mind simply our fervent hope and desire that God sends a speedy recovery to all ill patients who need their health restored.

והעלה ארוכה ומרפא לכל תחלואינו ולכל מכאובינו ולכל מכותינו

"and provide healing and cure for all our ailments, all our pains, and all our wounds"

The word תחלואינו refers to the common, ordinary illnesses which people occasionally suffer. Similarly, מכאובינו denotes normal aches and pains. But we also ask God to cure us from מכותינו – the injuries and illnesses which we bring upon ourselves. Many medical problems are self-inflicted, resulting from dangerous behavior, unhealthy eating, sleeping habits or insufficient exercise. We might have thought, at first glance, that we forfeit the right to ask God for good health if we cause harm to our bodies. But God's mercy extends so far that we are invited to ask Him to cure even those ailments which we have brought upon ourselves.

כי אל רופא רחמן ונאמן אתה

"for You are God, compassionate and faithful healer"

God is רחמן ("merciful") in the sense that, as mentioned, He is willing to heal even those maladies which we cause ourselves. Most physicians would not bother with a patient who neglects his health and does not take care of himself. But God patiently and mercifully cures even self-inflicted illnesses.

The word נאמן refers to consistency; a reliable person is somebody who can always be trusted to do a good job. God acts as our "healer" on a constant basis, at all times. We aren't even aware of the countless procedures being performed by our bodies at every moment of our lives, without which we would become ill, or worse. We rely on the Almighty to care for our well-being on a constant basis, at every moment, and in this sense He is a רופא נאמן – a most reliable healer.

ברוך אתה ה' רופא חולי עמו ישראל

"Blessed are You, Hashem, who heals the sick of His nation, Israel"

Why do we refer to God in this concluding blessing as the healer "of the sick of His nation, Israel"? Doesn't God heal all ill patients, regardless of their faith and nationality? Isn't He the one who cures all ailments, and not only those which affect Jews? Indeed, there have been Jews who felt offended by the text of this *beracha*, considering it exclusionary and even racist, and altered the text to suit their sensibilities.

We, of course, understand that the text of the *Amidah*, which was composed by the Men of the Great Assembly, a group of towering scholars that included several prophets, cannot be tampered with. We also believe that God undoubtedly heals both Jews and gentiles alike. In fact, the *beracha* of אשר יצר, which we recite several times a day, after each time we use the restroom, concludes by describing God as רופא כל בשר ומפליא לעשות ("who heals all flesh and performs wonders") – clearly emphasizing that He heals all human beings.

Why, then, do we describe Hashem here in the *Amidah* as רופא חולי עמו ישראל, the one who heals specifically the ill among the Jewish people?

One explanation is that this *beracha*, as mentioned above, was established primarily as a prayer on behalf of newly-circumcised infants. This prayer is thus specific to *Am Yisrael*, and we therefore refer to God here as the Healer of the Jewish people.

Furthermore, the first letters of the words רופא חולי עמו ישראל (רחע"י) have the combined numerical value of 288. The Arizal taught that there are 288 "sparks" within a person's soul, and when one of these sparks is not properly arranged within the soul, it causes illness. The text of this concluding *beracha* thus alludes to these 288 sparks which we ask Hashem to maintain in their proper arrangement to help us avoid illness. Indeed, several *siddurim* make a note that one should have this intention in mind while reciting this *beracha*.

There might also be another reason why we refer to God here as רופא חולי עמו ישראל. Undoubtedly, as mentioned, God mercifully cares for the ill patients of all nations. In this sense, He is the "doctor" of all mankind. But in a different sense, He is the "doctor" specifically of *Am Yisrael*. Most doctors work in an office and receive patients when they are ill and in need of treatment. Other doctors, however, are hired as the personal physicians of important public figures. The President of the United States, for example, has a personal doctor with whom he consults regularly, who oversees the President's health from close up, and who accompanies the President as a constant source of medical guidance. If we use the term "doctor" in the sense of a medical practitioner who tends to ill patients, God is רופא כל בשר, He is a devoted and competent "doctor" who lovingly treats all patients. But only for *Am Yisrael* does God serve as a close, personal physician, who accompanies them at all times to help them maintain good health. This unique relationship is reserved for the Jewish people, and it is in this sense that we describe the Almighty as רופא חולי עמו ישראל.

The Steipler Gaon *zs"l* offered a different explanation of this phrase. God created illness for the purpose of alerting us to spiritual ills that require our attention. When a person takes ill, he must respond by identifying the flaws in his soul that need to be corrected. Theoretically, then, only *Am Yisrael* should be affected by illness. It is only with us that God has established such a close relationship warranting a warning signal to repent. The only reason why people of other nations become sick is to avoid a *hillul Hashem*. If only Jews became sick, people would conclude that belonging to God's special nation brings a person suffering and misfortune. For this reason, it was necessary that all people – and not only the Jews – would be affected by illness.

On this basis, the Steipler Gaon explained the phrase רופא חולי עמו ישראל. Once God cures all the ill patients among the Jewish people, automatically, all people in the world will be cured. Members of other nations become ill only because Jews become ill. Therefore, when all Jews are cured, all ill patients throughout the world will be cured. We thus pray that God should cure all חולי עמו ישראל, all the patients among *Am Yisrael*, as this will have the result of eliminating illness from all mankind.

Earlier, in our discussion of the *beracha* for forgiveness (סלח לנו), we noted that the very fact that the Sages instituted that *beracha* demonstrates their confidence in God's willingness to forgive. *Halacha* strictly forbids reciting a *beracha* if there is any uncertainty as to whether it is warranted. Thus, if the Sages instructed us to recite a *beracha* describing God as "forgiving abundantly" (המרבה לסלוח), they must have known with absolute certainty that He is ready to forgive all sins.

The same is true regarding this *beracha* of רופא חולי עמו ישראל. *Hazal* instituted this *beracha* because God's healing is certain; prayers on behalf of an ill patient are indeed effective. It is therefore proper when reciting this *beracha* to have in mind one's family members or Torah scholars who have taken ill, or oneself, if he is ill. After the words ולכל מכותנו, one should add ופרט פלוני בן פלונית ("and especially so-and-so son of so-and-so"). Furthermore, when a family member is ill, Heaven forbid, and people inquire as to his well-being, one must be careful not to discourage them from praying. If he expresses too much optimism, saying things to the effect of, "He'll be ok", or "They think he's doing better", then people might be less inclined to continue praying on the patient's behalf. Prayer on behalf of the sick is immensely valuable, as evidenced by this *beracha* of the *Amidah*, and family members of an ill patient must therefore see to it that as many people pray for the patient as possible.

Finally, when we speak in this *beracha* of חולי עמו ישראל ("the sick of His nation, Israel"), we refer not only to the patients themselves, but also to their family members, friends and associates. When a person takes ill, he is not the only who suffers; those who know him and who depend on him also suffer as a result of the illness. We therefore pray that God assists all people who are affected by illness, and not only the patient.

This is also why the *misva* to visit a sick patient is commonly referred to in plural form – ביקור חולים. This obligation includes more than just paying the patient a visit, though this is certainly a central component of the *misva*. ביקור חולים entails offering assistance to everyone affected by the illness, such as giving the spouse rides to and from the hospital, running errands for the family, doing their carpool shift, and so on. Besides the anxiety and emotional distress that illness causes, it can also disrupt a family's functioning. Just as we pray to God to help everyone affected by an illness, similarly, we all bear the obligation to do our part in helping both the patient and all those around him to cope with the crisis.

The Ninth Beracha
ברך עלינו/ברכנו

The ninth *beracha*, in which we pray for our livelihood, features two different texts. The text of ברכנו is recited in the spring, summer and autumn, from Pesah until December 4th (sometimes, it is recited until December 5; in Israel, ברכנו is recited until 7 Mar-Heshvan). The text of ברך עלינו, in which pray for adequate rainfall, is recited during the rainy season.

This *beracha* is recited immediately following the prayer for health because one must be healthy before he can think about earning a living. Ill patients are too preoccupied with their illness to focus on their financial needs. In fact, many patients are in too much pain and discomfort to eat. Once a person regains his health and strength, and he sets out to earn a living, he looks to God and begs for assistance in His pursuit of an adequate livelihood.

"You shall Remember Hashem your God"

The concept underlying this prayer is that although we invest considerable work and effort in securing a livelihood, as we should, it is ultimately God who provides us with our needs. The success of our endeavors depends not on our skill and hard work, but rather on the Almighty.

It is told that the Brisker Rav once met a former student and asked him, "So, what do you do now?" The student responded by briefly describing the business he ran.

"Okay, but what are *you* doing?" the Rabbi repeated. The student, thinking that Rabbi had not heard his response, described in a louder voice the business that he ran.

"I heard you the first time", the Rabbi explained, "but you didn't answer my question. I asked you what you are doing, and you answered by telling me what Hashem is doing – giving you a livelihood through your business. What I want to know is what *you* are doing – what Torah you are learning, and what *misvot* you are involved in?"

Our success in earning a living is not our doing; it is God's work. Our achievements are in the areas of Torah and *misvot* – that success we can credit to ourselves. But our livelihood is given to us by God, after we do our part by making the effort.

Moshe Rabbenu explicitly teaches this perspective on livelihood in the Book of Debarim (8:12-18):

פן תאכל ושבעת ובתים טבים תבנה וישבת. ובקרך וצאנך ירבין וכסף וזהב ירבה לך וכל אשר לך ירבה. ורם לבבך ושכחת את ה' אלהיך... ואמרת בלבבך כחי ועצם ידי עשה לי את החיל הזה. וזכרת את ה' אלהיך כי הוא הנתן לך כח לעשות חיל...

Lest you eat and be satiated, and you build good houses and settle down, and you will have many cattle and sheep, and you will amass much silver and gold, and everything you have will be in abundance – and your heart will grow haughty, and you will forget Hashem your God…and you will say to yourself, "My strength and the power of my hand earned me all this wealth. You shall remember Hashem your God, for it is He who gives you the strength to achieve wealth…"

When *Beneh Yisrael* traveled through the wilderness, it was clear to them that they were supported by God. After all, they lived throughout this period in a place without food or water, and God supported them miraculously, providing them with manna from the heavens each morning and a supernatural well that traveled with them. But Moshe knew that once they entered the Land of Israel, built homes, developed farms and produced food through hard work and exertion, this recognition might fade. They might then credit themselves with their achievements, and overlook the fact that even when they work for their livelihood, it is Hashem "who gives you the strength to achieve wealth".

This is the great challenge of financial success: to humbly recognize that all that we have is a gift from God.

Raising Our Hands to the Heavens

One of the *misvot* which the Torah commanded in order to remind the farmer of this fundamental tenet is the obligation of *bikkurim* – to bring the first fruits that ripen to the *Bet Hamikdash*, and give them to the *kohen*. In Sefer Debarim (12:6; see Rashi), the Torah refers to *bikkurim* with the expression, תרומת ידכם, which literally means, "that which is raised by your hands". The farmer who brings *bikkurim*, the first of the fruits which he worked so tirelessly · to produce, essentially raises his hands to the heavens and declares, "My hands did not achieve this success. Everything I have came from the heavens – just like the manna!" This is the underlying message of *bikkurim*, and this is the Torah's outlook on *parnasa* (livelihood).

Each time we wash *netilat yadayim* in preparation for a meal, we raise our hands before drying them. Before we sit down to eat, we, like the farmer, raise our hands to the heavens to acknowledge that our food has been given to us by God. We remind ourselves that we cannot take the credit for the hearty meal we are about to eat, that our success is owed to the Almighty.

In fact, this message may likely lie at the heart of the *misva* of *netilat yadayim*. The Sages (see *Mishna Berura* 158:1) give two reasons for this obligation. The first is סרך תרומה, which means that *netilat yadayim* commemorates the time when the *kohanim* ate *teruma*, before which they were required to wash their hands to ensure ritual purity. The second reason for this *misva* is ידיים עסקניות הן, which literally means, "hands are busy". People's hands touch many different things over the course of their daily activity, and we must therefore wash them before eating to ensure cleanliness. But these two reasons may allude to a deeper message underlying *netilat yadayim*. We wash before eating for the purpose of תרומה, to recall the message of תרומת ידכם, of lifting our hands to the heavens and attributing our material success to God. This is necessary because ידיים עסקניות הן, our hands are "busy", working assiduously to earn a livelihood, and we might therefore come to mistakenly credit ourselves with our financial success. Before we sit down to a meal, we wash our hands and raise them, reminding ourselves that it is the Almighty who ensures the success of our hands' work.

This might also be the reason why the *kohanim* raise their hands as they recite *birkat kohanim*. They begin their blessing by praying, יברכך ה׳ וישמרך ("May Hashem bless you and protect you"), which the Sages interpret as a reference to material prosperity. The *kohanim* lift their hands to convey the message that our material blessings come from the heavens, from the Almighty, and the *kohanim* know this better than anybody else. The *kohanim* did not receive agricultural lands in *Eretz Yisrael*; they did not work to support themselves. They devoted all their time to studying and teaching Torah and serving in the *Bet Hamikdash*, and they were supported through the gifts given to them by the rest of the nation. They, more than anyone else, understood the message of תרומת ידכם, that a person's livelihood comes as a gift from heaven. They therefore lift their hands and pray that *Beneh Yisrael* be blessed by God with success and prosperity.

Appropriately, after God instructs Moshe with regard to the *misva* of *birkat kohanim*, He concludes, ואני אברכם ("and I shall bless them" – Bamidbar 6:27). The purpose of *birkat kohanim* is to lead *Beneh Yisrael* to the awareness that it is God who blesses them, who ensures the success of their endeavors so they can earn a respectable livelihood.

Faith and the Velocity of Money

Economists speak of a concept called "the velocity of money", which means that an economy is strong when money flows. If people are investing, lending, borrowing, buying and selling, an economy thrives. The market stalls when money does not flow as freely as it should, when people keep their money and refrain from buying and investing. This is how economic recession is born – when money doesn't flow. (This concept is indicated by the Hebrew word for coin – זוז – which means "move". Money, ideally, is something which "moves", constantly changing from one person to one another.)

What prevents people from spending? What is the underlying cause of this kind of financial stagnation?

The answer is that money stops moving when people are mistrusting. Lenders stop lending and shoppers stop shopping when they are anxious, when they do not trust the market, and therefore prefer to keep their cash.

This is well-known, basic economic theory. The more difficult question, however, which the economic experts are not able to answer, is, what makes people mistrusting? What causes people to become anxious and unwilling to spend or invest?

Rav Elchanan Wasserman explained that people who do not have faith in God do not have faith in other people, or in the market. The source of mistrust is the absence of trust in God. It is through faith in the Almighty that we are able to develop a feeling of trust in people and systems. Therefore, the most important solution to economic crisis is reinforced faith in God, recommitment to our belief in the Creator and His ability to care for and provide for His creatures. When people have faith in God, they will have faith towards each other, and the money will flow.

We will begin with the text recited during the summer months, and then proceed to the text recited during the rainy season.

ברכנו, ה' אלהינו בכל-מעשי ידינו
"Bless us, Hashem our God, in all our hands' work"

In ancient times, most work was done by hand, such as agriculture and craftsmanship. Although nowadays most people work with their minds, rather than with their hands, we nevertheless refer to work with the term מעשי ידינו, since working with one's hands this was the primary means of earning a living in antiquity.

The term אלוהינו refers to Providence, God's ongoing involvement in the world. We ask in this *beracha* that God should bless us with an awareness of אלוהינו, that we should always acknowledge that it is He who secures our livelihood. This phrase means that the Name of ה' אלוהינו should constantly be בכל מעשי ידינו, that it should accompany us throughout our professional life.

וברך שנתנו בטללי רצון ברכה ונדבה
"and bless our year with dews of favor, blessing and generosity"

The Sages teach us that the world cannot exist without the dew that forms on the ground in the morning. But there are different kinds of dew – that which is destructive for the produce, and that which helps the produce grow and develop healthfully. We therefore pray that God should bless us with the productive dew which the earth needs for its vegetation to grow properly.

ותהי אחריתה חיים ושבע ושלום
"it shall end with life, satiation and peace"

We pray that God should bless us with continuous prosperity that endures until the end of the year. Interestingly enough, we recite this prayer through the last day of the year – even during *minha* on Ereb Rosh Hashanah! Even if a person recites *minha* just moments before sundown on Ereb Rosh Hashanah, he prays in this *beracha* that should ensure our continued prosperity until the end of the year. This reflects our recognition of how quickly fortunes can change. It does not take long for a person to suddenly lose his livelihood or to suddenly earn a large fortune; often, this happens overnight, or even in an instant. Indeed, several years back, just before Rosh Hashanah 5769 (2008), the markets crashed, triggering a devastating economic collapse that caused thousands of people around the world to lose their jobs and savings. We therefore pray to God to bless us throughout the year, to the last moment.

In this phrase we also ask God for שבע, for the ability to feel satiated and content with what we have. No matter how much a person has, it does not help him if he does not feel content. It is told that Rockefeller would frequently say, "I just need a little more to feel content". Contentment is a precious blessing, as it allows a person to experience wealth even if he has little. King Shelomo teaches in the Book of Mishleh (13:25), צדיק אכל לשבע נפשו ובטן רשעים תחסר ("A righteous man eats to his soul's content, but the belly of the wicked is lacking"). The *sadikim* are blessed with the experience of satiation, whereas the wicked constantly feel that they lacking. We thus pray not only for a livelihood, but also for שבע, for the great blessing of contentment.

Why do we add here prayer for שלום, peace? Doesn't the *Amidah* conclude with a separate *beracha* in which we pray for peace? Why do we mention it here, as well?

In times of prosperity, it is easier for people to get along with one another peacefully. People feel content, happy and secure, and are not looking to fight or argue. Most conflicts in the home and in businesses erupt in times of financial hardship. When money is tight, people are anxious and irritable, and thus more prone to quarreling. It therefore says in Tehillim (147:14), השם גבולך שלום חלב חטים ישביעך – "who makes peace in your [Zion's] borders, who satiates you with the fat of wheat". An abundance of grain and wealth allows for peace and tranquility. We therefore plead to God to bless us with financial security for the sake of שלום, so that peace and harmony will prevail in our homes, communities and businesses.

כשנים הטובות לברכה
"like the good years, for blessing"

Rabbi Abraham, the son of the Vilna Gaon, commented that the word שנה ("year") relates to the Hebrew word לשנות – "to change". Things can drastically change over the course of a year. Even though God decrees our economic condition when the year begins, on Rosh Hashanah and Yom Kippur, it can still change during the year based on our conduct and prayers. We pray that any changes that occur during the year should be כשנים הטובות לברכה – positive changes, that our conditions should only improve and continue to improve, and not, Heaven forbid, deteriorate.

In the winter, we recite the following text:

ברך עלינו, ה' אלהינו, את השנה הזאת, ואת-כל-מיני תבואתה לטובה
"Bless for us, Hashem our God, this year and all its grain for goodness"

Why do we ask that God should bless the year "for goodness"? Isn't God's blessing by definition "good"? Why must we add this word?

For one thing, rainfall is only beneficial if it rains in the places where it is needed. If it rains over the ocean or in uninhabited regions, this does not help our water supply. We therefore beseech God to bless us with rainfall לטובה, in a manner that is useful and beneficial for our economy.

Additionally, wealth can often be a curse. As noted earlier, the *kohanim* bless the people, יברכך ה' וישמרך – "God shall bless you and protect you". This means that God should "bless" us with wealth and then "protect" us from ourselves. Wealth has the power to corrupt its owners, and make them arrogant, greedy and domineering. We pray that God should bless us with prosperity and success לברכה – in a manner that results in blessing, and not, God forbid, the opposite.

Furthermore, God will occasionally bless an unworthy person with worldly success in order to diminish from his reward in the next world, as it says in Tehillim (92:7), ...בפרוח רשעים כמו עשב. להשמדם עדי עד ("When the wicked sprout like grass...to destroy them for eternity"). Our prayer in this *beracha* is that God should bless us with material success לטובה, for goodness, without diminishing from the goodness that awaits us in the World to Come.

Another possibility is that we ask God to bless us with wealth so that we can use it לטובה, for goodness, for charitable purposes.

Finally, we pray that our wealth will not arouse other people's jealousy and cause them to initiate hostilities against us. Jealousy is a powerful emotion that drives people to irrational and destructive behavior, and thus success could very swiftly turn into a source of pain and anguish if it attracts attention and evokes envy. Kuwait, a small country in the Persian Gulf, is blessed with vast oil reserves, and this priceless treasure aroused the jealousy of its larger and more powerful neighbor, Iraq, which in 1990 launched an attack and conquered the country. We ask God that our material blessings shall always be לטובה, a source of peace and tranquility, and not the cause of conflict and hostility.

ותן טל ומטר לברכה על כל-פני האדמה

"and grant dew and rain for blessing on the surface of the land"

In the beginning of the *Amidah*, in the *geburot* section, we refer to rain with the term *geshem* (משיב הרוח ומוריד הגשם), whereas here we use the term *matar*. The word *geshem* denotes light rain showers, while *matar* refers to strong, steady rainstorms. We begin reciting משיב הרוח ומוריד הגשם immediately after Sukkot, when the עולי רגל, the Jews who had come to Jerusalem for the festival, are still making their way back home. We therefore pray only for גשם, light rain, so they will be able to travel easily and comfortably. In the winter, however, when we need rain for our water needs and the pilgrims have already reached their homes, we ask for מטר – significant rainfall.

How are we to understand the phrase על פני האדמה – "on the surface of the land"?

The Vilna Gaon explained this term as referring specifically to *Eretz Yisrael*. The earth, like human beings, has a *neshama*, a soul, a source of spiritual energy. In the human being, the soul is situated in the brain, and it is seen on the individual's face. Each person's face is unique, reflecting the uniqueness of his soul. When we meet a *sadik*, we can usually detect a certain shine or radiance emanating from the face, which is the result of the special power and force of their *neshama*. The earth is called אדמה, which relates to the word אדם (human being), because it, like a person, has a "soul". This spiritual quality of the earth is concentrated in the Land of Israel, which is thus called the פני האדמה – the "face of the earth". Therefore, when we pray for rain על פני האדמה, we ask that rain fall on the Land of Israel, the spiritual center of the earth.

ורוח פני תבל ושבע את העולם כלו מטובך

"and fill the face of the world, and satiate the entire earth with Your goodness"

After we pray for rain in *Eretz Yisrael*, we then ask God to provide adequate rainfall for the entire earth.

ומלא ידינו מברכתיך ומעושר מתנות ידיך

"and fill our hands with Your blessings and with the wealth of the gift of Your hand"

Each of these two phrases (ומלא ידינו מברכותיך and ומעושר מתנת ידיך) has three words which begin with the letters מ, י, מ – which spell the word מים ("water").

It is customary before reciting the Friday night *kiddush* to pour three drops of water in the cup of wine. When one pours these drops, he should have in mind the words, ומלא ידינו מברכותיך. The three drops of water symbolize our hopes that God should "fill our hands" with His blessings of rainfall and general prosperity.

Dedicated to

Rabbi and Mrs. Nechemia Drillman

Aryeh and Dena Loketch

The Tenth Beracha

תקע בשופר גדול

This *beracha* is the first blessing in the *Amidah* in which we pray for the Messianic Era. Specifically, we pray in this *beracha* for the ingathering of the Jewish exiles to the Land of Israel, which will be heralded by the sounding of the "great *shofar*".

We begin praying for the Messianic Era after the *beracha* of ברך עלינו, in which we pray for our livelihood, in order to show that we are not asking for Mashiah only for selfish reasons. Often, people begin longing for Mashiah when the markets crash, or when their business starts to decline. They pray for Mashiah to extricate them from their financial woes and guarantee their financial security. But this is not why we should be praying for Mashiah. We should want Mashiah for the Almighty's sake, to bring an end to evil and to publicize Divine Kingship throughout the world to all mankind. Therefore, it is only after we pray for our livelihood that we are ready to sincerely beseech God to bring the Messianic Era, when all people on earth will recognize His authority and dominion over the world.

Can Mashiah Come in Our Time?

A more fundamental question comes to mind when we consider the concept of praying for Mashiah. Our generation pales in comparison to previous generations of Jews. The spiritual level of the Jewish people today comes nowhere close to its level at the time of the Arizal and the Bet Yosef, for example. The level of their generation was far lower than that of the period of the *Rishonim*, the period of Rashi, the *Ba'aleh Hatosafot*, the Rambam and the Ramban. Extending back even further, the *Ge'onim*, like Rav Saadia Gaon, were much greater than the *Rishonim*, and the Talmudic scholars were on a much higher level than the *Ge'onim*.

We can only wonder, then, if Mashiah did not come during those periods, in the time of these towering, righteous personalities, how could we expect it to come in our generation? What right do we have to ask God to bring us Mashiah, as though our generation is more deserving of Mashiah than the Sages of the Talmud? The answer emerges from a comment made by the Arizal to his famous disciple, Rav Haim Vital. The Arizal said that God values the *misvot* performed in our generation more than those of past generations. The Jewish people have endured centuries of harsh exile, and have been subjected to influences and pressures that are in opposition to Torah. The centuries we have spent in exile have made it progressively more difficult for us to observe the Torah. Between the persecutions and the negative influences of the surrounding culture, maintaining the standards demanded by the Torah has become increasingly more difficult. Therefore, the *misvot* that we perform – even if they come nowhere near the level of past generations – carry far more weight than the *misvot* of our ancestors. It goes without saying that we are on a much lower level of Torah observance than the Talmudic Sages. But, living many centuries after them, we face much greater spiritual challenges, and God takes these challenges into account when evaluating our *misvot*, such that we can, indeed, be worthy of Mashiah's long-awaited arrival.

The Arizal made these comments in 16th-century Safed. Even then, he felt that God affords greater weight to the *misvot* performed at that time due to the pressures and challenges that the Jews confronted. Certainly, then, in our generation, which is characterized by decadence and immorality, when Torah observance is far more difficult than it ever was, every *misva* that we observe is cherished and valued by God, and helps us become deserving of redemption.

This concept underlies an enigmatic passage in the Midrash, which tells that R' Yossi ben Kisma's students asked him when Mashiah will arrive. He answered by citing a verse from Sefer Vayikra, from the beginning of Parashat Sav (6:2): זאת תורת העולה היא העולה על מוקדה על המזבח כל הלילה עד הבוקר ("This is the law of the burnt-offering – it is the burnt-offering which remains on the fire upon the altar throughout the night, until morning"). How does this verse answer the question of when Mashiah will come?

This verse speaks of the *misva* of הקטר חלבין ואימורין, the burning of leftover meat and fat on the altar during the night. Sacrifices were brought during the daytime hours, but any part of the sacrifices that was not consumed on the altar during the day was left on the altar to burn during the night. The Rabbis teach us that this procedure, of burning the leftover sacrificial meat, corresponds to Yaakov Abinu. The morning *tamid* (daily) sacrifice corresponds to Abraham, who established the morning *shaharit* prayer, the afternoon *tamid* corresponds to Yishak, the first to pray *minha*, and the nighttime burning of the leftover meat and fat corresponds to Yaakob, who initiated the *arbit* prayer service.

The ritual of הקטר חלבין ואימורין was the least dignified stage of the sacrificial process. The primary עבודה (service) was performed during the day, and it was only the leftovers that remained on the altar to be consumed during the nighttime. Why would this stage of the process specifically represent Yaakob, whom the Sages describe as בחיר האבות – the "choicest" of the three patriarchs?

The reason has to do with the symbolic meaning of the nighttime period, when the leftover meat and fats were burned on the altar. Nighttime symbolizes the darkness and suffering of exile, and for this reason the nighttime ritual in the *Bet Hamikdash* corresponds specifically to Yaakob Abinu, who spent 22 years in exile with Laban, and endured hardship and anguish for much of his life. In the *Mikdash*, the less prestigious and dignified עבודה is performed at night to symbolize the lower quality of Torah observance during the exile. The nighttime is followed by the morning sun – just as the exile is followed by the light of redemption. Although during exile our Torah observance is on a lower level, represented by the הקטר חלבין ואימורין, God affords immense value to the *misvot* we perform in exile, to our ability to withstand the unique pressures and challenges of our current situation, and thus renders us worthy of redemption.

This was R' Yossi ben Kisma's response to his students. Mashiah will come after the period of הקטר חלבין ואימורין, after a time when the Jews will perform *misvot* on a low, unimpressive level – because God will cherish those *misvot* which are performed in spite of immense spiritual challenges.

The answer, then, is that yes, indeed, we can earn Mashiah in our generation – and specifically in our generation. As Torah observance becomes increasingly more challenging, our *misvot* assume greater worth and value, rendering us deserving of Mashiah.

תקע בשופר גדול לחרותנו

"Sound the great *shofar* to herald our freedom"

To what *shofar* does this prayer refer, and what kind of "freedom" are we praying for in this *beracha*?

If we analyze the different situations in which we find the sounding of a *shofar*, we will discover that the *shofar* is something far more powerful than just an instrument, or a sound-making device. The *shofar* was sounded at the time of *Matan Torah* (Shemot 19:16), when *Beneh Yisrael* were cured of the "spiritual poison" injected by the snake when Adam and Hava committed their sin. The Sages teach us that the snake contaminated Adam and Hava and all their descendants by injecting within them spiritual impurities. When *Beneh Yisrael* stood at Mount Sinai and heard the sounding of the *shofar*, they were cleansed of this spiritual contamination. Unfortunately, these impurities returned as a result of the sin of the golden calf. King David alludes to this effect of *Matan Torah* when he writes, "אמרתי אלהים אתם ובני עליון כלכם, אכן כאדם תמותון" "I had said, 'You are Godlike – you are all higher beings'; alas, you shall die like human beings" (Tehillim 82:6). *Beneh Yisrael* were "Godlike" after *Matan Torah*, when they were purged of their *yeser hara* and sinful tendencies. Tragically, this status was lost as a result of the golden calf, and the people once again became like ordinary human beings.

The *shofar* thus has the capacity to free and release people from their "captivity". Just as the *shofar* is sounded at the onset of the *yobel* (jubilee year) to announce the freeing of servants (Vayikra 25:9), similarly, the *shofar* sounded at Mount Sinai freed *Beneh Yisrael* from their "servitude" to their base instincts and sinful inclinations. This is why the Torah describes the words of the *Aseret Hadibberot* (Ten Commandments) as being "חרות על הלוחות" "*harut al ha'luhot*" ("engraved upon the tablets" – Shemot 32:16). Our Sages teach that the word "*harut*" can also be read as "*herut*", or "freedom", alluding to the fact that a person achieves "freedom" through Torah. When *Beneh Yisrael* received the Torah, they heard the *shofar* which freed them from their spiritual captivity and granted them the freedom to reach great spiritual heights.

This is also why we sound the *shofar* on Rosh Hashanah, as part of our process of repentance. The *shofar* sounds have an effect similar to the effect of the *shofar* at Mount Sinai, purging us of our spiritual contamination so that we can repent and regain our state of purity.

We also find the *shofar* playing a vital role in the conquest of the Canaanite city of Jericho, as related in the Book of Yehoshua (chapter 6). When *Benei Yisrael* sounded the *shofar* around Jericho, the city walls crumbled, allowing the Israelite soldiers to enter and capture the city. The holy books explain that the walls of Jericho were sustained by the forces of spiritual impurity generated by the sins and corruption inside the city. The *shofar* sound extricated these forces from the walls, such that they could no longer stand. The walls thus collapsed and *Benei Yisrael* easily conquered the city.

For the same reason, some communities observe a custom to sound a *shofar* after a funeral. When a person passes away, harmful spiritual forces seek to attach themselves to the deceased's body. We therefore sound the *shofar* in an effort to chase away these harmful spirits and thereby protect the deceased.

In this *beracha*, we ask God to sound the "great *shofar*", the *shofar* that will bring us permanent freedom from everything that constrains us. We pray for freedom not only from the enemy nations, but also from our internal enemies, from our desires, our addictions, our evil inclinations, the *Satan*, from all the impure forces within us. But unlike the *shofar* that was sounded at *Matan Torah*, and the *shofar* that is sounded each year in the synagogue on Rosh Hashanah, which had or has only a temporary effect, we ask God to sound the "great *shofar*", the *shofar* which will permanently free us from our spiritual "captivity".

Furthermore, we ask for the sounding of the "great *shofar*" which will release every exile and every community of Jews from its particular form of "captivity". Every exile has its unique challenges, its unique manifestation of the *yeser hara*. In Soviet Russia, for example, the Jews' test was to remain faithful to their tradition despite anti-Semitic persecution. For American Jews, the greatest *yeser hara* is the lure of assimilation and the attraction of the indulgent lifestyle that characterizes contemporary American culture. The "great *shofar*" will rescue all Jews, wherever they are and whatever their situation, from their *yeser hara*, from the particular impure forces that threaten them.

In addition to its ability to bring us true freedom, the *shofar* sound also has the effect of mitigating God's attribute of strict justice. The verse says in Tehillim (47:6), עלה אלקים בתרועה – "*Elokim* rises through the *teru'a* sound". The sound of the *shofar* causes אלהים, the divine attribute of justice, to "rise" and give way to the attribute of mercy. Through the sounding of the *shofar*, God leaves the throne of justice, as it were, and sits on the throne of mercy.

This effect of the *shofar* is alluded to in the Hebrew word שופר. The middle two letters – ו,פ – have a combined numerical value of 86, which is the same numerical value as the word א-ל-ה-י-ם – the divine Name that signifies the attribute of justice. If we spell out the names of the letters the spell the word א-ל-ה-י-ם (אלף-למד-הא-יוד-מם), the combined numerical value becomes 300, represented by the letter ש at the beginning of the word שופר. Finally, if we calculate the numerical value of the word א-ל-ה-י-ם according to the "*hadraga*" system (א-אל-אלה-אלהי-אלהים), we arrive at 200, the value of the letter ר at the end of the word שופר. Thus, the sound of the *shofar* has the capacity to neutralize the power of all three kinds of דינים (harsh judgments) that can be issued against us. We pray to God to sound the great *shofar* that will usher in a period of unbridled mercy and compassion upon us and the Jewish people, through which we will be deserving of the in-gathering of the exiles and the final redemption.

What *shofar* will God sound at the time of the final redemption?

The holy books teach that this *shofar* will be the right horn of the ram which Abraham Abinu offered as a sacrifice in place of his son after the *akeda* (Bereshit 22:13). The left horn was the *shofar* sounded when our ancestors received the Torah at Mount Sinai, and the right horn is the *shofar* that will be sounded to herald the final redemption.

The first letters of the first five words of this *beracha* (תקע בשופר גדול לחרותנו ושא) spell the word בגלות ("in exile"), and thus allude to our hopes for our release from exile. The Hebrew word גלות ("exile") stems from the word לגלות, which means "to reveal" or "to disclose". God sent us into exile and scattered us throughout the world in order for us to "reveal" His presence in every location, at every place on earth. Whenever we study Torah or perform a *misva* in a given location, we fulfill the purpose of the גלות, by revealing God at that spot.

ושא נס לקבץ גליותינו
"and raise a banner to gather our exiles"

We pray in this *beracha* first for the sounding of the *shofar* (תקע בשופר גדול) and then for the raising of the "banner" to gather the exiles (ושא נס). However, in the Book of Yeshayahu (18:3), the prophet foresees the opposite sequence: כל ישבי תבל ושכני ארץ כנשא נס הרים תראו וכתקע שופר תשמעו ("All residents of earth and dwellers of the land – when the banner is raised upon the hills, you shall see, and when the *shofar* is sounded, you shall hear"). From this verse, it appears that the banners will first be raised, before the sounding of the great *shofar*.

The commentaries reconcile the text of this *beracha* with Yeshayahu's prophecy based upon the phenomenon of thunder and lightning. The thunder occurs first, and it generates the lightning. However, we see the lightning first because light travels faster than sound. Similarly, the sounding of the great *shofar* at the time of the redemption will occur before – and will in fact cause – the raising of the banner signifying our freedom. We therefore pray first for the sounding of the *shofar*, followed by the raising of the banner. Yeshayahu, however, describes what people will experience at that time, and he therefore first mentions the raising of the banner, which will be seen before the sounding of the *shofar*, because light travels more swiftly than sound.

וקבצנו יחד מארבע כנפות הארץ לארצנו
"and gather us together from the four corners of the earth to our land"

In the phrase יחד מארבע כנפות, the second, third and fourth letters of these three words, respectively, are חֶ-בֶ-ו, which comprise one of the Names of God. This Name is alluded to in a verse in the Book of Iyob (20:15), חיל בלע ויקאנו ("It swallowed power, and it expels it"), the first letters of which spell ח-ב-ו. As a result of a person's sins – particularly sins involving one's *zera*, his seed – the forces of impurity "swallow", or capture, his *kedusha*, his sacred qualities. We ask God to force the Satan to "expel" our *kedusha* and return it back to us. As discussed earlier, this is one of the functions served by the sounding of the *shofar*, and, therefore, this divine Name – ח-ב-ו – which alludes to this process of retrieving our status of *kedusha* from the forces of impurity, is embedded within this *beracha*.

We emphasize our desire to be gathered יחד, together, referring to the ingathering of the entire Jewish nation. As opposed to the redemption from the Babylonian exile, when only a percentage of the Jews returned to *Eretz Yisrael*, we long for the complete קיבוץ גליות, the time when all Jews around the world will be returned to their homeland, יחד – all together.

ברוך אתה ה' מקבץ נדחי עמו ישראל

"Blessed are You, Hashem, who gathers the distant ones of His nation, Israel"

The third letters of the words מקבץ נדחי עמו spell the divine Name of ח-ב-ו, and thus form yet another allusion to this Name, which, as discussed above, closely relates to the theme of the *shofar* sounding at the time of the redemption.

This phrase also alludes to the concept mentioned in the holy books that the Jewish people earn redemption through prayer, fasting and charity – as represented by the words קול ("voice" – prayer), צום ("fast"), ממון ("money" – charity), all three of which have the numerical value of 136. The final letters of the last four words of this *beracha* – מקבץ נדחי עמו ישראל – are צ,י,ו,ל, which have a combined numerical value of 136. This alludes to the fact that in order to earn redemption, we must commit ourselves to these three *misvot* – prayer, fasting and charity.

We refer to God here as gathering עמו ישראל – "His nation, Israel". The Gemara teaches in Masechet Sanhedrin (98a) that Mashiah will come either in a generation which is entirely righteous, or in a generation that is entirely sinful. Our hope, of course, is to earn redemption through our *misvot*, and not ever to reach the point when we are entirely sinful and God will be compelled, so-to-speak, to redeem us. We therefore pray that God should bring redemption to "His nation, Israel", to a Jewish nation that is devoted to Him, to His Torah. Through our involvement in קול, צום, ממון, we become deserving of redemption, and Mashiah can come to "His nation", to a Jewish people committed and faithful to the Almighty.

L'iluy Nishmat

Shlomo Joseph ben Regina
Lea bat Sarah
Regina bat Miriam
Fortuna bat Regina

The Eleventh Beracha

הָשִׁיבָה שׁוֹפְטֵינוּ

In this *beracha* we pray for the restoration of our judges, of the *Sanhedrin*, the highest body of Rabbinic authority which existed during the time of the *Bet Hamikdash*. In the absence of the *Sanhedrin*, the laws of the Torah cannot be properly enforced. Although we still, *baruch Hashem*, have competent Rabbis, scholarly halachic decisors, and even rabbinical courts, we do not have judges with the power and authority to enforce Torah law. The *Sanhedrin*'s absence undermines the quality of our collective religious observance, as violators are not deterred by the court's authority.

A famous incident that occurred in the 15th century demonstrates the importance that our *Hachamim* afforded to the institution of the *Sanhedrin*. There was a prominent Rabbi named Rav Yaakov Beirav, or the Mahari Beirav. He was born in Spain eighteen years before the expulsion, and after leaving Spain he traveled to several different cities, serving as the Chief Rabbi in Fez, Morocco and spending time in Cairo, Damascus and Jerusalem. Ultimately, he settled in Safed, and was one of the towering Rabbinic figures in Safed during the period of the Arizal. He was the teacher of Maran, Rav Yosef Karo, author of the *Shulhan Aruch*.

The Mahari Beirav decided that the time had come to reinstitute the *semicha*, the formal ordination of scholars from Rabbi to student that had begun with Moshe's ordination of Yehoshua, and was discontinued during the period of Roman persecution. Once the status of *semicha* was reinstated, a *Sanhedrin* could be appointed and the Jewish people would once again benefit from this body of Rabbinic leadership. The Rambam held that the *semicha* would be reinstated before the arrival of Mashiah, and the Mahari Beirav thus thought that he could hasten the coming of Mashiah by reinstating the *semicha*. He assembled twenty-five righteous scholars from the city of Safed, and they conferred *semicha* upon him, thus investing him with the authority to confer *semicha* upon others.

The decision to reinstate *semicha* triggered considerable controversy. The leading opponent to this movement was the Maharlbach – Rav Levi Ben Habib of Jerusalem (son of Rav Yaakob Ben Habib, author of the *En Yaakob*). Although the Maharlbach and the Mahari Beirav had befriended one another when they lived together in Jerusalem, the Maharlbach vehemently denounced the reinstating of *semicha*, and penned a long treatise explaining his position. Ultimately, the Maharlbach's position prevailed, and the *semicha* was discontinued.

Although the movement did not succeed, it demonstrates just how important the *Sanhedrin* was in the eyes of the great Rabbis, and how desperately they longed for its return.

A story is told of the Rebbe of Apta that highlights one of the many advantages of the Torah's legal system over the secular court system. A man once came to the Rebbe and ridiculed the concept of a *din Torah*, of bringing legal disputes to a Rabbi.

"I don't understand", the man said. "The secular legal system is so much better, so much more thorough. Each side hires a lawyer or a team of lawyers who study the case and present all sides of the argument. The court deliberates, presents its decision, and then the losing party can appeal to a higher court. By the time this process is finished, every possible angle is explored. Isn't this better than two people coming to the Rabbi, presenting their case, and then hearing the Rabbi's decision – a process that lasts all of an hour or so?"

The Rebbe answered by drawing an analogy to a wolf that slyly snatched a sheep from a herd when the shepherd wasn't looking. As the wolf sat down and prepared to eat its game, the lion, king of the jungle, came and demanded that it be given the sheep. The wolf, of course, refused, claiming that it seized the sheep and it therefore has exclusive rights to it.

Finally, the lion and the wolf agreed to go to the fox and ask it to settle their dispute. The fox heard both sides of the argument, and decided that they have no choice but to split the meat, and that it, the fox, should oversee the division to make sure that it is done precisely and equitably, and so, the fox placed some of the meat on one side of the scale and the rest on the other side. Seeing that the sides were not quite even, the fox ate some meat from the heavier side. This resulted in the other side becoming heavier, so the fox ate from that other side in an attempt to balance the scales. This repeated itself several times, until, finally, the fox had eaten all the meat, and there was no longer anything for the lion and the wolf to argue about.

The Rebbe explained that this is the problem with the secular court system. Very often, by the time the two parties finish with lawyer fees and court fees, they come to the realization that they would have been far better just leaving the matter alone. The battle over money itself costs so much money that it is often not worth the expense, time or aggravation. In the *Bet Din* system, the parties get clear, Torah guidance based on established halachic principles, without the hassle and costs that are often endured by going through the secular courts.

We therefore yearn for the restoration of the ancient Jewish court system, when halachic guidance was easily accessible for all questions, problems and disputes that could possibly arise.

השיבה שופטינו כבראשונה, ויועצינו כבתחלה
"Return our judges as [we had] originally, and our advisors, as [we had] in the beginning"

When we had the judges of the Sanhedrin, we also had access to "advisors", to scholars and leaders who could offer sound guidance and counsel on any matter. Good advice is something that all people crave, but is so difficult to come by in our time. Many people flock to self-proclaimed Kabbalists and fortune-tellers in a desperate attempt to receive guidance for life's vexing problems and the difficult decisions they need to make. We pray for the restoration of the Sanhedrin not only so that the laws of the Torah will once again be enforced, but also so that we can all regain access to the keen, sound guidance of truly wise scholars.

The word ויועצינו ("and our advisors") also alludes to the performance of the Torah's commands. The numerical value of this word is 248 – the number of the Torah's *misvot aseh* (positive commands). In our current condition, we are unable to properly observe all the *mitzvot*. The restoration of the *Sanhedrin* will give us the ability to once again fulfill all of God's commands, as we had done millennia ago. The 248 *misvot* are alluded to in the word ויועצינו because the best advice we can receive is to observe the *misvot*. More often than not, when we approach a Rabbi for advice in handling life's challenges, the advice is to recommit ourselves to the Torah's laws, to Shabbat, *kashrut*, family purity and so on. This is the most beneficial piece of advice that one could ever receive.

When we ask for the return of our judges כבראשונה, like we had originally, we refer to the first monarchs – David HaMelech and Shelomo HaMelech. The word כבראשונה is a variation of the word ראש, head, and refers to the first of something which continues – just like the head is the beginning of the body, which extends downward from the head. David HaMelech and Shelomo HaMelech were the ראש of the Jewish dynasty, which continued for many centuries after them and will be reinstated in the Messianic Era. The prayer for the return of our advisors כבתחילה refers to Moshe and Aharon, who were our first leaders, but were not monarchs and did not establish a permanent line of rulers.

והסר ממנו יגון ואנחה
"and remove from us distress and anguish"

Effective judicial and law enforcement systems help us all avoid "distress and anguish". They deter potential criminals and ensure that victims receive due compensation. In short, the restoration of the *Sanhedrin* will solve the difficult problems that plague our society and usher in a period of peace and contentment among people.

More generally, in this *beracha* we ask God to save us from any kind of emotional distress. If a person suffers from depression or anxiety, this is the section of the *Amidah* in which he should have in mind his request that God cure him from his emotional distress. Emotional disorders, like physical ailments, require the Almighty's help to be overcome, and this is the *beracha* in which we ask God to eliminate these disorders from the Jewish people.

Depression is one of the most dangerous weapons of the *yeser hara*. When a person feels depressed, he lacks the emotional energy to confront the challenges of Torah observances. He figures he has nothing to lose, and is thus capable of committing the most grievous offenses. Depression is therefore an illness which we must do everything we can to avoid and combat, and in this *beracha* we beseech the Almighty to assist us in this critical endeavor.

ומלך עלינו מהרה אתה ה' לבדך
"and soon reign over us, You, Hashem, alone"

Unfortunately, we all find ourselves under the "reign" of many different "kings". Our impulses, our desires, peer pressure, the natural lust for wealth – all these forces exert control over us and demand that we do certain things and act in certain ways. This is not how it is supposed to be. God is supposed to reign over us "alone", without any "competition" from other forces, pressures or people. As we pray for the restoration of Rabbinic authority, we also pray for the time when we will be freed from all kinds of "authority" and be subject only to the will of the King of kings, as determined by the *Sanhedrin*.

בחסד וברחמים, בצדק ובמשפט
"with kindness, compassion, righteousness and justice"

The combination of בצדק ובמשפט ("righteousness and justice") refers to המתקת הדינים, the "sweetening" of the harsh judgment. Even when we are deserving of punishment, God, in His infinite mercy, will lighten the sentence issued against us.

ברוך אתה ה' מלך אוהב צדקה ומשפט
"Blessed are You, Hashem, who loves righteousness and justice"

The Hafetz Haim noted that "righteousness" and "justice" do not really go together; in fact, these are two opposing attitudes. צדקה means treating people more kindly than they deserve, whereas משפט refers to the strict letter of the law. What do we mean when we say that God loves both צדקה and משפט?

The Hafetz Haim explained that God "loves" when we react with צדקה to the way people treat us, while acting with משפט in our behavior towards others. When our friends, family members or neighbors treat us with less respect than we feel we deserve, or if they act in a way that we feel is not 100 percent fair, we should respond with צדקה – forgivingly. It is wrong to fuss and fret over every infraction, every small offense that is committed against us. But in the way we treat our peers, we must exercise the quality of משפט, strict justice. Even though we react tolerantly and forgivingly, this does not mean we should demand the same of our peers. We are to act with utmost care and concern for the feelings and property of other people, even while we show flexibility and tolerance when it comes to our property and honor.

This was the outstanding quality of Abraham Abinu, which he sought to transmit to his progeny, as the verse states in the Book of Bereshit (18:19): כי ידעתיו למען אשר יצוה את בניו ואת ביתו אחריו ושמרו דרך ה' לעשות צדקה ומשפט ("I know about him [Abraham] that he will instruct his sons and daughters after him to observe the ways of God, to perform righteousness and justice"). Abraham embodied this unique quality which God "loves" – the quality of tolerating other people's wrongs while ensuring not to act wrongfully toward them.

The Mishna in Pirkeh Abot (5:5) lists the ten miracles that occurred in the *Bet Hamikdash*, including the phenomenon of עומדים צפופים ומשתחוים רווחים – the people stood crowded together in the Temple courtyard, yet when they bowed, there was ample space for all of them. One Rabbi commented that there is a deeper message underlying the Mishna's comment. When people are עומדים, when they stand firmly in place, without showing flexibility and tolerance, then צפופים – life becomes "crowded" and uncomfortable. But when people are משתחוים, when they "bow" and are willing to give in for the sake of peace, then רווחים – the world is a far more pleasant and comfortable place to live.

God loves this combination of צדקה ומשפט, and this combination must therefore characterize our approach toward interpersonal relations. Such an approach will help make the world a much better place, a place where people live and work together happily, without constant strife and friction.

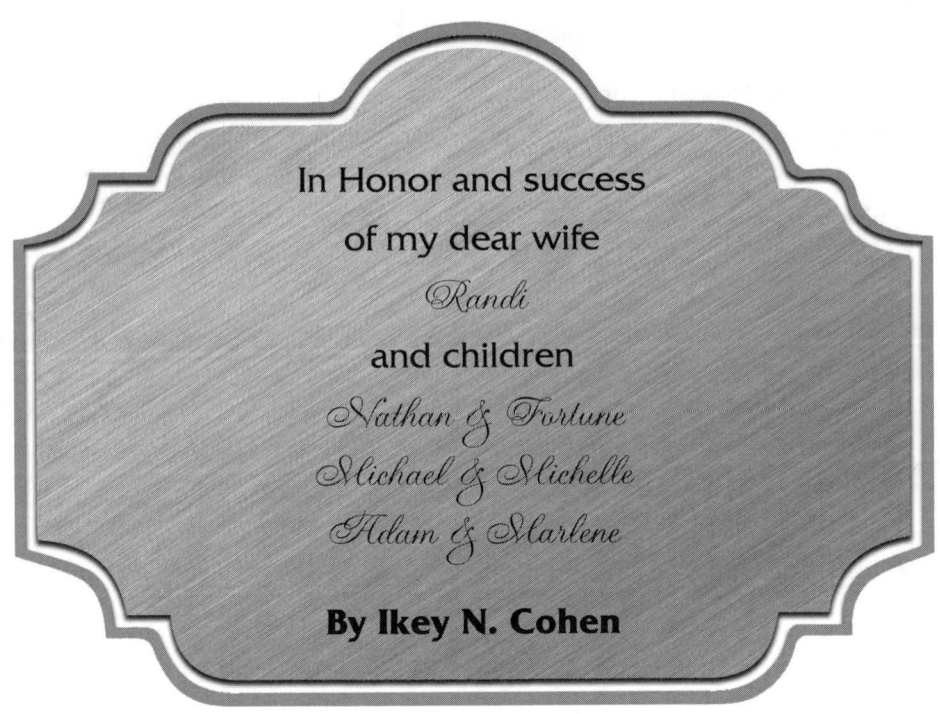

In Honor and success
of my dear wife
Randi
and children
Nathan & Fortune
Michael & Michelle
Adam & Marlene

By Ikey N. Cohen

The Twelfth Beracha

למינים ולמלשינים

In this blessing of the *Amidah* we pray for the downfall of several groups of enemies who pose grave threats to the Jewish people. The Talmud (Berachot 28) tells that this *beracha* was not included in the original *Amidah* prayer. The original *Amidah* prayer consisted of only eighteen *berachot* – which is why we commonly refer to this prayer as "*shemona esreh*" ("eighteen") – but the current version contains nineteen *berachot*, as the blessing of למינים was added by the sages of Yavneh after the Temple's destruction.

A Rabbi or a Poet?

The Gemara relates that when Rabban Gamliel, the leading rabbinical authority of the time, decided that this *beracha* must be added, he convened the greatest scholars of the time and asked which of them was capable of composing the text of this *beracha*. One scholar, a *Tanna* by the unusual name of Shemuel Ha'katan, stood and announced that he is prepared and qualified to assume such a responsibility.

Why did Rabban Gamliel convene the generation's leading Rabbis for this purpose? Why didn't he simply approach a talented poet, inform the poet of the desired content of this *beracha*, and then ask him to compose a text?

The answer is that a poet is precisely who Rabban Gamliel did not want for this job. The original eighteen *berachot* were composed by the Men of the Great Assembly, a group of towering luminaries which included three prophets – Hagai, Zecharya and Malachi. This text was written with *ru'ah ha'kodesh*, and it contains infinite depth and meaning that underlie the words. The sages and prophets who composed the *Amidah* prayer possessed the knowledge and insight necessary to produce a sacred text endowed with deep spiritual meaning on many different levels. If a new *beracha* was now being introduced centuries later, it had to meet this lofty standard. Its composition required a righteous scholar on or near the level of the Men of the Great Assembly, so that this *beracha* would possess the same spiritual power and meaning as the rest of the *Amidah*.

Rabban Gamliel therefore assembled a group of accomplished sages, and Shemuel Ha'katan was deemed worthy to undertake this holy task. His credentials are indicated elsewhere in the Talmud, in Masechet Sanhedrin (11a), where we read that Shemuel Ha'katan was among seven scholars whom Rabban Gamliel once convened to discuss matters relevant to the Jewish calendar. Issues relating to the calendar were decided upon exclusively by the nation's greatest sages, and Shemuel Ha'katan's inclusion in this meeting thus testifies to his unique stature as a Torah scholar. Furthermore, the Gemara there comments that Shemuel Ha'katan was worthy of the level of prophecy achieved by Moshe Rabbenu, and it was only due to his generation's unworthiness that he was denied this exalted stature. Shemuel Ha'katan was thus clearly qualified for the task of formulating the text for a new section of the *Amidah* prayer.

"Shemuel the Small"

But there is also another reason why specifically Shemuel Ha'katan was deemed worthy of composing this *beracha*. The Talmud explains that he was called "Shemuel Ha'katan" ("Shemuel the Small") because "he made himself small", meaning, he was exceedingly humble and unassuming. Case in point, in the aforementioned passage in Masechet Sanhedrin, the Gemara relates that eight Rabbis arrived at Rabban Gamliel's meeting to discuss the calendar, despite the fact that only seven had been invited. Shemuel Ha'katan, in his extraordinary humility, voluntarily excused himself from the meeting, not wishing to embarrass the uninvited attendee.

Why was humility such a critical credential for this job? Why was it necessary to choose specifically the humblest scholar for the task of composing the *beracha* of למינים?

The Mishna in Masechet Yoma (18b) tells that during the times of the Second Temple, the Rabbis of the *Sanhedrin* would meet with the *kohen gadol* each year before Yom Kippur to prepare him for the special Yom Kippur service. During this session, they would make him swear under oath that he would not deviate from the procedure they taught him. The post of the high priesthood was occasionally held by members of the heretical Sadducee sect, which rejected the rabbinic tradition concerning the details of the Yom Kippur service. The Rabbis therefore had no choice but to demand an oath of compliance.

Interestingly enough, the Mishna relates that after the *kohen gadol* swore, both he and the Rabbis wept. He wept, quite obviously, because he was suspected of heresy. But why did the Rabbis weep? The Mishna explains that they wept because they suspected somebody who may have been innocent. True, they were compelled to impose this oath upon the *kohen gadol* in light of the rampant rejection of traditional norms, but this had to be done with a degree of pain. Even in situations that warrant suspicion, one may not relish the opportunity or enjoy the self-righteous feeling of pointing fingers and making accusations. This must be done with absolute sincerity and purity of heart; the need to suspect other people must cause a person grief and anguish.

Similarly, the Hafetz Haim lists numerous conditions that must be met for a person to be allowed to speak *lashon ha'ra* (negative speech) about his fellow. One condition is that the speaker must not enjoy the experience of relaying negative information about another person. Even when it is necessary to speak *lashon ha'ra*, this must be done uncomfortably, with an element of unease. One should never celebrate or welcome an opportunity to speak negatively about his fellow Jew.

This is why Shemuel Ha'katan's humility rendered him worthy of composing the *beracha* of למינים. In *Pirkei Abot*, we read about the different proverbs or teachings that various *Tanna'im* would frequently say. It is told there that Shemuel Ha'katan would often repeat the verse in Mishle (24:17), בנפול אויביך אל תשמח – "When your enemy falls – do not rejoice". Shemuel Ha'katan exemplified the humility required when struggling against ruthless foes. Of course, we must fight with vigor and determination against those who seek our physical or spiritual destruction. But this fight must be fought with absolute sincerity, purely for the sake of God, without any tinge of arrogance, vengeance, or personal vendetta. As such, we must not relish the defeat of our enemies; we should feel pained and distraught by the need to fight. This is what Shemuel Ha'katan, the humblest of the sages, preached: "When your enemy falls – do not rejoice".

And so, he was chosen to compose the prayer for our enemies' downfall. This *beracha* is a necessary evil, so-to-speak. All the other blessings pray for an ideal; in this blessing, we ask God to do something which we would prefer we would not need Him to do – destroy our spiritual detractors. Therefore, specifically Shemuel Ha'katan, who championed and embodied the value of humility, and abhorred triumphalism and self-adulation in response to victory, was able to compose the *beracha* of ולמינים. He was the one who knew the way to appeal to God sincerely, and with a pure heart, to defeat those who wage war against the Torah.

It is customary for *paytanim* (Rabbis who compose hymns) to embed their name somewhere in their hymns. For example, in the famous לכה דודי hymn which we sing each Shabbat, the letters that begin the first four stanzas spell the name שלמה, alluding to Rabbi Shlomo Alkabetz, the Kabbalist who composed this prayer. The Ben Ish Hai noted that Shemuel Ha'katan, too, made an allusion to his name in this *beracha*. The final four words of this *beracha* – שובר **א**ויבים ו**מ**כניע **מ**ינים – begin with the letters ש,א,ו,מ,מ, and the *beracha* begins with the letter ל. These five letters are the letters that spell the name Shemuel. (Later, we will see that there are versions of this *beracha* in which the final word is זדים, and not מינים.)

Shemuel Ha'katan's authorship of this *beracha* is also alluded to in the Torah. In the last of Bilam's prophecies, he exclaims, אוי מי יחיה משמו אל (Bamidbar 24:23). This literally means, "Alas! Who can withstand they whose name [ends with] *el*", referring to the fact that the divine Name of אל is embedded within the name of *Am Yisrael*, thus giving them immense power. The Ben Ish Hai, however, writes that this may also be read as מי יחיה משמואל – "Who can withstand Shemuel?!" Bilam foresaw the prayer against the enemy nations that would be composed by the great sage Shemuel Ha'katan, and which Jews would recite several times a day throughout the centuries. He recognized the power of this prayer and its eventual success in causing the downfall of the Jewish people's enemies, none of whom can even hope to withstand the power of *Bene Yisrael*'s prayers to the Almighty.

למינים

"For the heretics"

This term refers to those who deny the fundamental tenets of Jewish faith – especially the existence of God, the divine origin and immutability of the Torah, and the authenticity of the oral rabbinic tradition – and who seek to disseminate their heretical beliefs among the Jewish people.

The Rambam, in Hilchot *Tefila* (2:1), provides the historical background to this prayer for the downfall of the *minim*:

בימי רבן גמליאל רבו האפיקורוסין בישראל והיו מצירין לישראל ומסיתין אותן לשוב מאחרי השם. וכיון שראה שזו גדולה מכל צרכי בני אדם עמד הוא ובית דינו והתקין ברכה אחת שתהיה בה שאלה מלפני השם לאבד האפיקורוסין וקבע אותה בתפלה כדי שתהיה ערוכה בפי הכל.

During the time of Rabban Gamliel, there was a proliferation of heretics among Israel, and they caused Israel distress and lured them to turn away from God. Seeing that this is greater than all human needs, he and his court went ahead and established a blessing in which it is asked of God to destroy the heretics, and he instituted it as part of the prayer so that it would be familiar to everyone.

The heretics in Rabban Gamliel's time posed a grave threat to the Jewish people, as they exerted great efforts to spread their beliefs. They ridiculed the rabbis, denied the authority of the halachic tradition, and caused masses of Jews to reject Torah authority. This threat to the Jewish faith prompted Rabban Gamliel to add this *beracha* to the *Amidah*, so that everyone would pray that the efforts of the *minim* would not succeed.

The Rambam describes this request as גדולה מכל צרכי בני אדם – "greater than all human needs". If we would be asked to identify the most important of the nineteen blessings of the *Amidah*, many of us would likely point to the *beracha* of רפאנו, in which we pray for good health, or perhaps ברכנו, the prayer for livelihood. The more idealistic among us might choose את צמח דוד or תשכון בתוך ירושלים, in which we pray for our national redemption. But for the Rambam, the *beracha* of ולמינים is the most important of all the blessings of the *Amidah*, the one in which we pray for the "greatest human need". This is because the *beracha* of ולמינים prays for our protection from false ideologies. In essence, this is the prayer for *emuna*, for faith. We beseech God to foil the efforts of those who wage war against the Jewish faith and seek to replace it with competing beliefs. This is, indeed, the Jewish people's most pressing need, and this *beracha* therefore expresses the most urgent of all the requests submitted to the Almighty in the *Amidah*.

The supreme importance of this *beracha* is subtly indicated by its punctuation. When we look inside the *siddur*, we will notice different *nekudot* (vowel punctuation) underneath the Name of Hashem in the conclusion of each *beracha* of the *Amidah*. The *beracha* of אתה חונן, for example, concludes with the blessing, ברוך אתה ה' חונן הדעת, and God's Name in this phrase is punctuated with the *patah* vowel (יְהֹוַה). According to Kabbalistic teaching, this vowel corresponds to the *sefira* (emanation) of חכמה (wisdom), and is thus used in the context of this *beracha*, in which we pray for wisdom. In the next *beracha*, the blessing in which we pray for help in repentance, the Name is punctuated with the *sereh* vowel (יְהֹוֵה). The *sereh* represents the *sefira* of *bina* (understanding), which is the basis of repentance. The pattern continues in the *beracha* of סלח לנו, where we find Hashem's Name in the conclusion punctuated with a *segol*, (יְהֹוֶה), the symbol of kindness, which is of course the basis on which we plead for forgiveness. Likewise, in the conclusion of the *beracha* of ראה נא בעינינו, the Name is punctuated with a *sheva*, (יְהֹוְה), which expresses the divine attribute of גבורה (power) and is thus appropriate for the prayer for victory over our enemies.

Revealingly, the vowel punctuation chosen for the conclusion of the twelfth *beracha*, the blessing of למינים, is the *kamatz*, (יְהֹוָה), which signifies the highest of all the *sefirot*, the *sefira* of כתר. The word כתר means "crown", and it signifies that which lies above us, beyond our grasp and our comprehension. This *sefira* alludes to *emuna*, our faith in God and our tradition that is not contingent upon human logic and rationale. It therefore corresponds to the *beracha* of למינים, in which we beseech the Almighty to help us in strengthening and fortifying our *emuna*, so that we do not fall prey to the relentless efforts of our theological opponents to engender skepticism and lead us to reject our tradition.

The prayer for the downfall of the *minim* is thus a prayer for the spiritual health of the Jewish people. We ask God to ensure our protection from false ideologies, that we will be firm and resolute in our resistance to anti-Torah beliefs, no matter how vigorously their proponents work to disseminate them.

ולמלשינים
"and for the informers"

The phenomenon of מלשינים has, unfortunately, a long and tragic history among the Jewish people. Over the centuries, communities have fallen victim to Jewish collaborators who revealed information, or spewed lies, about their fellow Jews in exchange for money, prestige or other favors from the non-Jewish government.

The Gemara tells that R' Shimon bar Yohai once spoke critically about the Roman government during a private meeting among the rabbis. One of his students, astonishingly enough, reported his comments to the authorities, forcing the great sage to hide in a cave with his son for fourteen years. There are many accounts from the Middle Ages, too, of Jews who betrayed their people for personal gain. In 1250, a Jew in England handed over details of the Jewish community's finances to the officials of King Henry III, and told them that the Jews were capable of paying twice the amount of taxes that they were paying. Three hundred years later, in 1553, Jews brought incriminating lies about the Talmud to Pope Julius III, which resulted in the burning of all editions of the Talmud throughout Italy. During the period of the Spanish Inquisition, it was common for Jewish collaborators to inform the authorities of Jews who secretly practiced Judaism. So much so, in fact, that until today, the Spanish word for "evil" begins with the prefix "malo", from the Hebrew word "*malshin*" ("informer").

In the early 16th century, a Jew who assumed the name Antonius Margarutha, and who was the son of the renowned Torah scholar Rav Yaakov Margoliyot, wrote books that cast allegations against the Talmud and lobbied against the Jews of Regensburg, Germany. His efforts led to the Jews' expulsion from the city. Closer to modern times, there were Russian Jews who reported to the Czarist government officials the Jews who evaded conscription and who lived in regions which the government set off limits to Jews. A Jew named Jacob Broffman claimed to prove that the Jews were running a state within a state that posed a threat to Russia.

For good reason, Rabbis and other Jewish leaders treated this offense with utmost severity. The Rambam, in Hilchot Hobel U'mazik, ruled that a *moser* (informer) has no share in the world to come, and that it is permissible to kill him. Indeed, although capital punishment was officially discontinued toward the end of the Second Temple era, there were occasions where communities executed informers. Rabbi Yosef ibn Migash (Spain, 1077-1141) once ordered that an informer be hung at the time of the *ne'ila* prayer on Yom Kippur. When asked about the timing of the execution, he explained that it would provide the community with an extra *zechut* (source of merit) during the final moments of judgment. There are reports of communities punishing informers by branding their foreheads with hot iron, and others that would sever the ears, hands and legs of these offenders. In the famous German Jewish communities of Worms and Mayence, a special curse was declared each week in the synagogue condemning Jews who committed this crime against their nation.

The Hatam Sofer writes that the *malshinim* are actually responsible for our ongoing exile and the delay in our national redemption. We read in the Book of Bereshit (15:19-21) of God's promise to Abraham Abinu that his descendants would inherit the lands of ten nations. As we know, however, *Beneh Yisrael* ultimately dispossessed only seven nations. The Sages explain that the three nations of Edom, Amon and Moab were allowed to remain on their lands, and the Jewish people will take possession of those territories only at the time of the final redemption. Amon and Moab were granted rights to their lands until the Messianic Era in the merit of their ancestor Lot, Abraham's nephew. Rashi, in his commentary to Debarim (2:5), writes that Lot earned this reward when he joined Abraham and Sara in Egypt to escape the drought that ravaged Canaan. Abraham and Sara lived in Egypt under the guise of brother and sister, afraid that otherwise Abraham would be killed by an Egyptian desiring Sara's beauty. Lot, to his credit, kept the secret and resisted the temptation to divulge the truth in exchange for money. God rewarded Lot for his discretion and restraint by protecting his descendants' territory from *Beneh Yisrael* until the time of the final redemption.

As long as there are Jewish informers betraying their own people, the Hatam Sofer notes, Lot's descendants are entitled to their territory in reward for their ancestor's loyalty to Abraham. If we have informers among us, then we have no right to the territory of Lot, who refused to expose the truth about Abraham and Sara's relationship. Once we eliminate the *malshinim* from our midst, we will then be deserving of the region assigned to Lot, and the final redemption will then unfold.

For this reason, the Hatam Sofer explained, the *beracha* of למינים, in which we pray for the downfall of the *malshinim*, is recited shortly before the *beracha* of תשכן בתוך ירושלים, in which we pray for the final redemption. We pray that we will purge the *malshinim* from our midst so that we will be rendered worthy of finally possessing the lands of Lot's ancestors with the arrival of Messianic Era.

אל תהי תקוה
"there shall be no hope"

We pray that the sinister efforts of these groups of wicked people should be fruitless, and have not even a hope of succeeding. This phrase also alludes to the eternal condemnation that is decreed upon the מינים and מלשינים. The Rambam writes that these wicked people are sentenced to eternal punishment; even if *Gehinam* would at some point stop burning, they would continue enduring retribution for their sins. We thus proclaim that such people will have "no hope", as they will forever be condemned to suffer punishment as a result of their efforts against the Jewish people.

וכל הזדים כרגע יאבדו
"and all the evildoers shall be destroyed in an instant"

The term זדים refers to those who recognize the existence of God, but nevertheless wage battle against Him and the Jewish people, such as Pharoah and Amalek. We ask that they be eliminated "in an instant", without requiring a lengthy process of redemption and salvation. The Soviet Union existed for seven decades, and yet disappeared overnight, virtually "in an instant". We ask the Almighty that all His enemies who wage war against His beloved nation shall similarly meet their downfall "in an instant".

וכל אויביך וכל שונאיך מהרה יכרתו
"and all your enemies and foes shall swiftly be eliminated"

Many *siddurim* print underneath or near these words various names of evil angels and harmful spiritual forces, such as ס"מ. The enemies that wage war against us in this world receive their strength from the "enemy angels" in the heavens. When war erupts here on earth, it is actually the culmination of a process of hostilities that began in the heavens, with the angels of different nations battling against one another. For this reason, Rav Haim ben Attar writes, *(the Or Ha'haim)* after the name. the Torah describes going out to battle with the phrase כי תצא למלחמה על אויביך ("When you go out to war against your enemies" – Devarim 21:10), implying that the war is already underway, and *Bene Yisrael* go to the war in progress. Rav Haim ben Attar explains that by the time *Bene Yisrael* begin making their way to the battlefield, the war has already been raging between the various forces in the heavens.

This phrase in the *Amidah* – וכל אויביך וכל שונאיך מהרה יכרתו – brings to mind the prayers we recite on Rosh Hashanah as we eat the *simanim* – the special foods that symbolize our aspirations for the new year. These include prayers such as שיכרתו שונאינו, that our enemies shall be destroyed and eliminated. In these prayers, too, we have in mind not only the actual enemies of the Jewish people here on earth, but also the harmful angels and other spiritual forces in the heavens that seek our destruction, including the evil angels that are created as a result of our misdeeds.

ומלכות הרשעה מהרה תעקר ותשבר, ותכלם ותכניעם, במהרה בימינו
"and You shall swiftly uproot and demolish the evil kingdom, and eliminate and subdue them, speedily and in our days"

We ask God to foil the efforts of not only the individuals who threaten us, but also the governments, the establishments that promote false ideologies and seek to disseminate them throughout the world. Governments wield considerable power, and thus governments representing false beliefs pose an especially grave threat to the faith in the true God. We must therefore beseech the Almighty to frustrate their efforts to supplant the true faith with their false ideologies.

This prayer for the failure of these governments is actually alluded to in the Torah. Toward the end of the Book of Vayikra, in Parashat Behar, we find a section dealing with the laws of reclaiming lands and people that were sold due to financial pressures. If a person fell upon hard times and was forced to sell his property, or himself as a servant, there are various *halachot* that apply, starting with the obligation for his kinsmen to reclaim the person's property or freedom. The *Ba'al Haturim* notes that the word *ge'ula* ("redemption"), in its various forms, appears nineteen times in this section, corresponding to the nineteen blessings of the *Amidah* prayer. The twelfth instance of *ge'ula* in this section appears in reference to a Jew who was forced to sell himself into the service of an idol-worshiper:

וכי תשיג יד גר ותושב עמך ומך אחיך עמו ונמכר לגר תושב עמך או לעקר משפחת גר. אחרי נמכר גאולה תהיה לו...

"If a foreign resident among you gains the upper hand, and your brother becomes impoverished with him, and is sold to a foreign resident among you, or to an idolater from a foreign family – after he is sold, he shall be redeemed...(Vayikra 25:47-48)

The Torah in this context uses the word עקר in describing the idolatrous master of the impoverished Jew. The commentators explain that the Hebrew root ע.ק.ר. means "uproot", and it is used in reference to idolatry because it will one day be eliminated and eradicated from the earth. The Torah uses this term specifically in this context, regarding a Jew sold into the service of idolatry, because this situation in particular arouses God's anger against the world's idolatrous nations. When a Jew is forced to place himself into the service of an idolater and thus comes directly under his sphere of influence, God's anger is kindled, and He reaffirms His promise, as it were, to eradicate paganism from the face of the earth.

Accordingly, these verses correspond to the twelfth *beracha* of the *Amidah*, when we pray ומלכות הרשעה מהרה תעקר, petitioning God to eliminate the powerful governments that exert pagan influence upon us. We beg the Almighty to foil these efforts and protect His children from falling under the web of idolatry and other false ideologies. We ask that He soon fulfill His promise of עקר משפחת גר, to "uproot" the pagan governments so that innocent Jews will not fall prey to their efforts to spread their beliefs throughout the world.

We ask that all these enemy nations be eliminated במהרה בימינו, immediately. Every moment that they prosper and enjoy success, God's Name is desecrated in the world. We therefore beseech God to bring an immediate end to their success, so that His Name will, once and for all, be recognized and exalted throughout the earth.

ברוך אתה ה' שובר אויבים ומכניע זדים
"Blessed are You, Hashem, who breaks enemies and subdues the evildoers"

There is a difference of opinion among the halachic authorities concerning the precise text of this concluding phrase, and Hacham Ovadia Yosef *zt"l* devotes a lengthy essay to this subject in his work *Yehave Da'at*. Rav Haim Palachi, and many others, maintain that the proper text is ומכניע זדים, and this is, indeed, the text in many of our *siddurim*. The Ben Ish Hai, however, held that the final word of this *beracha* should be מינים, and not זדים.

Refuah Shelema to:

Leah bat Virginie
and
Tzadok Israel ben Yehudit

Sam Flaster

The Thirteenth Beracha

על הצדיקים

In this *beracha* we ask God to bless and reward all the righteous members of the nation, specifying different groups of Jews who are especially deserving of His compassion and grace.

על הצדיקים ועל החסדים
"Upon the righteous and the pious"

What is the difference between a צדיק and a חסיד?

The most common understanding is that a צדיק is somebody

who faithfully and meticulously fulfills all his religious duties, upholding every letter of the strict *halacha*, whereas a חסיד goes even further. The חסיד, knowing what God wants from us, extends beyond the strict call of duty, accepting upon himself additional measures of stringency and special piety that are not required according to *halacha*.

The Abudarham adds further insight into this distinction between the צדיק and the חסיד. He claims that a צדיק is somebody who was always righteous and observant, who already during childhood did as he was told, behaved properly, and observed all the *misvot*. A חסיד, by contrast, is a בעל תשובה, a Jew with a far-from-perfect past who made the necessary changes and now lives a life of devotion to Torah. The חסיד undertakes special measures of piety because of his past experiences, because of his natural tendency to sinful behavior. Just as a recovering alcoholic must dissociate himself from people who drink and ensure to never pass by a bar alone, similarly, the penitent sinner must erect "fences" in the form of special personal measures of piety to keep a safe distance from temptation.

Our Sages (Menahot 29b) teach us that the Almighty created this word with the letter ה', which has a wide open area on the bottom, symbolizing the ease with which a person can "fall" out of this world and plummet into the abyss of sin. As the Mishna in Avot (4:28) warns, הקנאה התאוה והכבוד מוציאין את האדם מן העולם – "Jealousy, lust and honor can expel a person from this world". But the letter ה' also has an opening on the side, through which a person can return after he has fallen. A separate "entrance" is needed because after a person has "fallen" into sin, he cannot return the same way he left. A sinner who wishes to return to religious observance must chart a new course, along which he steers clear of the areas in which he stumbled the first time around. The חסיד, who wishes to return to God after having committed sins, must undertake special measures of stringency to ensure that he stays on the course of *teshuba* and does not fall back onto the path of sin.

In this *beracha* we pray for both the צדיקים and the חסידים, for all the righteous people of *Am Yisrael*, that they should be blessed with joy and success, and always remain steadfast in their commitment and devotion to the Almighty.

ועל שארית עמך בית ישראל
"and upon the remnant of Your nation, the House of Israel"

This refers to the entire nation, who has survived the centuries of persecution against the Jews. Alternatively, it might refer specifically to the "remnants" of the previous generation, the older members of our nation who have remained unwaveringly loyal to the Torah throughout their lives.

ועל זקניהם
"and upon their elders"

In some *siddurim* this phrase is omitted, but Hacham Ovadia Yosef *zt"l* ruled that it should be included in this *beracha*. The term זקן in this context means זה שקנה חכמה – "he who has acquired wisdom" – referring to the Torah scholars. We ask that our Torah sages will be rewarded in full for their tireless efforts to acquire Torah scholarship. This phrase also refers to all those who serve the community, in whatever capacity, such as the Rabbinic judges, the *gabba'im* in the synagogue, and others who care for vital communal needs. We beseech God to reward them all for their devoted service to the community and to *Am Yisrael*.

ועל פליטת בית-סופריהם
"and upon the vestige of their house of scribes"

This might refer to the סופרים, the scholars and scribes who write books, Torah scrolls, *tefillin*, *mezuzot* and so on. Some explain the term פליטת as denoting frailty, which is used here to describe the scholars who often suffer physical weakness due to their rigorous schedule, which allows little time for relaxation, sleep and eating.

Another possible explanation of the term סופרים is that it refers to the schoolteachers, whose job has always been viewed as among the most vital roles in *Am Yisrael*. We pray to God to reward our devoted schoolteachers for their patience and dedication in teaching and nurturing the next generation of Torah Jews.

ועל גרי הצדק
"and upon the righteous converts"

Unfortunately, many people who convert to Judaism do so for the wrong reasons, such as for marriage, money and the like. In this *beracha* we pray for the success and welfare of the גירי הצדק, those who have been driven by a sincere commitment to the truth about God and a desire to serve Him as members of *Am Yisrael*. The term גירי הצדק refers to converts such as the sailors in the story of Yona, whose boat was struck by a violent storm that followed them wherever they sailed. They cast Yona from the boat, and the storm immediately stopped. They then brought him back to the ship, at which point the storm erupted again, until they threw the prophet back into the water. They saw the truth of God and divine justice with their own eyes, and the Sages say that they went to Jerusalem and became righteous converts.

These are the types of converts for whom we pray in this *beracha* – those who convert with pure sincerity, out of a desire to become faithful servants of the Almighty.

ועלינו
"and upon us"

We ask God that as He rewards the exceptional members of our nation, He should remember us, as well, and grant us reward for our good deeds, even if our merits pale in comparison to those of the groups mentioned earlier in the *beracha*.

יהמו נא רחמיך ה' אלהינו
"You shall have compassion, Hashem our God"

The divine Name of הוי"ה signifies the attribute of kindness, whereas אלוקים expresses the attribute of strict justice. When the two Names are combined, as in this phrase (ה' אלוקינו), the reference is to המתקת הדינים, the "sweetening" of judgment by God's attribute of kindness. This is, essentially, what רחמים ("compassion") means; it is the result of God's attribute of kindness being introduced to negate the effects of the harsh judgment against us.

ותן שכר טוב לכל-הבוטחים בשמך באמת, ושים חלקנו עמהם
"and grant a proper reward to all who truly trust in Your Name, and make our portion with theirs"

We ask God to grant us a portion in the eternal world together with the righteous *sadikim* and other groups listed above. The obvious question arises, doesn't a person have to earn his portion? How can one pray for a reward on par with the reward given to the great *sadikim*? What right do we have to ask for a portion together with the righteous members of our nation?

The Arizal explained that there are certain sinners who forfeit their share in the world to come due to their wrongdoing. The portions that had been allocated to these individuals are therefore transferred and added onto the portions received by the souls in the next world. If the sinner then repents and thus becomes worthy of his share, the one who was given his portion does not necessarily have to relinquish the extra portion that he had received, and God therefore must find a different portion for the repentant sinner. The Arizal claimed that when we pray, "make our portion with theirs", we ask that if at some point we forfeit our share in the world to come, the forfeited share should be transferred to one of the *sadikim*. The *sadikim* are pious and selfless, and will not insist on retaining the share if we subsequently repent and thus become eligible to regain our portion in the next world.

ולעולם לא נבוש, כי בך בטחנו

"and forever we shall not be ashamed, for we have trusted in You"

Embarrassment in this world is always temporary. If a person experiences shame, the emotional pain might endure for several days, or at worse several years, and it eventually fades away. The incident is forgotten, and people grow accustomed to the embarrassing situation, and the sting of humiliation thus naturally abates. In the next world, however, humiliation is eternal. The shame we will experience in the world to come will remain forever; the stains of our wrongdoing will accompany us for all eternity.

The Talmud (Kiddushin 81a) tells the story of a certain sage named Rav Amram Hasida, who once rescued five young Jewish women from captivity and hosted them on the second floor of his home. At night, he would have the large, heavy ladder that connected the two floors removed, so that he would not have access to the area where the girls slept. One night, however, he happened to wake up and noticed one of the attractive young women on the second floor. He took the ladder and started walking up in order to commit a sin. He suddenly stopped himself by shouting, "There is a fire in Amram's home!"

Immediately, his neighbors rushed inside his home – only to find Rav Amram on a ladder leading up to five attractive women, and of course there was no fire.

"Why did you say there was a fire?" the neighbors asked.

"I saw a fire beneath me", he explained, "the fire of *Gehinam!*" He proceeded to tell the people who had gathered in his home that he was prepared to endure the humiliation of this experience – having the entire neighborhood seeing the great Rabbi starting to make his way to the five women – in order to spare himself eternal humiliation in the world to come. Rav Amram understood the difference between fleeting moments of embarrassment during our lifetime and the eternal embarrassment suffered by a sinner in the next world.

We therefore pray to the Almighty in this *beracha*, ולעולם לא נבוש – that we should not experience eternal shame in the next world, that we should always have the wisdom and self-discipline to avoid wrongdoing and thereby avoid eternal embarrassment.

The request ולעולם לא נבוש may also mean that we hope never to resent the embarrassment caused to us by others. The *Sefer Ha'hinuch*, amidst his discussion of the prohibition against taking revenge from one's fellow, notes the fundamental relationship between avoiding revenge and *bitahon*, faith in the Almighty. If a person truly believes that everything that happens to him has been ordained by God, he harbors no feelings of resentment or vengeance toward those who have wronged him. King David, for example, was ruthlessly cursed, heckled and humiliated by a man named Shim'i ben Geira. This was during David's most painful and humiliating moment, when he was forced to flee Jerusalem due to the revolt mounted by his own son, Abshalom. David's servant offered to kill Shim'i, but David urged him to desist, noting that this was Hashem's will, that he should suffer this humiliation (Shemuel II 16:10-11).

This should be our response, as well, to the harm and embarrassment that people cause us. If we truly believe that this is God's will, that He ordained that this should happen, then we will not be disturbed at all when people offend us. We will not feel any shame or emotional discomfort whatsoever, and will instead remain perfectly calm and at ease, knowing with full confidence that this was what God wanted to happen.

We ask the Almighty to bless us by helping us engender this level of trust and faith in Him, whereby we are capable of accepting and tolerating the taunts, insults and aggravation that we so often experience. We pray that לעולם לא נבוש, we should feel ashamed, because בך בטחנו, we will trust and believe with our heart and soul that everything that transpires is the will of God, who loves us and whose every deed is done for our ultimate benefit.

The Fourteenth Beracha

תשכן בתוך ירושלים

In this *beracha* we pray for the rebuilding of the *Bet Hamikdash*, which will herald the arrival of the Messianic Era and the end of all the Jewish people's troubles. In this sense, the *beracha* of תשכן בתוך ירושלים is the most important blessing of the *Amidah* prayer, as the fulfillment of this request holds the key to the solution of all the difficult problems and hardships facing us, both individually and collectively.

The first *Bet Hamikdash* was built by King Shelomo, and it stood for 410 years until it was set ablaze by the Babylonian legions during the time of the wicked emperor Nevuchadnesar. The Second Temple was built under the leadership of Ezra HaSofer during the period of benevolent Persian rule, and it stood for 420 years, until its destruction at the hands of the Roman Empire. The Torah alludes to these *Bateh Mikdash* in the opening verse of Parashat Tesave (Shemot 27:20), where God instructs Moshe to have *Beneh Yisrael* provide olive oil for the *menorah*, and He describes the oil as כתית ("crushed olives"). The numerical value of this word is 830, alluding to the 420 years of the First Temple and the 410 years of the Second Temple. Earlier, in Parashat Teruma (25:8), Hashem says that the purpose of the *Mishkan* (and, later, of the *Bet Hamikdash*) is ושכנתי – that God should reside among *Beneh Yisrael*. This word may be read as a combination of the words שכן ת"י – "resided 410", referring to the 410 years of the First Temple. This word may also be read as ושני ת"כ – "and the second, 420", hinting to the 420 years of the Second Temple.

The Rabbis teach us that the first two *Bateh Mikdash* laid the groundwork and prepared us and the world for the Third and final *Bet Hamikdash*. A farmer who wishes to plant a strong, sturdy tree that produces an abundance of high quality fruits may have to first plant a lower quality tree to prepare the ground. After the tree produces fruit, he will uproot the tree and plant another in its place. Then, after the second tree has matured and produced fruit, he will uproot it and plant in its place the third and final tree, now that the ground is ready to support it. Similarly, the city of Jerusalem, and the entire world, needs to be prepared for the Third Temple. It will be such a majestic structure, and the divine presence will be sensed so profoundly in that building, that the world needs to first undergo a process of preparation. The 830 years during which the world had a *Bet Hamikdash* laid the groundwork in preparation for the third and final *Mikdash*, which we pray will be rebuilt in our time.

God thus instructs preparing oil כתית למאור ("crushed olives, for lighting"). The 830 years represented by the word כתית will serve

למאור, to prepare the earth for the great light of the *Shechina* which will be revealed through the Third Temple.

We read in Tehillim (127:1), "If Hashem does not build a house, then its builders labored on it for naught". We beg the Almighty to restore the Temple, to build the final, eternal *Bet Hamikdash*, for otherwise, the first two Temples will have been "for naught", they will have served no purpose. "If Hashem does not build a house" – if He does not bring us the Third Temple, then "its builders labored on it for naught" – the effort invested in building the first two *Bateh Mikdash* will have been done in vein. The descent of the Third Temple will affirm the value and importance of the first two Temples, which prepared us for the revelation of God's glory in the eternal *Mikdash*.

Can Our Generation be Worthy of the *Bet Hamikdash*?

Our Sages teach that the Third Temple will differ fundamentally from the first two *Bateh Mikdash*. Whereas the first two Temples were built by human laborers, the Third Temple will be built by God, in the heavens. *Beneh Yisrael* proclaimed in the song sung after the splitting of the sea, מקדש ה' כוננו ידיך – "The Temple that Your hands, Hashem, have built" (Shemot 15:17). This refers to the Third Temple, which will be built by God, and not by people.

Actually, it is already being built currently. Each prayer we recite for the rebuilding of the Temple, and every *misva* we perform, contributes to the building effort. Thus, for example, the Gemara writes that anyone who celebrates with a bride and groom at their wedding is credited with building one of the ruins of Jerusalem. While the precise connection between the Temple and this *misva* of שמחת חתן וכלה (celebrating with a bride and groom) remains unclear, it emerges from the Gemara's comment that we can "build" the Temple through our *misvot*. Several truckloads of materials are brought to a construction site to provide the necessary equipment and supplies needed for the building. Each *misva* we perform and prayer that we recite adds some "materials" to the "construction site" in the heavens. The "building project" is already well underway, thanks to the countless *misvot* that have been performed and prayers that have been recited by Jews throughout the millennia. We are active participants in this project, and play a crucial role in advancing the process of rebuilding the *Mikdash*.

This answers a basic question that often weighs heavily on people's minds. Can Mashiah really come in our time? If the Temple was not rebuilt in the periods of the great *sadikim*, in the time of the *Tanna'im* and *Amora'im*, or of the *Rishonim*, then how can we be so arrogant to think that we will be deserving of the Temple's restoration?

The answer is simple. Each generation, and in fact each individual, contributes to the building project through his *misvot*. The generations of *sadikim* undoubtedly made enormous contributions toward this effort, but we make contributions of our own. Each *misva* brings us a bit closer to the desired goal. Thus, we are certainly capable of finishing the project that previous, worthier generations were unable to complete. There is only a small bit left to complete – and we, through our *misvot*, are able to realize this goal through our prayer, Torah and *misvot*.

King David's Gates of Repentance

If, indeed, the Third Temple will descend "prefab" from the heavens, the question arises as to how we will fulfill the Torah obligation to construct a *Mikdash*. The Torah explicitly writes in the Book of Shemot (25:8), ועשו לי מקדש ושכנתי בתוכם ("They shall make for Me a Sanctuary, and I shall reside among them"), which the Rabbis understood as introducing the eternal obligation to build a *Mikdash*. How do we fulfill this *misva* if the Third Temple will be built by the Almighty and descend onto Jerusalem readymade?

One answer, proposed by the Maharil Diskin, is that only the skeletal structure of the Temple will descend readymade from the heavens. God will leave plenty of work for us, and we will fulfill our *misva* by completing the interior of the *Bet Hamikdash*. This is why we pray in the holiday liturgy, והראנו בבנינו ושמחנו בתיקונו – "Show us its building, and bring us joy through its completion". We ask God to show us בנינו, the structure of the *Mikdash*, and then grant us the joy of תיקונו, of being involved in completing and perfecting the building.

There is, however, another answer to this question. The prophet Yirmiyahu, in describing the fall of Jerusalem in the Book of Echa (2:9), writes, טבעו בארץ שעריה – "Its gates sank into the ground". The gates of the *Bet Hamikdash* were not burned along with the rest of the building. They rather "sank into the ground". They were buried deep underneath the ground of the Temple Mount, and in the Messianic Era, they will resurface. Those gates will be reinstated in the Third and final *Mikdash*, and will represent the "manmade" component of the Temple. Even though the Almighty Himself will construct the Third Temple, the Jewish people will be considered the builders since the doors will have been made by King David.

The halachic basis for this notion is the Gemara's ruling in Masechet Bava Batra (53b) concerning the case of a house built on ownerless property.[5] The Gemara establishes that if one person builds a house on such property, but the door is placed by somebody else, the second person is considered the rightful owner of the property. A house without doors is worthless, and therefore it is the one who affixes the door whom *Halacha* considers the rightful owner.

Applying this rule to the *Bet Hamikdash*, the Third Temple will be attributed to King David, as his doors will be affixed to the building. Even though God builds the building, it is considered King David's project, as he built the building's doors. For this reason, the verse in Tehillim (30:1) speaks of חנוכת הבית לדוד – "the dedication of David's house", referring to the Third *Bet Hamikdash*. The *Mikdash*

---

5. Specifically, the Gemara speaks of property that had belonged to a convert to Judaism. After conversion, a convert is no longer considered related to his family members. If he does not marry and have children after conversion, he has no inheritors after his death, and thus his property is ownerless.

is considered King David's, because the doors to the Temple will be his. In the next verse, King David exclaims, ארוממך ה' כי דליתני (literally, "I shall exalt You, O God, for You have lifted me"). He praises the Almighty כי דליתני – because He kept his "door" (דלת), the gate to the *Bet Hamildash*, on account of which he is considered the true builder of the even the Third and final *Mikdash*.

The Sages (Midrash Tanhuma Naso 28) describe King David as the exemplar of *teshuba*, repentance. They explain that a person of his level of piety would not ordinarily commit the kind of sin he committed with Batsheba, but God arranged for this incident to happen in order to demonstrate the power of repentance. King David was allowed to commit this offense in order to serve as an eternal, inspiring example of *teshuba*, of humble confession and firm resolve to rectify the negative effects of sin. This quality of King David is symbolized by the "gates" that he constructed. King David built the door that led to the *kodesh ha'kodashim*, the inner sanctum of the Temple. This chamber was accessed only once a year, on Yom Kippur, the day of *teshuba*, when the *kohen gadol* entered to beg for forgiveness on behalf of the people. Both literally and figuratively, it is King David, the paradigm of repentance, who built the "gates of repentance", the door to God's inner chamber, where He awaits for us to return and repent.

The Gemara in Masechet Hagiga (12b) comments that God has two chambers in the heavens – an outer chamber, which is characterized by an aura of glory and euphoria, and inner chamber, where the Almighty "cries", as it were. The Rabbis explain that the outer chamber is where the Almighty meets with the holy *sadikim*, who lived piously throughout their lives. This is the room of majesty and splendor, where the *sadikim* are greeted with the honor and glory they deserve. God's innermost chamber, however, is reserved for the *ba'aleh teshuba*, those who had fallen and struggled to pick themselves up, who were not perfect, who worked and toiled to grow and improve. This inner chamber is a place of "crying", where the *ba'aleh teshuba* shed tears of remorse. The Sages (Berachot 34b) famously comment, מקום שבעלי תשובה עומדים אין צדיקים גמורים יכולים לעמוד בו – "The place where *ba'aleh teshuba* stand – the completely righteous are not allowed to stand there". God lovingly invites the *ba'aleh teshuba* into his private chamber, whereas the *sadikim* are assigned the outer room.

The *kodesh ha'kodashim* corresponds to God's heavenly "inner chamber". It is the chamber of repentance, the chamber of tearful remorse, regret, prayer and supplication. The gate to this chamber was built by King David himself, the exemplar of repentance, the man who showed us how to return to the Almighty through sincere prayer and *teshuba*.

The Temple will be built by God, but it will require as well the "gates of repentance". The *Mikdash* cannot be completed without our *teshuba*, without passing through the "gates" of King David. As we pray for the Temple's restoration, we must also resolve in our hearts to do our share in bringing our nation's final redemption through sincere and wholehearted *teshuba*, as taught to us by King David.

The aforementioned verse in Echa tells that when the gates of the Temple sank into the ground, their bolts were shattered (טבעו בארץ שעריה אבד ושבר בריחיה). Without a bolt, a door cannot be locked. Throughout the millennia of exile, King David's gates, the gates of repentance, have remained opened. Indeed, the Sages (Berachot 32b) famously teach, שערי דמעות לא ננעלו – "The gates of tears have not been locked". Even after the Temple's destruction, we have a way back to the Almighty through the gates of tears, through sincere, heartfelt remorse and repentance. These are the gates built for us by David, the exemplar of repentance, and through which we must pass in order to bring about the long-awaited restoration of our Temple.

תשכן בתוך ירושלים עירך כאשר דברת
"Reside in Your city, Jerusalem, as You said"

The Gemara in Masechet Ta'anit (5a) states that there is a

heavenly city of Jerusalem parallel to the city of Jerusalem here on earth. We pray that God should take residence in the heavenly Jerusalem – "Your city, Jerusalem" – which will prepare us for the second and final stage, the *Shechina*'s revelation in the earthly city of Jerusalem.

Alternatively, this passage is a prayer to God to maintain His ongoing residence in the earthly Jerusalem, even in its current state of desolation. God warns in the Book of Vayikra (26:31), והשימותי את מקדשיכם – "I shall lay your Sanctuary desolate". The Sages inferred from this verse that even in its state of שממה ("desolation"), the Temple is still called a מקדש (from the word קדש, holiness), meaning, it still retains its status of sanctity. This is why it is halachically forbidden to walk on the Temple Mount today, despite the absence of the *Mikdash*. The site of the Temple remains holy, even though our enemies have constructed a house of foreign worship on that site. We ask God in this *beracha* תשכון בתוך ירושלים, that He should maintain His presence in Jerusalem even in our current state of exile. We add, כאשר דברת – "as You said" – referring to the aforementioned verse in Vayikra, והשימותי את מקדשיכם, where God indicated to us that He would remain present in Jerusalem even in its state of destruction.

וכסא דוד עבדך מהרה בתוכה תכין
"and speedily establish the throne of Your servant, David, in its midst"

During the time of the Arizal, there were those who argued that this passage should be omitted from the *beracha* of תשכון בתוך ירושלים. They noted that King David's reign is the theme of the next *beracha*, the *beracha* of את צמח דוד, whereas this *beracha* speaks about the rebuilding of the *Mikdash*, which does not directly relate to the theme of the Davidic dynasty. In fact, the story is told of a man who came to the Arizal, and upon looking at the man's forehead, the Arizal immediately recognized that he does not pray properly. He asked the man if he omitted the clause וכסא דוד עבדך מהרה בתוכה תכין from the *Amidah* prayer, and the man replied in the affirmative. The

Arizal told him that it is recognizable on his forehead that he had never prayed a proper *Amidah* in his life.

The question, then, arises, why do we add this clause in the context of תשכון בתוך ירושלים?

The Arizal answered by noting that this *beracha* mentions not David, but rather כסא דוד, which literally means "David's throne". This term, the Arizal explained, actually refers to Mashiah ben Yosef, the "messiah" from the tribe of Yosef who will come and lay the groundwork for the arrival of Mashiah ben David, a descendant of King David who will reinstate the Jewish dynasty. Our Sages teach that there is a possibility that Mashiah ben Yosef will be killed by Armilus, an enemy of the Jewish people, as he fulfills his mission. When we pray here for the restoration of the Temple, we pray as well for the כסא דוד, the for Mashiah ben Yosef who will prepare the throne of King David with the unfolding of the Messianic Era. We beseech Hashem to protect Mashiah ben Yosef from Armilus during the turbulent events that will precede the rebuilding of the Temple. Indeed, many *siddurim* add a comment in parentheses next to this phrase that one should have in mind to pray for the protection of Mashiah ben Yosef from Armilus.

The phrase וכסא דוד עבדך מהרה בתוכה תכין also alludes to the concept that God's "throne" is "incomplete" during the period of exile. As long as the *Bet Hamikdash* lay in ruins, God's kingship over the world is not apparent, and thus His throne is deficient, as it were. The Sages inferred this notion from the verse, כי יד על כס י-ה (Shemot 17:16), in which God refers to His throne with the word כס, a shortened version of the full word, כסא. God's Name is also "incomplete", as it were, during our period of exile, as indicated in this same verse which uses the Name י-ה, an abbreviated form of the Name י-ה-ו-ה. At the time of final redemption, God's Name will be completed; י-ה will be restored to its complete form of י-ה-ו-ה. The Ba'al Shem Tov explained the verse ימלא ה' כל משאלותיך (literally, "Hashem shall fulfill all your wishes" – Tehillim 20:6) to mean ימלא

ה' – completing the divine Name of ה-ו-ה-י – shall be כל משאלותיך – all a person's requests and aspirations. Our primary goal and objective should be to complete God's Name, to bring Him glory and worldwide recognition by bringing our nation's redemption. We therefore pray for the restoration of כסא דוד עבדך, the throne of the Almighty, which is represented by the throne of King David.

ובנה אותה בנין עולם
"and build it as an eternal structure"

Since the Third Temple will be built by God Himself, it will endure eternally. The first two *Bateh Mikdash* were built by human beings, and therefore just as humans are mortal, the Temples did not last for eternity. But the Third Temple will remain forever, just as God exists forever.

במהרה בימינו
"speedily and in our days"

While the simple meaning of this phrase is that we pray for the privilege of seeing the Temple's restoration בימינו, in our days, it may also mean that the Temple will be rebuilt through, or as a result of, ימינו – the way we spend our days.

The *Zohar* teaches that the righteous *sadikim* fill their days with Torah and *misvot*. They do not squander even a single day, utilizing each one to its fullest as an opportunity to study Torah, perform *misvot*, and help other people. The day then rises to the heavens and comes before the Almighty to testify that it had been properly utilized by the *sadik*. God stores the day, so-to-speak, in a special "vault" in the heavens, and when the *sadik* dies, all his days are brought to him and they form special garments for his soul. The *Zohar* concludes by warning those who waste their days on vanity that they will have no "clothing" for their souls in the afterlife. Time is our most precious commodity, and the righteous ones among us are wise enough to fill their time with meaningful and constructive pursuits, rather than squandering it. The Torah thus describes Abraham Abinu as בא בימים (Bereshit 24:1), or "coming with his days". Abraham left the world accompanied by all his days. Every day he lived joined his soul to testify to the proper use of his time here on earth.

The stores sell two kinds of calendars. In some, the customer is expected to tear off each day after it passes, whereas in the other, each day's page remains, and the person simply turns to the next page. One Rabbi commented that it is far preferable to purchase the second kind. We do not believe that a day is "torn", that each day that passes is simply discarded and never thought of again. For us, each day has eternal value because of what we accomplish on that day. It is not "torn off"; it stays with us, forever – assuming we use it productively.

We therefore pray that God should rebuild the *Mikdash* בימינו, through our days, through our proper use of our time. As we conclude this *beracha*, we acknowledge that the restoration of the Temple depends largely on ימינו, on the way we use the time we are given here on earth.

Hacham Ben Sion Abba Shaul *zt"l* noted how people often complain on fast days about the length of the day. Apparently, the days are long, there is plenty of time for us to study significant portions of the Torah, to devote time to our families, to visit sick patients in the hospital, to volunteer for communal needs, and so on. People complain that they do not have enough time, but this is because so much of their time is wasted on vanity. It is by using our time constructively, for meaningful and valuable purposes, that we become worthy of redemption and the restoration of the *Bet Hamikdash*.

ברוך אתה ה' בונה ירושלים

"Blessed are You, Hashem, who builds Jerusalem"

We describe Hashem as בונה ירושלים, in the present tense, because He builds Jerusalem already in the present. As mentioned, the construction of the Temple is already well underway, as each *misva* we perform and every *tefila* we recite contributes to the ongoing process, which will culminate in the descent of the completed *Mikdash* from the heavens to the sacred site of the Temple in Jerusalem.

לעילוי נשמת
דוד אברהם נתנאל
בן
הרב יעקב יוסף צבי

The Fifteenth Beracha

את צמח דוד

After we pray for the restoration of the *Bet Hamikdash*, we pray for the other major component of our national redemption – the restoration of מלכות בית דוד, the Davidic dynasty through the arrival of Mashiah, the Messianic King, a scion from the line of David who will reinstate the Jewish monarchy.

Anticipating *Mashiah*

Our Sages (Shabbat 31a) teach that each of us, after leaving this world, will be asked the question, צפית לישועה – "Did you anticipate salvation?" We will be judged as to whether or not we longed for the arrival of Mashiah. When we recite this *beracha* in the *Amidah*, we are reminded of this obligation to believe in and anticipate redemption. In fact, the Arizal comments that when a person recites the words toward the end of this *beracha*, כי לישועתך קוינו כל היום ("for we long for Your salvation all day"), he should have in mind to fulfill the *misva* of longing for the Mashiah. Of course, one does not fulfill this *misva* unless he sincerely feels such a longing, and harbors genuine hopes and aspirations to see a redeemed world under the leadership of the Messianic King.

The great Sages of Israel anticipated the arrival of Mashiah in a very real and genuine way. When Rabbi Levi Yishak of Berditchev sent invitations to his daughter's wedding, he wrote on the invitation that the wedding will take place on Mosa'eh Shabbat Nahamu, in the rebuilt city of Jerusalem. He then added in parentheses that if, Heaven forbid, Mashiah does not come before the wedding date, then the affair will take place in a banquet hall in Berditchev. He truly believed that Mashiah could arrive at any moment, and truly wished for Mashiah to come, and therefore planned to make his daughter's wedding not in his town in Europe, but in the rebuilt city of Jerusalem.

Another story is told of the Yismah Moshe, whose son studied in a yeshiva in a different town and would return home for Shabbat each week. One Friday, as the Rabbi studied in his room, the rest of the family noticed that the son had not yet returned from yeshiva, and they grew concerned. Finally, shortly before the onset of Shabbat, the young man arrived. The family members, relieved and overjoyed that the boy had returned safely, exclaimed, "He's here! He's here!"

Suddenly, the Rabbi burst out of his study, put on his hat, and rushed to the front door.

"He's here... Where?" he asked.

The family members pointed to his son, and explained that they were referring to him.

"Oh", the Rabbi said, disappointed. "When I heard you shout, 'He's here!' I assumed you meant that Mashiah arrived.

To the Yismah Moshe, Mashiah was not some kind of hypothetical possibility; it was real. He truly expected Mashiah to arrive any day, and therefore when his family excitedly shouted, "He's here!" he instinctively assumed that Mashiah had come.

The Hafetz Haim was famous for (obviously, among many other things) anticipating the arrival of Mashiah. As a *kohen*, he felt obliged to prepare himself to perform the priestly duties that will be assigned to the *kohanim* in the *Bet Hamikdash*. Thus, for example, whenever he would travel by carriage, he would tell the driver to start driving, and then run and jump onto it. He explained that he adopted this practice because of the Gemara's comment כהנים זריזין הן – the *kohanim* performed their duties in the Temple with energy and vigor. In order to prepare himself for the priestly service, the Hafetz Haim trained himself to be energetic, so he could perform the *avoda* (service in the Bet Ha*Mikdash*) in the proper manner when the Temple is rebuilt.

This is the meaning of צפית לישועה – anticipating the arrival of Mashiah as a real event that could occur at any moment.

Bringing Redemption

But in addition to longing for Mashiah, we must also work toward bringing Mashiah. It is disingenuous to pray את צמח דוד עבדך, and beg Hashem to bring us the redemption, without committing ourselves to doing what needs to be done to make *Am Yisrael* worthy of redemption. We must take concrete, significant measures to render our nation deserving of Mashiah and of the restoration of Jewish kingship.

To identify more clearly the measures needed to help bring our redemption, we need to first understand and appreciate the precise effects of the Temple's destruction. The Rabbis teach that the heavenly angels lost two of their wings with the destruction of the Temple. The prophet Yeshayahu (6:2) describes the angels as equipped with six wings – two that cover the face, two that cover the legs, and two that are used for flying. These six wings correspond to the six words of the phrase ברוך שם כבוד מלכותו לעולם ועד ("Blessed is the Name of the majesty of His glory for all eternity"). This is the phrase that Yaakob Abinu proclaimed on his deathbed, after receiving his sons' confirmation that they were fully devoted to God. It is also the phrase we recite after mistakenly reciting a ברכה לבטלה, an unwarranted *beracha*. If a *beracha* was not warranted, then it remains motionless; it has no means of rising to the heavens and coming before God's throne. We therefore recite the phrase ברוך שם כבוד מלכותו לעולם ועד, which corresponds to the angels' wings. This recitation appends "wings" to our *beracha*, enabling it to soar to the Heavenly Throne and come before God.

But while Yeshayahu beheld a vision of angels with six wings, the prophet Yehezkel (1:6) described the angels as having only four wings. The reason for this discrepancy is that Yehezkel beheld his prophecies after the Temple's destruction, when the angels had only four wings.

Some Rabbis explained that the two lost wings are those which correspond to the middle pair of letters in the phrase of ברוך שם, namely, the words כבוד מלכותו. The Temple's destruction marked the loss of כבוד מלכותו, the glory of God's Kingship. When *Am Yisrael* went into exile, the *Shechina* also went into exile, as it were. God's kingship and majesty was no longer apparent, and therefore the angels lost the wings of כבוד מלכותו, the wings that represent the glory of divine kingship. We thus pray in the festival prayer service, גלה כבוד מלכותך מהרה, asking Hashem to reveal כבוד מלכותך, the majesty of His kingship which was lost as a result of the Temple's destruction.

The concept of כבוד מלכותו refers specifically to the decline of standards of morality. The verse states in Tehillim (45:14),

כל כבודה בת מלך פנימה – "All the honor of a princess is inside". This is the verse that expresses the ideal of modesty, the purity and sanctity of *Am Yisrael* in the area of relationships between men and women. It exhorts the Jewish woman to be private and modest, rather than seek the attention of men outside her home. This phrase, כל כבודה בת מלך פנימה, contains an allusion to כבוד מלכותו, the divine kingship that was lost as a result of the Temple's destruction and the Jewish people's exile. God's kingship is undermined by promiscuity, by the kind of decadence and immorality that unfortunately characterizes contemporary society. As indicated in the verse in Tehillim, כבוד מלכותו is expressed through modesty and discretion; vulgarity and indiscretion in the area of intimate relations expresses the precise opposite, the rejection of divine kingship and keeping the divine presence distant. God abhors immodesty, and He keeps distant from the Jewish people, as it were, when we do not conduct ourselves at the proper standard of morality. He will restore כבוד מלכותו when we act in a manner that reflects the splendor of divine kingship.

Yaakob Abinu foresaw the sharp decline in standards of morality that would occur in the final period before *Am Yisrael*'s redemption. As he lay on his deathbed, he expressed to his sons his wish to reveal את אשר יקרא אתכם באחרית הימים – "that which will occur to you at the end of days" (Bereshit 49:1). The word יקרא relates to the word קרי, which refers to the impurity and contamination brought by immorality. Yaakob Abinu warned that באחרית הימים, just before the end of the exile, the Jewish people will deteriorate in the area of קרי, and conduct themselves immodestly and unbecomingly in the area of intimacy. Unfortunately, we are seeing the fulfillment of this prophecy in our time. We cannot expect the gentile nations, or even Jews with little or no Torah background, to uphold the Torah's standards of morality, but we can and must demand these standards of ourselves. And, sadly, we have fallen very far from the standards demanded by *Halacha*. Too many parents are reluctant to admonish their daughters to dress appropriately, and too many men – both married and unmarried – are not careful regarding what they look at and to what they are exposed through the technology in their homes. Our carelessness in this regard, and the alarming deterioration that has been steadily progressing in recent generations – especially among the Torah observant community – serves to keep כבוד מלכותו away from us, and keep the *Shechina* in exile, rather than bringing the redemption closer.[6]

It is hypocritical to pray for redemption without exerting effort to bring the redemption. If we truly anticipate and desire the arrival of Mashiah, then we must work to improve ourselves specifically in the area of modesty, to raise the standards of *kedusha* in our homes and our communities.

Bringing redemption also requires renewed commitment to Torah study. There are some Rabbis who maintain that the "missing wings" of the angels are those which correspond to the final two words in the phrase ברוך שם – the words לעולם ועד. The first letters of these words, ל and ו, have the combined numerical value of thirty-six – the numbers of *masechtot* (tractates) in the Gemara. Furthermore, the six words of ברוך שם correspond to the six books of the Mishna, the final two of which are קדשים and טהרות. These two books deal with the laws of sacrifices and ritual purity, which, generally speaking, have no practical application after the Temple's destruction. These are the two "wings" that were lost when we went into exile, and we restore those wings, and bring our nation's redemption, by recommitting ourselves to mastering all six sections of the Mishna, and all thirty-six tractates of Gemara. Our advanced Torah learning, especially the Talmud, will help restore the missing "wings" and bring our final redemption closer.

---

6. The six weeks of שובבי"ם – when we read the first six *parashiyot* of the Book of Shemot – are especially suited to atone for, and to correct, sins of this nature. These six weeks correspond to the six primary ערי מקלט, the cities of refuge for inadvertent killers. Like the six cities, these six weeks serve as "refuge" for people struggling with the *yeser hara* of immorality. Similarly, the forty-two days of שובבי"ם correspond to the other forty-two cities of refuge. Furthermore, Hacham Baruch Ben Haim z"l would often tell his students that the verse of שמע ישראל contains six words, which correspond to the six primary cities of refuge, and the paragraph of ואהבת has forty-two words, corresponding to the other forty-two cities. The Sages comment that one who feels the evil inclination overpowering him should recite the *shema*. This recitation serves as a kind of "refuge" for those seeking to escape the clutches of temptation and sin.

The final two "wings" also refer to the sin of שנאת חנם, baseless hatred, on account of which the Second Temple was destroyed. When Yaakob Abinu sent Yosef to check on his brothers, a mission which resulted in their selling him into slavery, he said to Yosef, הלוא אחיך רועים בשכם לכה ואשלחך ("Indeed, your brothers are shepherding in Shechem; I shall now send you…" – 37:13). The word בשכם is an acronym representing the words ברוך שם כבוד מלכותו, and the next two words, לכה ואשלחך, begin with the letters ל and ו, which represent the final two words – לעולם ועד. Latent in Yaakob's instruction to Yosef is a hint to the loss of לעולם ועד, that these two wings have been separated from the other four. The act of שנאת חנם that was about to unfold, the sin of brothers mistreating each other, results in the loss of the final two wings, לעולם ועד. Our efforts to bring redemption must also include a renewed commitment to dealing kindly, patiently and forgivingly with our fellow Jews, avoiding anger and resentment, and working toward establishing and maintaining friendly, congenial relations with all Jews, no matter how different they may be from us. This will help restore the lost "wings" and accelerate the process of the Redemption of Israel.

את צמח דוד עבדך מהרה תצמיח
"Speedily make the plant of Your servant, David, sprout"

We refer to Mashiah in this *beracha* with the name צמח, the name which Mashiah is called in the prophecy of Zecharya (3:8), הנני מביא את עבדי צמח ("I am hereby bringing My servant, Semah"). Mashiah has several different names, and the Hebrew word משיח may in fact be read as an acronym representing four of Mashiah's more common names – מנחם, שילה ינון, חנינא. The different names represent different aspects of Mashiah's character. Great people are often complex people; they excel in numerous different areas. The Messianic King is therefore assigned several different names, to reflect the many different facets of his extraordinary character.

The word את is often used "לרבות", meaning, to indicate that something else is included in the context under discussion. In this instance, the word את serves as an allusion to Mashiah ben Yosef, the messiah from the tribes of Yosef who will arrive before the Messianic King from the Davidic dynasty. We pray for both messiahs, as both signify critical stages in the process of our nation's redemption.

We describe the unfolding of our redemption with the verb תצמיח ("sprout"). Our redemption resembles the process of the growth of a tree. When a seed or even a sapling is planted in the ground, it takes a good deal of time for the tree to grow, develop and bear fruit. The agricultural process requires patience, hard work and faith that the time and effort will pay off in the end. Similarly, we cannot expect all our nation's problems to be solved overnight. Our redemption will "sprout", progressing step-by-step, and we must continue investing the necessary effort to move the process along, with patience and faith that we will, eventually, witness the final stages of the Messianic process. When we pray that this process should unfold מהרה ("speedily"), this does not mean that we want the redemption to occur in an instant, like a flash of lightning. Rather, as the Vilna Gaon explains, it means that each stage should pass quickly, and not be delayed unnecessarily.

וקרנו תרום בישועתך
"and raise his horn, through Your salvation"

The dynasty of King David is referred to as an animal horn, a symbol of durability. A horn is the only part of the animal that does not decay and remains strong and firm forever. Unlike the reign of King Shaul, whose kingship was short-lived, King David's royal dynasty will endure for eternity. Therefore, when the prophet Shemuel anointed Shaul as king, he used oil from a פך, an earthenware jug (Shemuel I 10:1), which breaks when it is dropped. When anointing David, however, Shemuel used a utensil called a קרן (Shemuel I 16:13), foreshadowing the endurance and permanence of King David's reign, as symbolized by an animal's horn.

Additionally, the horn is a symbol of a gradual process. When an animal is born, its horns are very small, but they gradually grow over the course of the animal's life. The term קרן is therefore used in reference to the process of redemption, which will unfold gradually, one step after another. In this sense, the term קרן may also be understood to mean קרני אור, rays of sunlight. Sunrise does not occur in a single instant; it would be too difficult for our eyes if the thick nighttime darkness would suddenly give way to the brilliant midday light. God therefore arranged for sunrise to develop over a period of time, beginning with the appearance of light on the eastern horizon, which slowly increases until the sun appears, and the light gradually grows stronger as the sun rises through the sky. Likewise, we would not be able to suddenly adjust to the brilliant "light" of our national redemption. God has the process unfold gradually, allowing us to grow accustomed to each stage before the onset of the next phase, until we are finally ready for the final stage.

כי לישועתך קווינו כל היום
"for we have longed for Your salvation all day"

We pray and beg for redemption because we long for redemption, and if we do not feel a longing for redemption, then this *beracha* reminds us of the obligation to long for Mashiah, that we, our lives and the world are woefully deficient in the absence of the *Bet Hamikdash* and the reign of King David's dynasty.

There are different reasons why people long for Mashiah. Many people yearn for our redemption because they are beset by personal hardships, such as debt and illness, and they realize that Mashiah's arrival will herald the resolution to all these and other thorny challenges that people confront in their lives. Others may yearn for redemption because they long to see departed loved ones, with whom they will be reunited at the time of the resurrection. But the primary reason to pray and long for redemption is לישועתך – for the sake of God's salvation, as it were. As long as the Jewish people are in exile, the *Shechina* is in exile, so-to-speak. God's glory is undermined, and will be restored only with the redemption of Israel. This should be our primary motivation for praying for Mashiah, and we therefore emphasize in this *beracha* כי לישועתך קוינו כל היום, that we pray because we yearn to see the Almighty's salvation, so-to-speak, the restoration of God's glory as all the world's inhabitants will recognize His kingship and authority.

At the same time, however, the phrase כי לישועתך קוינו כל היום also alludes to the salvation from all our private, individual troubles and concerns. It is written in several *siddurim* that when one recites this passage, he should have in mind to pray for the resolution of all the problems facing all members of our nation, such as health issues, financial difficulties, infertility, family problems, spiritual struggles, and so on.

ברוך אתה ה' מצמיח קרן ישועה
"Blessed are You, Hashem, who makes the horn of salvation sprout"

When a seed is planted in the ground, it decays before it begins to grow and sprout in the form of a plant. The process of "מצמיח", the "sprouting" of Jewish redemption, proceeds in a similar manner. Before the redemption surfaces, there is a process of "decay", of spiritual and moral decline. The religious crises that we witness in our day, the defection of Jewish youths from our community and tradition, the relentless assault on Jewish values and laws, the breakdown of the Jewish family, the decline in morality and restraint – this is all part of the "decay" that precedes redemption. When we recite this *beracha*, which reminds us that redemption unfolds like the development of a seed, we are reminded that the problems we witness and experience are actually the incipient stages of our national redemption, and that the "plant" of the Messianic Era will soon rise above the surface, bringing salvation and respite from all our challenges and hardships.

The Sixteenth Beracha
שמע קולנו

The *beracha* of שמע קולנו marks the conclusion of the בקשה section of the *Amidah*, the section in which we present our requests. In this *beracha* we plead to God to accept all our prayers, regardless of whether we are deserving of a favorable response.

שמע קולנו ה' אלהינו
"Hear our voice, Hashem our God"

We ask Hashem to hear our "voice", not our "speech". Speech is something intelligible, a series of words that can be understood, whereas a voice is incoherent. The phrase שמע בקול – "hearing a voice" – refers to accepting something that does not necessarily make logical sense. For example, after Sara demanded that Abraham send away Hagar and Yishmael, God instructed Abraham שמע בקולה ("heed her [Sara's] voice" – Bereshit 21:12). Sara's request made no sense to Abraham. As bastions of *hesed*, Abraham and Sara were "in the business" of welcoming people, extending loving kindness to all, not driving family members away from the home. But God told Abraham to follow Sara's instruction, to hear her "voice", even though he could not make any rational sense out of it.

Similarly, God tells Yishak of the reward he and his descendants will receive עקב אשר שמע אברהם בקולי – on account of the fact that Abraham "heard My voice" (Bereshit 26:5), referring to the command of *akedat Yishak*. Quite obviously, the command to slaughter Yishak on an altar, especially after God had promised that a great nation would emerge from him, made no sense to Abraham at all. But He nevertheless heeded the Almighty's "voice", He accepted a command that he could not possibly understand.

When we say the words שמע קולנו, we acknowledge the fact that it might not "make sense" for God to accept our prayers. We are unworthy of having our requests granted, and the prayers themselves are often not recited the way they should be. But as we conclude this section of the *tefila*, we beg from the depths of our hearts that God should fulfill our wishes even if there is no logical reason to, and even if we are undeserving of a favorable response.

אב הרחמן חוס ורחם עלינו
"Merciful Father – be gracious and have compassion on us"

The word חוס denotes the special feelings of care and concern that one feels towards something or someone in whom he's invested, such as a parent's concern for a child. God says to the prophet Yona (4:11), ואני לא אחוס על נינוה העיר הגדולה – "Shall I not have compassion for Nineveh, the great city..." As the Creator of all people, God naturally tends to treat us compassionately. Even if the people of Nineveh did not, strictly speaking, deserve a second chance, God nevertheless forgave them because they were, after all, His creations. חוס thus refers to compassion that stems from a certain sense of connection that one feels to the other.

רחם, by contrast, refers to compassion due to the person's plight. When we see a homeless person, we are moved to offer assistance even though we have never met this person before or have any connection to him, simply out of pity for the suffering he endures.

We ask God to grant our requests, despite our unworthiness, for two reasons: first, we are His creatures, and members of His beloved nation, and, second, we are desperate and helpless, incapable of meeting our needs without His assistance.

וקבל ברחמים וברצון את תפלתנו, כי אל שומע תפילות ותחנונים אתה
"and mercifully and willfully accept our prayers, for Your are a God who hears prayers and supplications"

The term תפילות refers to the fixed, standard prayers that we recite, whereas תחנונים denotes our additional, personal supplications. The Sages teach that this *beracha* of שמע קולנו is the appropriate place to insert any kind of personal prayer that one wishes to recite to God, in any language, in any text. In this *beracha*, one may ask for anything, whether it is success in the business meeting later that day, that one's child should receive a good grade, for the health of an ill family member, for a spouse, and so on. Particularly, it is worthwhile to insert in שמע קולנו a prayer for one's livelihood, and in fact, the Hida formulated a special text of a prayer for *parnasa* that one should recite in this *beracha*. Before reciting this special prayer, though, it is proper to first recite a prayer sincerely asking God to forgive one's sins.

The *Aruch Ha'shulhan* writes that it is improper to recite this voluntary prayer at every prayer service, as this would appear disrespectful to the *Ansheh Kenesset Hagedola*, who formulated the *Amidah* text. If a person recites an additional text in every prayer, he gives the impression that the original text is inadequate and requires modification. Therefore, although it is laudable to recite the Hida's prayer for *parnasa* in שמע קולנו, one should occasionally omit this prayer, out of respect for the great *sadikim* of the *Ansheh Kenesset Hagedola* who did not include this text when formulating the *Amidah*.

Furthermore, one should not prolong his *Amidah* recitation through additional supplications in שמע קולנו if this will cause him to miss the recitation of *Nakdishach* with the congregation. Joining the congregational recitation of *Nakdishach* is more important than voluntary prayers, and therefore one should not insert additional supplications at the expense of *Nakdishach*. Instead, one may add voluntary prayers at the very end of the *Amidah*, before reciting עושה שלום, as at that point one may recite *Nakdishach* with the congregation, since he is considered to have completed the *Amidah*. Likewise, the *Aruch Ha'shulhan's* ruling, that one should not add voluntary prayers in each and every *Amidah*, does not apply once one reaches the end of the *Amidah* and has recited the verse יהיו לרצון אמרי פי. At this point, one may add voluntary supplications without restriction.

ומלפניך מלכנו ריקם אל תשיבנו
"and do not send us away from You empty-handed, our King"

Even if God will not answer all our prayers, we beseech Him to at very least grant us one request, so we do not "return empty-handed", so that we come away from our prayers with at least one of our wishes fulfilled.

We refer to God here as מלכנו, "our King", because a king has the authority to overrule a court's decision. With His absolute power, God is able to grant our wishes even if we don't deserve anything.

חננו וענננו ושמע תפלתנו
"pity us, answer us, and hear our prayers"

The word חננו relates to the word חנם, which means free. Acknowledging our unworthiness, we beg the Almighty for a מתנת חנם, a handout, to give us what we do not deserve.

כי אתה שומע תפלת כל פה
"for You hear the prayer of every mouth"

Prayer, by definition, must come from the heart. It is not about saying words, but rather about using words to express the emotions of the heart. Unfortunately, however, we often end up mouthing the words of the prayer service without any feeling or emotion. In our final plea before proceeding to the next stage of the prayer service, we describe God as hearing תפלת כל פה – the prayer of every mouth. He looks kindly upon even the prayers that were recited only with the lips, and not with the heart, and we beg Him to compassionately accept our words, even if they were not recited with the feeling and emotion that we should have during *tefila*.

This expression also emphasizes the fact that God listens to every mouth's prayer regardless of how it is articulated. He accepts prayers in any language, and on any level of eloquence. Even a simple, plain request in English is treasured by God, and potentially worthy of acceptance.

ברוך אתה ה' שומע תפלה
Blessed are You, Hashem, who hears prayer"

We refer to prayer here with the singular form, תפלה, as opposed to the plural form – תפילות – which was used earlier in this *beracha*. Our Rabbis teach us that the angels take all the prayers of all Jews and make them into a "crown" which they then bring to the Almighty. Eventually, all our *tefilot* merge into a single תפלה which is brought before God and lovingly accepted.

Additionally, the phrase שומע תפלה alludes to the individual attention that each of us receives from God. Although there are likely many thousands of Jews across the world praying at the same time, Hashem gives each person His complete, undivided attention, so-to-speak, as though he is the only person speaking to God at that moment. When we pray, we must feel that God is focusing exclusively on us and on our prayers, eager to hear each and every word.

Refuah Shelema to:

Leah bat Virginie
and
Tzadok Israel ben Yehudit

Sam Flaster

The Seventeenth Beracha

רצה

The seventeenth *beracha* begins the third and final section of the *Amidah*, in which we make our "concluding statements" to the Almighty after having submitted all our requests.

רצה ה' אלהינו בעמך ישראל ולתפלתם שעה
"Be pleased, Hashem our God, with Your nation, Israel, and heed their prayers"

Before taking leave of God's presence, we reiterate our plea that He accept our prayers even if they are imperfect and unworthy of acceptance.

והשב העבודה לדביר ביתך
"and return the service to the sanctuary of Your abode"

It is likely that this passage was added after the Temple's destruction; otherwise, it seems difficult to understand why Jews during the time of the *Bet HaMikdash* would pray to God to restore the *avoda*, the ritual service of the Temple. Alternatively, it is possible that this passage was, in fact, included in the original text of the *Amidah* formulated in the beginning of the Second Temple. The *Shechina* was not present in the Second Temple at the same level in which it was manifest in the First Temple. Possibly, this clause is a prayer that God should restore His *Shechina* to the *Bet HaMikdash* in full force, to the level at which it was present in the First Temple.

Most of the prayers we recite focus on our own personal needs – our health, financial success, children, and so on. As we conclude the *Amidah*, we add a request "on God's behalf" so-to-speak, praying for the *Shechina*'s return to the Temple. We in effect say to Hashem, "We are not only praying for ourselves – we are praying for You, too! Therefore, in this merit, accept our prayers and respond favorably"!

The Hida writes that when a person recites these words, he should have in mind the particular sacrifices that would be brought on that particular occasion. In *shaharit*, one should have in mind while reciting these words that our prayers should be regarded as the morning daily *tamid* offering, and at *minha* one should have in mind that the prayers should be treated as the afternoon *tamid*. During *arbit*, one should request in his mind that our prayers be accorded the status of the חלבים ואימורים, the parts of the animal sacrifices that burned on the altar throughout the night. Furthermore, a person should have in mind at this point that the prayers he recites should count towards whatever personal sacrifices he is required to bring for transgressions that he has committed.

ואשי ישראל ותפלתם מהרה באהבה תקבל ברצון

"and You shall quickly and lovingly accept the fire offerings of Israel, and their prayers, willfully"

This is among the more difficult passages of the *Amidah* prayer, as it appears that we pray for the acceptance of אשי ישראל – the sacrifices. Of course, we do not offer sacrifices, due to the absence of the *Bet Hamikdash*. What, then, do we mean when we ask God to accept אשי ישראל?

Some explain that the phrase ואשי ישראל actually belongs to the previous clause, which we should read as follows: והשב העבודה לדביר ביתך ואשי ישראל ("return the service to the Sanctuary of Your abode – as well as the fire offerings of Israel"). This reading, of course, significantly affects the punctuation of this *beracha*, requiring us to read the words ואשי ישראל together with והשב העבודה לדביר ביתך. In most of our *siddurim*, however, a comma is placed after the words והשב העבודה לדביר ביתך, before ואשי ישראל, indicating that אשי ישראל begins a new clause, such that we ask the Almighty to accept our offerings. Our question, then, resurfaces: how can we pray for the acceptance of our sacrifices, if we do not offer sacrifices?

Some explain, quite simply, that אשי ישראל do not refer to sacrifices, but rather to our prayers, which are recited in place of the sacrifices. After all, even when a person brought a sacrifice, the primary component was the *kavana*, his intention, his feelings of devotion to God expressed through the sacrifice. Prayer, too, is an expression of genuine feelings of devotion to God, and therefore אשי ישראל might simply be just another way of saying "prayer".

But if so, then why do we ask God to accept אשי ישראל and ותפלתם? Is this not redundant?

The answer is that these terms refer to two different kinds of prayer. אשי ישראל refers to the obligatory daily prayer services, whereas ותפלתם denotes to the voluntary prayers that we recite outside the framework of the formal, fixed service. We ask the

Almighty to lovingly accept both our obligatory prayers, as well as the voluntary supplications that we make on many occasions throughout the day.

There is, however, a much different approach to explain this passage. The Sages teach that the angel Michael has an altar in the heavens, upon which he offers to God the souls of the *sadikim*, through which *Am Yisrael* earns atonement for its sins. These sacrifices, of course, are unaffected by the Temple's destruction, and they continue even today. We thus ask the Almighty to eagerly accept אשי ישראל, the souls of the righteous members of *Am Yisrael* that are offered on our behalf. According to this interpretation, the word מהרה does not, of course, mean that we pray for the quick death of the *sadikim*, Heaven forbid, but rather that once a *sadik* dies, his soul should be immediately placed upon Michael's altar, without delay, to bring us atonement. (It should be noted that the custom of many Ashkenazim is to omit the word מהרה from this passage.)

The *Noda Be'yehuda* noted that according to this reading, we can understand why this passage also mentions ותפלתם. Our Sages (Berachot 8a) teach that a person's prayers are answered only if he prays with a *minyan* in the synagogue. According to the *Noda Be'yehuda*, a righteous person's soul is brought upon the heavenly altar after his death only if he had prayed in the synagogue with a *minyan*. This is why we recite here in the *Amidah* that אשי ישראל, the offering of the souls, will be accepted together with תפלתם. This means that a person's soul is offered before God after his passing only if he had prayed in the manner in which payers are accepted – meaning, only if he had prayed with a *minyan*.

Another interpretation may be suggested in light of the tradition that even today, Eliyahu the Prophet offers sacrifices to the Almighty on our behalf at the site of the ruins of the *Bet Hamikdash*. (The Sages teach that the site of the *Bet HaMikdash* retains its status of halachic sanctity even today, such that sacrifices may still be offered at the site. Eliyahu Ha'navi is identified as Pinhas, the grandson of Aharon, and he was thus a *kohen* who is eligible to perform the ritual service.) We ask God to accept those sacrifices that His prophet, Eliyahu, offers on our behalf each day.

ואתה ברחמיך הרבים תחפץ בנו ותרצנו
"In Your abundant mercy, desire us and be pleased by us"

Rabbenu Yona writes in his work *Sha'areh Teshuba* that the *sadikim* aspire to more than simply complying with God's commands to avoid punishment. Their goal is תחפוץ בנו, that Hashem should be pleased with them. A good employee, for example, does not want only to keep his job so he can receive his paycheck. He wants to please his boss, to have his boss pat him on the back, compliment him for his work, and tell him how much he means to the company. Similarly, we ask God to confirm that He is pleased with us – and not just that He is not angry with us.

Occasionally, God sends us signals indicating that He is pleased with us. These signals come in the form of manifestations of individual divine providence that we all experience at various times throughout our lives, or sudden, unexpected blessings that we receive. When these events happen, we feel as though God is standing next to us telling us that He is happy with our work, that He is pleased with us and wants to do something special for us, and it is this kind of relationship – whereby we not only fulfill our duties, but please the Almighty – that we should be aspiring to.

ותחזינה עינינו בשובך לציון ברחמים
"and our eyes shall behold Your return to Zion with compassion"

We do not pray simply for the *Shechina*'s return to Jerusalem, but rather for the privilege of beholding the *Shechina*'s return with our own eyes, in fulfillment of the prophecy of Yeshayahu (52:8) כי עין בעין יראו בשוב ה' ציון – "for they will see God's return to Zion with their very eyes".

Why is it so significant to actually behold Hashem's return to Jerusalem?

If a person experiences salvation on his own merits, he is deserving of seeing the events which God brought about to save him. If, however, a person is saved undeservingly, such as through the merits of another person, he is not entitled to see the act of deliverance.

The clearest example of this rule is the story of Lot and his wife, whom God mercifully rescued from the city of Sedom. Lot and his family were rescued only in the merit of his uncle, Abraham; if not for Abraham's merit, Lot and his wife would have perished along with the rest of the condemned city. They were not deserving of being rescued in their own right. For this reason, the angel that rescued them instructed them not to turn around to watch the city's downfall (Bereshit 19:17). As they were not deserving of being saved, it would be arrogant for them to see their townspeople die.

This principle might also underlie the dispute among the Sages concerning the "צהר" that God commanded Noah to build into the ark (see Rashi to Bereshit 6:16). One view claims that Noah was to build a window, whereas others explain this term as referring to a special kind of jewel that provided illumination. It is likely that this debate hinges on the more famous debate (cited by Rashi on Bereshit 6:9) as to whether Noah was truly righteous, or righteous only in comparison with his sinful contemporaries. If Noah was, indeed, a *sadik*, then he was permitted to witness the death wrought by the flood, and hence God instructed him to build a window in the ark. If, however, Noah was not truly deserving of being saved, then he would be forbidden from having a window in the ark enabling him to see the destruction.

We therefore pray that we should be worthy of redemption on our own merits, such that we are given the privilege of beholding God's salvation and His return to Jerusalem with our very eyes.

Guarding One's Eyes

How does one become worthy of beholding the *Shechina*'s return at the time of the Messianic Era?

Our Rabbis teach that whoever guards his eyes from improper sights is rewarded with the privilege of beholding the *Shechina*. Our eyes will be worthy of seeing the divine presence only if we ensure to protect them from impurity, from sights we are forbidden to see.

שמירת העיניים, guarding the eyes from improper sights, is one of the most important keys to achieving *kedusha*. The verse states in the Book of Iyob (5:7), כי אדם לעמל יולד ("for a person is born to toil"). The word עמל represents the words עין (eye), מאור ("light", referring to the *berit mila*), and לשון (tongue). A person's primary work during his lifetime is to control these three parts of the body – his eyes, his mouth, and his *berit mila*. This is how a person achieves *kedusha* and lives a life of purity and spiritual greatness.

The eyes, especially, are the windows to a person's soul, and must therefore be treated with special care and attention. For this reason, Torah leaders are sometimes referred to as עיני העדה, the "eyes" of the nation. It is because they shield their eyes from inappropriate sights that they are given the wisdom and insight to see what ordinary laymen cannot, and the ability to access the depths of the Torah.

Masechet Bava Kama begins with the laws of *nezikin* (torts), and the first category of *nezikin* discussed is שור המזיק, which literally refers to an ox that causes damage. However, the word שור also refers to sight, as in Bilam's prophecy – אשורנו ולא קרוב ("I behold it, though it is still distant" – Bamidbar 24:17). The Torah similarly writes in the Book of Bereshit (49:22), בנות צעדה עלי שור, which means that the Egyptian woman gazed at Yosef. By opening the discussion of *nezikin* with the topic of שור המזיק, the Sages allude to the fact that the primary source of *nezikin*, of damage, is the eyes, seeing improper sights. For this reason, the Talmud states that one who wishes to be a חסיד, a pious person, should study the laws of *nezikin*. Piety begins with avoiding the damage caused by inappropriate sights, which are destructive to a person's soul.

The Gemara in Masechet Bava Mesia (107b) tells about Rav who walked through a cemetery, and commented that ninety-nine of the people buried there died as a result of עין הרע (the evil eye), and only one died from natural causes. If a person does not protect his eyes from improper sights – as most people, unfortunately do not – then he becomes vulnerable to the effects of the עין הרע, to the "evil eye" of others. If he uses his eyes indiscriminately, then he exposes himself to the harmful effects of the eyes of other people. Thus, most people meet their end through exposure to the "evil eye". But the converse is also true. R' Yohanan is cited as commenting that as a descendant of Yosef, he, like Yosef, was not vulnerable to the harmful effects of the עין הרע. R' Yohanan was very careful with his eyes, just as Yosef resisted temptation and did not look upon Potifar's wife. They were thus shielded from the עין הרע, from the negative view of other people.

Additionally, one who avoids improper sights is given the ability to see other people in a positive light. Eyes that have been protected from harmful sights are able to see the favorable and admirable aspects of other people, whereas eyes that have been exposed to improper sights are "impaired", and denied the ability to see the positive qualities of others.

The Ben Ish Hai writes that before a person recites *kiddush* on Friday night, he should look at the *kiddush* cup, first with his right eye, and ten with his left eye. Each time, he should think of the numerical value of the word עין – 130, which is five times the numerical value of the divine Name of הוי"ה (26x5). The Ben Ish Hai writes that looking at the *kiddush* cup in this way and with this intention serves to repair the spiritual damage caused by viewing improper sights. Needless to say, this "repair" is meaningless if a person makes no effort to guard his eyes, if he watches television or views the internet indiscriminately, or looks freely at the barrage of improper sights that unfortunately flood our streets. It is only through a sincere, concentrated effort to protect one's eyes that he is able to keep his soul pure and spiritually intact.

One might wonder why viewing inappropriate sights has such a devastating effect on a person's soul. After all, if there is no physical contact between a person and the one whom he looks upon, how could this possibly affect him? How could the soul be harmed through mere seeing?

In truth, seeing is a form of contact. Sometimes where we're sitting in a traffic jam we can "feel" the driver in the car next to us staring at us. The eyes have a certain power that can be "felt", albeit in a different way than direct physical contact. This explains God's otherwise peculiar response to Moshe's plea to be allowed to enter *Eretz Yisrael*. Moshe recites 515 prayers begging to go into the land – and God answers that he may not go into the land, but he may climb onto a mountain and look at the land. How would seeing *Eretz Yisrael* provide any consolation to Moshe, who so desperately wanted to go there? The answer is that seeing has a stronger effect than we might think. By gazing upon the Land of Israel, Moshe felt, at least in one sense, as though he was actually there.

And so, indeed, seeing is akin to touching. When we look upon something, we absorb it, we bring it into our souls, and we must therefore ensure to look upon only that which we would want to absorb and allow entry into our inner beings.

Tradition teaches that anytime a person feels tempted to look at something inappropriate, but he retrains himself and does not look, that moment is an עת רצון, an especially auspicious time for prayer, to have one's wishes granted. At that moment, God pays special attention to one's prayer, and offers an opportune moment to grant his requests.

This is how important it is to shield one's eyes from improper thoughts. Through שמירת עיניים, we earn special merit to have our prayers answered, and will also be granted the privilege to see the *Shechina* return to Jerusalem, with our very eyes.

ברוך אתה ה' המחזיר שכינתו לציון
"Blessed are You Hashem, who returns His divine presence to Zion"

Every night, the *Shechina* returns to the ruins of the Temple and weeps, as it were, over the loss of the *Bet HaMikdash*. We therefore conclude this *beracha* in the present tense – "who returns His presence to Zion" – because even now, during our period of exile, God returns to Zion every night. He has not forgotten about the *Mikdash*, and will soon return there permanently, with the rebuilding of the third and final Temple.

In Honor of our new Daughter

Mazal bat Leah

Thank you to Rabbi Mansour for constant devotion

and commitment to our

community and individual family.

Leah and Joey Habert

and Family

The Eighteenth Beracha

מודים

The Purpose of Creation

There are a number of indications that this *beracha* of the *Amidah*, the *beracha* of *modim*, is unique. For one thing, we are required to bow when reciting *modim* – a property that this *beracha* shares with only one other *beracha*, the opening *beracha* of the *Amidah*. This already suggests something different about this *beracha*. Additionally, the *Mishna Berura* cites a view that if one does not concentrate on the meaning of the words while reciting *modim*, he does not fulfill the *misva* of prayer – which is also a quality that is unique to this *beracha* and the first *beracha* of the *Amidah*. Although *Halacha* does not follow this opinion, the fact that such a view exists reflects the unique status of the *beracha* of *modim*. Furthermore, during the *hazan*'s repetition of the *Amidah*, each member of the congregation is required to recite a different version of *modim* (called "*modim de'Rabbanan*") while the *hazan* recites this *beracha*. When it comes to the other blessings of the *Amidah*, the *hazan*'s recitation suffices for the entire congregation. But *modim* is different. Each congregant must personally recite *modim* to express his gratitude to the Almighty – as the *hazan*'s recitation does not suffice.

The reason for this *beracha*'s uniqueness becomes perfectly clear once we consider the singular importance of הכרת הטוב, gratitude, which we express in this *beracha*.

The Ramban, in a famous passage in his Torah commentary (end of Parashat Bo), writes that the purpose of all the *misvot*, and in fact the purpose of the world's creation, is for us to not only recognize and believe in God, but to give praise and express gratitude to Him for all He does. Gratitude is not just a value, not even just an important value – it is the purpose of creation itself!

In the Book of Debarim (beginning of Parashat Ki-Tabo), the Torah introduces the command of *bikkurim*, which requires bringing one's first fruits to the *Bet HaMikdash* and expressing gratitude to the Almighty for a successful crop. The Torah refers to the fruits as ראשית כל פרי האדמה ("the first of all the fruits of the ground" – Debarim 26:2). The word ראשית is familiar to us from the first verse in the Torah – בראשית ברא אלוהים את השמים ואת הארץ (literally, "In the beginning, God created heaven and earth"). Our Sages teach that the word בראשית means בשביל ראשית – "for the purpose of ראשית". God created the world for the purpose of ראשית, the *bikkurim* – meaning, for the message embodied by the *bikkurim*. We are brought into this world to feel grateful to God for all He gives us.

As such, *modim* is not just one of the nineteen *berachot* of the *Amidah*. Through the recitation of this *beracha*, we fulfill the primary purpose for which we were created.

The *Beracha* of Moshe Rabbenu

The exemplar of הכרת הטוב was Moshe Rabbenu. When he was forced to flee Egypt, he arrived at a well in Midyan, where he rescued Yitro's daughters from a group of bullying shepherds who had chased them from the well. When Yitro's daughters reported this incident to their father, they said that an איש מצרי ("Egyptian man") had rescued them (Shemot 2:19). This has been explained to mean that when the young women thanked Moshe for his assistance, he refused to take credit. Instead, he advised the women to express gratitude to the איש מצרי, the Egyptian man whom Moshe had killed because he was beating an Israelite slave. This incident caused Moshe to flee Egypt and come to Midyan, and it was thus "thanks" to the violent Egyptian taskmaster that Yitro's daughters were saved.

This is how far Moshe's sense of gratitude extended – that he was able to acknowledge and appreciate the role of the taskmaster in helping him rescue Yitro's daughters.

Later, after God appeared to Moshe and commanded him to return to Egypt and lead *Beneh Yisrael* to freedom, Moshe requested permission from his father-in-law, Yitro. Although God commanded him to leave, and his mission involved the rescuing of millions of oppressed slaves, Moshe nevertheless insisted on asking Yitro for permission to leave. Yitro had taken him in when he was a helpless, lonely fugitive, and he felt a debt of gratitude. He thus could not bring himself to leave Midyan before receiving Yitro's permission.

Moshe's sense of הכרת הטוב extended even to inanimate objects. He refused to cast his staff upon the water in Egypt to turn it into blood, because he felt indebted to the water for rescuing him when he was an infant. It was therefore Aharon, and not Moshe, who transformed the water into blood. Moshe similarly refused to bring about the second plague, the plague of frogs, as it also entailed stretching his staff over the water. He likewise did not bring the plague of lice, which affected the earth of Egypt, as he had used the earth to hide the body of the Egyptian taskmaster whom he killed. This is how far Moshe went in feeling grateful and appreciative – to the point where he felt indebted to the river and to dirt, and was unwilling to "harm" them even for the purpose of delivering *Beneh Yisrael* from slavery.

For good reason, then, the *beracha* of *modim* which we recite three times each day is associated with Moshe Rabbenu. The Sages comment that Moshe Rabbenu foresaw the time when the *misva* of *bikkurim* would not apply, after the destruction of the *Bet HaMikdash*, and he therefore established the three daily prayers in place of *bikkurim*. Of course, as the Gemara teaches, the three patriarchs – Abraham, Yishak and Yaakob – instituted the daily prayers, well before Moshe Rabbenu. Clearly, then, Moshe Rabbenu did not establish the daily prayers. Rather, he instituted the blessing of *modim*, the expression of gratitude to the Almighty, in place of *bikkurim*. During the times of the *Mikdash*, people expressed gratitude to Hashem for their livelihood by offering the first fruits to the Temple. Foreseeing the Temple's destruction, and thus the inability to bring *bikkurim*, Moshe Rabbenu established the daily recitation of *modim*, a verbal declaration of gratitude to God to take the place of *bikkurim*. Appropriately, it was Moshe, the bastion of הכרת הטוב, who instituted the daily expression of gratitude, the requirement to turn to Hashem three times each day to simply say, "Thank you" for all He does for us.

Modim is the *beracha* of Moshe Rabbenu, the section of the *Amidah* through which we seek to emulate our great prophet and teacher, who set for us an inspiring example of acknowledging the kindnesses performed for us, and feeling and expressing our debt of gratitude.

Gratitude for Everything, Big and Small

There is a common and unfortunate misconception that the requirement of הכרת הטוב refers to gratitude for the "big things", for the major, or unexpected, blessings we receive in life – such as a promotion, a family *simha*, or the recovery of a seriously-ill family member. People often overlook the obligation to feel grateful to Hashem for all we have in life – even the so-called "little things".

There is a well-known halachic obligation of ברכת הגומל which requires one to recite a special *beracha* of thanksgiving to Hashem after experiencing one of four kinds of personal salvation: recovery from serious illness, release from prison or captivity, safe arrival after an overseas journey, and safe arrival after a journey through a desert. This *beracha* must be recited in the presence of a *minyan*, and it is preferable to have at least two Rabbis included in the *minyan*. A person reciting this *beracha* might mistakenly think that he owes a debt of gratitude to God only for this particular event which he experienced. He is therefore urged to invite two Rabbis, spiritual guides, to be present when he recited ברכת הגומל. They serve the crucial role of teaching and instructing him to feel grateful for all that he has, for everything he has received, for all the blessings in his life. These major events – such as recovering from a grave illness – must be an occasion to reflect upon all that the Almighty does for a person every day, and indeed at every moment, of his life. The recitation of ברכת הגומל should therefore be done in the presence of Rabbis who will remind the individual of the debt of gratitude he owes to the Almighty for all he has, and not only for the salvation he has just experienced.

For the same reason, the Torah requires that the meat of the *korban toda* (thanksgiving offering) be eaten only on the day of its offering. Whereas the meat of other sacrifices may be eaten for two days, the meat of a thanksgiving offering becomes forbidden the morning after the day of its offering – even though the *korban toda* is the largest sacrifice. The Torah wanted the person bringing a thanksgiving offering to invite guests to publicize the event he is celebrating, and to include Rabbis in his guest list. The Rabbis will speak at the celebration and admonish the individual – and all the guests – of the obligation to feel grateful for all they have.

Saying "Thank You" at the Checkout Counter

Rav Alexander Ziskind of Horodna devotes a section of his work *Yesod Ve'shoresh Ha'aboda* to the concept of הכרת הטוב, and describes how he would turn to God and say, "Thank you" at many points throughout the day. For example, each day he thanked Hashem for giving him an office, a room where he can be alone to concentrate on his studies and developing his relationship with his Creator. How many of us feel grateful for having an office? A quiet room for study or work is not something to be taken for granted. Hashem gave us an office – we must be grateful!

Rav Alexander Ziskind further describes how he would thank the Almighty each time he received a letter from his son informing him that he and his children are well. Upon hearing of the well-being of his son, daughter-in-law and grandchildren, he would turn to Hashem to give praise and express his gratitude. How many times do we pick a phone, ask our child or other family member, "How are you?" and hear, "*Baruch Hashem* well"? Do we stop for a moment to thank Hashem? Or do we just take it for granted that our children, parents and siblings are healthy and have food and shelter?

Rav Alexander Ziskind also writes that he would make a point of thanking Hashem every Friday, when he put on his Shabbat suit. He knew of many *sadikim* who were unable to afford special clothing for Shabbat. But he was fortunate enough to have a special Shabbat suit – and so he said, "Thank you", each and every week. He also expressed his gratitude each time he put on his heavy winter coat before going outside into the cold. Not everybody could afford warm winter gear. If God has given us sweaters, warm boots and a cozy jacket – we must thank Him!

Another remarkable example mentioned by Rav Alexander Ziskind was the gratitude he experienced whenever he had the ability to join the congregation in reciting *kedusha* or answering to *kaddish*. He normally took a very long time to recite the *Amidah*, which usually meant missing *kedusha* and sometimes even *kaddish*. On those rare occasions when he had the opportunity to recite *kedusha* and answer *kaddish*, he thanked Hashem for this privilege.

Rav Alexander Ziskind also thanked God for his memory. Especially as he aged, and remembering became more difficult, he expressed his gratitude to the Almighty each time he was able to remember something without special effort. Yes, even our memory is sufficient cause to thank our Creator!

Rav Alexander Ziskind tells of situations when he carried his snuffbox with him in the street, and it slipped out of his hands and fell to the ground. When he saw that the box was still intact and did not break, he thanked Hashem. Do we thank God whenever we drop our cell phone and it doesn't break?

In this chapter he also describes how he would thank Hashem in the store. If he needed to buy something, and he went to a store to make a purchase, he thanked God that he had the money to buy what he needed. He knew of *sadikim* who couldn't afford even simple household items. The fact that he could go the supermarket and make a purchase was not taken for granted. He would stop, say a brief "thank you" to God, and then proceed with his purchase.

We go the supermarket countless times, put our groceries in the shopping cart, go to the checkout counter, and pull out our credit card or checkbook. Do we ever stop for a moment to thank Hashem for enabling us to do this? We are surely aware that many people do not have this luxury of buying the food and household items that their families need. Yet, we forget to thank Hashem for this ability that He graciously gives us.

Modim is our opportunity to reflect on any of the innumerable kindnesses that God performs for us each day. Of course, it is impossible to think of everything that God has given us, certainly in the few moments we spend reciting *modim*. Rav Avigdor Miller therefore advised that we think of one blessing in our lives for which we must be grateful as we recite this *beracha*. When we reach *modim*, we should pause for a moment, contemplate one of the countless blessings in our lives, and then recite the *beracha* with this blessing in mind. This simple method will, without question, profoundly enhance our recitation of *modim*, and, moreover, enhance our overall sense of appreciation and gratitude to God. This will, in turn, make us more positive, optimistic and upbeat people, capable of recognizing and celebrating all that we have in life, rather than feeling deprived over that which we do not have.

Make No Assumptions

Why do most of us fail to feel grateful for what we have in life? Why are we thankful only for the dramatic, momentous or unexpected events, but not for the everyday blessings such as health, food, clothing and shelter?

The answer relates to the halachic concept known as חזקה, or presumed status. *Halacha* allows us to make certain assumptions based on the status quo. If, for example, a pair of *tefillin* was written and checked by a qualified, God-fearing scribe, we may assume that it has retained this status and nothing has changed. One is not required to have his *tefillin* checked each morning before he wears it for the *misva*; he may rightfully assume that its status today is the same as it was yesterday, and the day before.

Unfortunately, most of us make the mistake of applying the notion of חזקה to our state of well-being. Since our heart has been beating properly every moment since we were conceived, we naturally assume that it will continue beating properly now, and in a moment from now, and tomorrow and the next day. Since the day we were born, we always had food to eat and a sturdy roof over our heads. By instinct, we assume that this will continue today, and next week, next month, next year, and next decade.

This mistaken assumption is what blinds us to our debt of gratitude to God for all we have. King David concluded the Book of Tehillim with the words כל הנשמה תהלל י–ה (literally, "Every soul shall praise God"). The Sages interpreted the word נשמה in this verse to mean נשימה – "breath". King David here instructs us to give praise and thanksgiving to the Almighty על כל נשימה ונשימה, for every breath we take. We must not assume that just because we've been breathing since birth, we will continue breathing at the next moment. Each breath we breathe is a new gift from God. What happens at this moment is not a function of what happened the previous moment. The fact that we enjoy generally good health and general financial stability right now has no bearing on what will happen one moment from now. Each moment of life, each breath, is an independent blessing from God.

In order to feel grateful, we cannot misapply the notion of חזקה. The concept of חזקה works in *Halacha*, but not with regard to our state of well-being. We cannot assume that yesterday's status will be continued today. Each day, and each moment, stands independent of the one that preceded it.

This fundamental basis of the concept of הכרת הטוב is expressed in a fascinating Mishna in *Pirkeh Abot* (2:9), which tells of the five disciples of Rabban Yohanan ben Zakai. Rabban Yohanan asked his students to identify the most important value for a person to embrace, and the most grievous quality from which one must distance himself. Generally, the students named two opposite qualities. R' Eliezer, for example, named "a good eye" as the most important virtue, and "an evil eye" as the gravest negative attribute. Curiously, however, one of the students, R' Shimon ben Netanel, responded by naming two attributes that appear to have little to do with one another. As the most important attribute to embrace, R'

Shimon pointed to הרואה את הנולד, which literally means foreseeing future developments and considering the consequences of one's decisions and actions. But when asked to identify the quality from which one must distance himself, R' Shimon named הלווה ואינו משלם – borrowing without repaying. What connection is there between failure to repay loans and foreseeing the consequences of one's actions?

Failing to repay a loan signifies the height of ingratitude. If somebody was kind enough to lend money, the most elementary standards of gratitude dictate, at very least, returning the borrowed funds. The flipside of ingratitude, R' Shimon taught, is הרואה את הנולד – perceiving everything as נולד, as happening anew at each moment. Feeling grateful stems from recognizing that we receive all we have at every moment of our lives, that there is no necessary continuity from one moment to the next. A person needs to be seeing everything in life as נולד, as given to him at this moment, which naturally engenders a genuine sense of appreciation for the blessings in his life.

Making a List

There is another reason why we often fail to sense and express our gratitude to Hashem – because we feel deprived. Too many of us focus on what we do not have, rather than on what we have. It is difficult to feel grateful when we feel shortchanged. We do not thank God sufficiently because we are too busy complaining to Him. Preoccupied as we are with all the things that we want but do not have, we feel underprivileged. It is therefore not at all surprising that we do not say, "Thank you" to God as often or as sincerely as we should.

One Rabbi suggested rectifying this problem with a surprisingly simple exercise. The next time a person feels angry at God, and feels that He is unfairly depriving him of what he rightfully deserves, he should take a piece of paper and make two lists, side-by-side. The first list should include everything that God has given him in his life, and the other should include everything he wants but does not have.

If he then honestly compares and evaluates the two lists, he will find that God has given him virtually everything he needs and wants – life, generally good health, a roof over his head, food and clothing, family and friends, and so on. Most of what he wants but does not have is really not that necessary; for the most part, these are luxuries that he could reasonably do without.

When Rabbi Avigdor Miller would pass by a pharmacy, he would walk up to the window and take note of all the medications the store advertised. He would look at each one, think for a moment, and then say, "Thank you Hashem for not making me require this medication". These medicines were manufactured because there are ill patients who need them. Rabbi Miller was wise enough to take a moment to appreciate the fact that he was spared from all these ailments. So many things can go wrong with the human body, and we must be grateful for each and every moment that the body functions properly.

This applies to finances, as well. We always complain that we do not have enough money. But if somebody would come along and offer us $1 million for one of our ears, would we give away our ear? Of course not. What this demonstrates is that we are worth $1 million and much more – but we prefer, rightfully so, to keep our vital assets rather than cash them in. Similarly, we all feel we can use some more cash, but we don't sell our home and move into a small two-bedroom apartment. We have the money we want, but we use it for our important needs. This must be our perspective on wealth – focusing on all that we have, rather than on what we do not have.

This focus is a prerequisite for experiencing and expressing gratitude. It requires taking a moment, or several moments, to recognize the fact that God has given us virtually everything we could ask for. We therefore have much for which to be grateful.

Gratitude as Confession

There is another insight into the value of הכרת הטוב that is worth exploring before delving into the text of this *beracha*. Rav Yitzchak Hutner noted that the word מודה actually bears two meanings – confess and thank. There is a good reason, Rav Hutner explained, why these two concepts are closely associated with one another. Namely, one must "confess" before he can thank. In order to feel grateful, one must first acknowledge that a favor has been done. If one feels independent and self-sufficient, and denies that he has received assistance or a gift, then he quite obviously cannot feel appreciative. Gratitude begins with confession – admitting that one has been the beneficiary of somebody else's goodwill.

Part of the challenge of *modim* is the need to "confess", to humbly recognize God's role in absolutely everything that we have. Sincere gratitude is a humbling experience, and this is part of the reason why this *beracha* earns such a special place in the *Amidah* service. It requires us to acknowledge our helplessness, to "confess" our debt of gratitude to the Almighty for everything in our lives. *Modim* thus requires us to recognize God's role in our lives, to reflect upon and consider how much He has done for us, and continues to do for us, at each and every moment.

מודים אנחנו לך
"We thank you"

The word מודים can mean "thank", but can also mean "bow". Indeed, we bow when reciting this word, and we therefore declare that we bow – מודים – in humble submission and gratitude to God.

שאתה הוא ה' אלהינו ואלהי אבותינו
"that You are Hashem our God, and God of our forefathers"

The first thing for which we thank Hashem is the fact that He is our God, meaning, that we recognize Him as the one true God. Had we been born and raised in a different setting, we would be living our lives without knowing that there is a God whom we must serve. We are grateful, first and foremost, for the knowledge we have been given of the Almighty's existence and kingship.

לְעוֹלָם וָעֶד

"forever"

We are not only grateful for having Hashem as our God, but, even more so, for His guarantee that He will always be our God. The Christians and Moslems recognize that the Jews were the chosen nation, but they claim that God has since rejected the Jews and chosen them, instead. We, however, know that God made an eternal promise to our ancestors that He would never exchange us for another people, and for this we are grateful.

The eternity of our stature as God's chosen nation was established at the time of *Matan Torah*, when we received the Torah at Sinai. It is commonly understood that the event at Mount Sinai was a "wedding" between God and the Jewish people, when both parties eagerly expressed their willingness to join into a special bond and covenant with each other. The Talmud, however, teaches that this is only partially correct. We are told that God lifted Mount Sinai over the heads of *Am Yisrael*, threatening to drop it on them and crush them if they refused to accept the Torah. *Beneh Yisrael*'s agreement to this relationship was thus coerced. In a certain sense – astonishing as it may sound – God "forced Himself", as it were, upon our ancestors at Mount Sinai. This was not a mutually consensual relationship; rather, one party forced it upon the other.

Herein lies the basis of our eternal relationship with God. The Torah (Debarim 22:29) commands that if a man forces himself upon a girl, he must marry her and may never divorce her. Once a girl is violated, she is unlikely to find a husband, and the Torah therefore commands the assailant to marry the young woman and care for her forever. God, as it were, forced us into a relationship with Him at

Sinai, and, as such, is barred, so-to-speak, from ever "divorcing" us. His commitment to us, to be our God and care for us as His special nation, is everlasting, and will never be broken.

צורנו

"our Rock"

"Rock" is used here as a metaphor signifying a source of protection. When we face problems and crises, God is the "rock" that shields us from harm and guarantees our safety.

צור חיינו

"Rock of our lives"

God is the protector of our lives; whenever our lives are threatened, we know we can turn to the Almighty for help.

A secular physician in Israel once reported that his religious patients cope with and recover from illness more easily than his non-observant patients. He explained that religious patients generally react to a diagnosis with hope and optimism. Regardless of the situation, they have somewhere to turn – Hashem. God-fearing patients sit in the waiting room reading Tehillim, and even if they cannot understand the words, they find comfort and peace of mind knowing that they have an address, they have someone at their side ready to help. This keeps them relaxed and at ease, an emotional condition that makes the process of treatment and recovery so much smoother and easier.

This observation was already made many centuries earlier, by the Rambam, who worked as a physician and served as the personal doctor of the Sultan. In a letter written to the Sultan, the Rambam points to anxiety, anger, stress and depression as the sources of the vast majority of physical ailments. He adds that people who are God-fearing and place their trust in the Almighty are, by and large, spared from these harmful emotions. Since they trust in God, and confidently believe that He controls all events and everything He does is ultimately for their benefit, they do not experience distress, fear and frustration as others do. The Rambam thus strongly advised the king to follow this example and place his trust in God, if for no other reason than as a medical precaution, to spare himself the harmful health effects of anxiety and stress.

God is thus צור חיינו, the protector of our lives. Our lives are prolonged by our belief in Him as our Creator and our King.

מגן ישענו אתה הוא
"shield of our salvation; it is You"

God is our מגן, our "shield", our source of protection, and in that capacity He brings us salvation during times of crisis. "It is You" – no other being or force provides us with protection.

לדר ודר נודה לך ונספר תהלתך
"for every generation we shall thank You and tell Your praise"

At this point in the *beracha*, we turn to God and make a promise – that we will, forever, give Him praise and speak of His greatness. We commit to accustom ourselves to observing and speaking about God's greatness and the kindnesses that He showers upon us. In order to fulfill this promise, we must regularly take note of God's involvement in our lives, and the countless blessings that He bestows upon us at every moment.

This phrase also expresses our commitment to study Torah, as its wisdom is the greatest possible praise of God and His greatness.

A number of books mention that people who have been unable to beget children should have special concentration when they recite the words לדר ודר נודה לך. They should have in mind their desire to ensure that God's praises will be spoken לדר ודר, in future generations, and to that end they desire and pray for children.

על-חיינו המסורים בידיך
"for our lives that are given over into Your hands"

Our lives, and our daily sustenance, are all dependent upon the Almighty's grace.

ועל נשמותינו הפקודות לך
"and for our souls that are entrusted with You"

The word פקודות relates to the Hebrew word פקדון, which means "collateral". When a person borrows money, he gives collateral to the lender so that if he fails to pay the debt, the lender will keep the collateral in lieu of payment. Our souls return to God each night when we go to sleep, and serve as "collateral". If we fail to pay our "debts" by fulfilling our responsibilities, then He can keep our soul in the heavens rather than returning it to us in the morning, Heaven forbid, and yet, even though the soul ascends to the heavens each night with – unfortunately – a large registry of sins that were committed over the course of the day, God lovingly returns our soul in the morning, willing to give us a second chance. We therefore thank Hashem for נשמותינו הפקודות לך – our souls that He has every right to keep as collateral for our mounting debt, and yet He lovingly returns to us each and every morning.[7]

Alternatively, this clause refers to the time of תחיית המתים, the resurrection. When a person dies, the soul departs only temporarily from the body. This is why we customarily refer to death with the term פטירה, which connotes a temporary departure. The soul departs the body and leaves behind a small "charge" with which God will resurrect the body at the time of תחיית המתים. Just as when a car battery loses its power, it might still retain a small amount of voltage

---

7. One Rabbi commented that we must follow God's example of patience and compassion in dealing with borrowers. It often happens that borrowers are delinquent and do not repay their debts on time. If we expect God to return our "collateral" each morning despite our mounting debt, then we, too, must show patience and indulgence and allow borrowers the time they need to repay their loans.

which allows it to be jump-started, similarly, God will "jump-start" the body at the time of the resurrection. We therefore thank Hashem for continuing to care for the souls after death, in preparation for their ultimate resurrection in the future. The departed souls are "entrusted" with God from the moment of death until the time of תחיית המתים.

The word נשמותינו in this clause might also mean נשימותינו – "our breaths". We recognize that our ability to breathe at every moment is a magnificent and precious gift from the Almighty. We often take breathing for granted, until we find ourselves in high elevations, such as in places in Colorado and in Mexico City, where the air is thin and it is difficult to breathe until one grows accustomed to the conditions. The human body's respiratory system is a remarkable phenomenon. The lungs contain 300 million tiny air sacks, which, if they would be stretched out, would spread over 70 square meters. These air sacks fill with air each time we inhale, and then supply oxygen to every blood cell in our body, while expelling the harmful carbon dioxide. We thank Hashem for providing us with the oxygen we need to live, and with the truly sensational bodily system that He put in place to enable our bodies to receive and process the oxygen in the air.

Our circulatory system, too, is an extraordinary manifestation of divine grace. There is no man-made pump in the world that can pump continuously, every moment, for 120 years. Nor are there pipes that can have liquid run through them without pause for many decades. Burst water pipes are a regular occurrence in virtually every city around the world, and yet, the veins in our body remain intact throughout our lives. We thus thank Hashem for נשימותינו – for each and every breath, for every second that He enables us to live.

ועל נסיך שבכל-יום עמנו
"and for Your miracles that occur for us each day"

The word נס refers to supernatural events. In this *beracha*, we acknowledge the fact that such miracles occur each and every day. The continued existence of the Jewish people, despite millennia of exile and persecution, is nothing short of a miraculous phenomenon that defies every law of history. Similarly, the survival, success and growth of the modern State of Israel is a modern, supernatural miracle that we take for granted, but must not be overlooked. One observer commented that if all the enemies of the Jewish State in the Middle East would march together to Jerusalem and spit all at once, they would literally drown the city. The country is surrounded on all sides by virulent enemies, and yet it survives and flourishes. This is just one of the many supernatural events that occur each and every day – ועל נסיך שבכל יום עמנו – for which we give thanks to the Almighty in this *beracha*.

Another daily miracle is our ability to resist and withstand the *yeser ha'ra*. It is supernatural and miraculous without question, that we remain committed to our religious traditions, observe the Torah in all its detail, and make time for prayer and Torah learning, despite all the spiritually hostile pressures that abound. The *yeser ha'ra* is stronger, more potent and more clever today than ever before. Is it not miraculous that we are nevertheless able to remain faithful to the Torah, each of us on his level? For this miracle, too, we give thanks to Hashem.

ועל נפלאותיך וטובותיך שבכל עת, ערב ובוקר וצהרים
"and for Your wonders and favors at all times – evening, morning and afternoon"

The term נפלאות refers to the miracles of which no one is aware. King David urges us to praise Hashem who is עושה נפלאות גדולות לבדו – "performs great wonders, alone" (Tehillim 136:4). This refers to the "wonders" that occur לבדו, when God is "alone", as it were, with nobody around to witness the event. At all times – "evening, morning and afternoon" – God performs miracles that literally save our lives, but nobody is aware of them. We occasionally hear on the news about a would-be terrorist who was noticed and captured by security personnel on his way to a suicide bombing mission, but we do not hear of the would-be terrorist whose explosives detonated in his garage and killed him. This is just one example. Every day, throughout the day, God is at work protecting us in ways that we cannot even imagine.

The classic example of this kind of miracle is the story of Bilam. The king of Moav, Balak, summoned Bilam, a non-Jewish prophet, to place a curse upon *Beneh Yisrael*, and if Bilam had succeeded, the entire Israelite nation would have been annihilated. God intervened to save *Beneh Yisrael*, and He transformed Bilam's curse into a blessing. Nobody – except Bilam and Balak – was aware of this miracle. Until God told Moshe to record this incident in the Torah, nobody had known what had happened. *Beneh Yisrael* slept peacefully in their tents while God saved them from annihilation. This is a classic instance of נפלאותיך, of a wonder performed by God without anybody knowing it.

A person walks into the synagogue, or another room, and is about to sit down when his friend calls to him from the back of the room. Instead of sitting down, he goes to his friend to speak with him, and ends up sitting there. Little did he know – or will he know – that the chair on which he was about to sit was ridden with germs, and if he had sat down, he would have caught the flu and been incapacitated for a week. So often, and in ways we cannot imagine, God protects us without our ever realizing it.

הטוב, כי לא כלו רחמיך, המרחם, כי-לא תמו חסדיך
"The good one – for Your compassion is unending; and the compassionate one – for Your kindness is unlimited"

God deals with us kindly and compassionately forever. A parent deals kindly and compassionately with his or her children, but the parent eventually ages and is then unable to help the child. The Almighty, however, does not age, and continues dealing kindly with us forever, without limit. Additionally, parents do not have the resources to dispense unlimited kindness to their children. Finite amounts of time and money limit the extent of parents' favors for their children, whereas God's resources are unlimited, and He can therefore dispense boundless kindness to us and to all people.

Furthermore, people are limited in their emotional capacity to feel pity. If a poor individual approaches us on Friday afternoon, explaining that he cannot afford food for Shabbat and asking for $50, most of us will feel compassion and give him $50. If he approaches us again the next week on Friday, we will probably give him another $50. But when this repeats itself week after week, we will, sooner or later, lose patience and refuse to give him money. God is not like that. We can approach Him repeatedly, without limit, to ask for assistance, and He will happily give it. There is no limit to His compassion, because there is no limit to His patience and His desire to give us what we need.

Another difference between human and divine compassion is that a human being's compassion is often a selfish feeling. We give to and help a person in need to assuage the uncomfortable feelings of pity and guilt that we experience. Selfish compassion is, by definition, limited. But God is genuinely compassionate; He wants to give purely for the sake of giving. This sort of kindness and mercy is limitless and everlasting.

Finally, human beings rarely feel compassion for somebody who does not deserve to be helped. The Almighty, however, has pity on us and seeks to alleviate our troubles even if we are undeserving of His assistance. Regardless of whether we are worthy, He mercifully steps in to provide us with our needs and help resolve our troubles.

כי מעולם קוינו לך
"for we have forever longed for You"

Throughout the generations, Jews have turned to God for assistance, and He has provided it.

ועל כולם יתברך ויתרומם ויתנשא תמיד, שמך מלכנו לעולם ועד

"For all of them, Your Name, our King, shall always be blessed, glorified and exalted, forever"

יתברך means that all people on earth shall recognize the Almighty as the source of all blessings. We pray that Hashem's kindnesses shall be recognized by all of humanity. Similarly, we pray that God's Name shall יתרומם, meaning, that all people will acknowledge the fact that God's greatness far exceeds any expressions of praise that can be formulated. We also pray ויתנשא – that all will recognize that God's greatness exceeds that of the angels and all other beings.

וכל החיים יודוך סלה

"and all living beings shall thank You, sela"

Even the animal kingdom will recognize God's greatness and express gratitude to Him.

ויהללו ויברכו את שמך הגדול באמת לעולם כי טוב

"and they shall praise and bless Your great Name, sincerely, forever, for it is good"

God's Name is synonymous with goodness; He is pure goodness, and all creatures must therefore give Him praise.

האל ישועתנו ועזרתנו סלה האל הטוב

"the God who is our salvation and assistance, sela, the good God"

ישועתנו refers to the help that God gives those who are incapable of helping themselves, such as incapacitated ill patients, whereas עזרתנו refers to God's role in ensuring the success of the efforts that we make in working to solve our problems.

Hanukah and Purim

עַל הַנִּסִּים

On Hanukah and Purim, we insert at this point in the *Amidah* the special paragraph of *Al Ha'nissim* to express gratitude for the great miracles God performed for us on these occasions. This paragraph is naturally inserted here, as part of the *Modim* section, in which we give thanks to God for "Your – נִסֶּיךָ שֶׁבְּכָל-יוֹם עִמָּנוּ, וְעַל נִפְלְאוֹתֶיךָ וְטוֹבוֹתֶיךָ שֶׁבְּכָל עֵת, עֶרֶב וָבֹקֶר וְצָהֳרִים miracles that [You perform] for us each day, and for Your wonders and kindnesses that [You perform] at every moment – evening, morning and afternoon". On Hanukah and Purim, after thanking God for the miracles He performs on a daily basis, we thank Him as well for the special miracles that He performed for our ancestors during the time of the Hashmonaim and during the time of Mordechai and Ester.

Al Ha'nissim begins with a generic expression of gratitude that we recite on both Hanukah and Purim. We then proceed to describe the particular miracle that occurred, in the בימי מתתיה paragraph on Hanukah, and בימי מרדכי ואסתר on Purim.

על הנסים, ועל הפרקן, ועל הגבורות, ועל התשועות
"For the miracles, the redemption, the manifestations of power, and the salvations"

What exactly is the difference between the words פורקן ("redemption") and תשועות ("salvations")?

The term פרקן refers to the general redemption, whereas ישועה or תשועה is used in reference to the particular events that comprised the redemption. For example, the Exodus from Egypt was a פרקן, an event of redemption for *Am Yisrael*, but the subsequent miracles – the manna, the well of water, and so on – were specific ישועות that were necessary as part of the redemption. Similarly, if a gravely ill patient survives an illness, the survival is considered a פרקן, but his overcoming the day-to-day challenges along the road to full recovery is described with the term ישועה. We thus thank Hashem not only for saving us from our troubles, but also for each individual act of ישועה that He performs as part of the general process of redemption.

ועל הנפלאות, ועל הנחמות
"and for the wonders and consolations"

A person needs consolation when he feels that all hope is lost, when he finds himself in a grave crisis that has no solution. Hashem, through His wonders, brings us consolation in situations that appear hopeless. The struggle against the Greeks, and Haman's decree of annihilation, seemed like hopeless situations for the Jewish people, but God demonstrated that even under such circumstances He is capable of providing a solution.

בימים ההם בזמן הזה
"in those days, at this time"

This refers to more than the fact that the miracles occurred during this period on the calendar. Our Rabbis teach us that the festivals on the Jewish calendar bring certain spiritual forces to the world. For example, when we describe Pesah as זמן חרותנו, "the time of our freedom", it means not only that our ancestors were released from bondage on this date, but also that Pesah is a time especially conducive to achieving freedom over one's sinful inclinations and tendencies. Likewise, Sukkot is זמן שמחתנו, our occasion of joy, the time when we are given special capabilities to achieve genuine joy and satisfaction in life. On Hanukah and Purim, too, we are given the special spiritual powers that our unique to these holidays.

בימי מתתיה
The Hanukah Insert

בימי מתתיה בן יוחנן כהן גדול חשמונאי ובניו
"In the times of Matitya, son of Yohanan the kohen gadol, the Hashmonai, and his sons"

Our custom is to pronounce the name "Matitya" (מתתיה), and not Matityahu (מתתיהו). (Incidentally, Matitya was not the *kohen gadol*; his father, Yohanan, was the *kohen gadol*.)

In the corresponding section for Purim, we mention Mordechai and Ester without naming their parents. Why then, here, do we make a point of mentioning that Matitya's father was Yohanan?

One answer is that Yohanan, like Matitya, was a righteous *saddik*, and Matitya thus benefited from זכות אבות – the merit of his righteous forebears.

Additionally, a deep connection exists between the names "Matitya" and "Yohanan", which both directly relate to the miracle of Hanukah. The name "Matitya" means מתת י-ה – a gift of God. It signifies the recognition one must have that everything in his life has been granted as a generous gift from the Almighty. The name "Yohanan" similarly represents the expression י-ו חנן – "God graciously gives". It also alludes to the acknowledgment of everything one has as a gracious gift from Hashem.

When a person recognizes that even the "natural" phenomena that he experiences and derives benefit from, such as his livelihood, his home, his family, the sunrise, and so on, is given to Him by God, then God is prepared to give Him gifts even beyond the constraints of the natural order. Matitya was deserving of God's miraculous intervention because he embodied the ideal of מתת י-ה, of recognizing that even the so-called "ordinary" things in his life are gifts from the Almighty which was a message he learned from his father, Yohanan. If a person recognizes the natural phenomena as gifts from God, then he is deserving of additional gifts, even beyond the normal limitations of nature.

כשעמדה מלכות יון הרשעה על עמך ישראל לשכחם תורתך
"when the wicked Greek Empire rose up against Your nation, Israel, to have them forget Your Torah"

The Greeks sought to eradicate Judaism. Whereas Haman – like Hitler, many centuries later – campaigned against the Jewish people, regardless of their faith, practices or lifestyle, the Greeks waged war against the religion. Their goal was to make the Jews forget the Torah, and replace it with Greek scholarship and culture. This is the reason why Purim is celebrated primarily through physical indulgence – eating and drinking – while on Hanukah we celebrate by reciting *hallel* and singing praises to God. On Purim we celebrate our physical survival, and so our celebration focuses upon physical activities, whereas on Hanukah we celebrate our spiritual triumph, and we therefore direct our attention toward spiritual pursuits.

The Greeks' efforts to make the Torah forgotten nearly succeeded. The Ramban describes how the vast majority of the Jews at the time of the Greek persecution assimilated, and the Torah was as close to disappearing from the earth, Heaven forbid, as it ever was throughout Jewish history. The fact that Torah study and observance has survived and continues to thrive is a truly extraordinary miracle.

As part of our commemoration of this miracle, there is a custom in many yeshivot to send gifts to the Rabbis on Hanukah. This holiday celebrates our victory over those who tried לשכחם תורתיך, to make us forget the Torah, and we therefore sense special feelings of gratitude to the Rabbis and teachers, who devote their lives to teaching Torah and ensuring that Torah will never be forgotten.

ולהעבירם מחקי רצנך
"and to turn them away from the statutes that You willed"

The focal point of the Greeks' campaign was the חוקים, those *misvot* which we cannot understand, whose rationale eludes human comprehension. The Greeks were philosophical, and were driven by reason and logic. They could not tolerate a creed that required following laws which do not make sense according to human logic. It was therefore the חוקים that drew their fierce opposition and that became the focus of their persecution against the Jewish people.

It says in Tehillim (119:155), רחוק מרשעים ישועה כי חקיך לא דרשו – "Salvation is distant from the wicked, because they do not study Your statutes". If a person rejects the חוקים, the *misvot* whose logic he cannot grasp, refusing to extend beyond the limited confines of logic and reason, then Hashem will similarly care for Him only within the narrow limits of the natural order. The Almighty brings ישועה, miraculous salvation, only to those who commit themselves to all the *misvot*, including the חוקים. As they extend beyond the limits of reason, God, too, will not limit Himself to the confines of nature, and will perform miracles to save them from their troubles.

ואתה, ברחמיך הרבים, עמדת להם בעת צרתם

"and You, in Your abundant mercy, stood with them in their time of distress"

We emphasize that the victory was the result of divine compassion, and not the strength or talents of the Hashmonaim. The triumph over the Greeks was due to God's compassion, love and devotion to the Jewish people.

רבת את ריבם, דנת את דינם, נקמת את נקמתם

"You waged their fight, judged their case, and exacted their revenge"

Hashem brought retribution upon the Greeks as נקמתם – the revenge of the Jewish people. Although the Greeks' campaign was a battle against the Almighty Himself, He got involved not for His own honor, but rather for the sake of *Am Yisrael*. This resembles the war which *Beneh Yisrael* fought against Midyan, as told in the Book of Bamidbar (chapter 31). When commanding *Beneh Yisrael* to wage this battle, God referred to it as נקמת בני ישראל ("the revenge of *Beneh Yisrael*" – 31:2), but the Torah says that *Beneh Yisrael* participated in this effort לתת נקמת ה' במדין – to exact God's revenge (31:3). God wages the battles against our enemies for our sake, while we fight for the sake of His honor.

מסרת גבורים ביד חלשים, ורבים ביד מעטים

"You placed the mighty in the hands of the weak, the many in the hands of the few"

Our Sages describe the Hashmonaim as חלשים, "weak". They were not mighty, powerful warriors. Unfortunately, the secular elements among the Jewish nation misrepresent the Hanukah story and portray the Maccabees as large, muscular, intimidating soldiers, and they celebrate Hanukah as a holiday of Jewish military and athletic prowess. This is a grave injustice to Jewish tradition, and undermines the entire message of the holiday, which is expressing gratitude to God for this miraculous victory. There is no greater distortion of history than using the word "Maccabee" – which is an acrostic representing the phrase מי כמוך באלים יי' ("Who is like You among the mighty ones, Hashem!") – as a symbol of physical might and athletic capability. The Hashmonaim defeated the Greek Empire miraculously, through God's assistance. They were militarily feeble, but spiritually powerful, and this is how they achieved victory.

The Hashmonaim were not only weak, but also מעטים – few in number. As mentioned, the vast majority of the Jewish people had assimilated, and many Jews took no interest and did not participate in this campaign against the Greeks. The Jewish army was thus grossly outnumbered by the Greek forces, and yet they miraculously overpowered them.

The simple meaning of this phrase – "You placed the mighty in the hands of the weak, the many in the hands of the few" – is that the Jews overcame the Greeks *despite the fact* that they were weak and fewer in number. Some, however, explain that to the contrary, this means that the Jews were victorious precisely *because* they were weak and fewer in number. (This phrase would then be consistent with the subsequent phrase – "the wicked in the hands of the righteous, the impure in the hands of the pure, and the cynics in the hands of those involved in Your Torah" – which clearly means that the Hashmonaim won *because* they were pure, righteous and involved in Torah.) A soldier who realizes that he is physically and militarily inferior to the enemy has no choice other than placing his trust in God, and praying to Him for assistance. It is specifically as a result of the Hashmonaim's disadvantage that they won – because their military inferiority compelled them to turn to God and beg His assistance.

We read in Tehillim (33:17-18), שקר הסוס לתשועה וברב חילו לא ימלט. הנה עין ה' אל יראיו למיחלים לחסדו – "A horse is a false source of salvation; even with all his might, he will not escape. Indeed, God's eyes are upon those who fear Him, to those who long for His kindness". The soldiers without the powerful artillery and equipment are forced to look to the Almighty for assistance, thus giving them – ironically – a distinct advantage on the battlefield.

ורשעים ביד צדיקים, וטמאים ביד טהורים, וזדים ביד עוסקי תורתך
"the wicked in the hands of the righteous, the impure in the hands of the pure, and the cynics in the hands of those involved in Your Torah"

The phrase עוסקי תורתך refers to the investment of effort into Torah study regardless of the outcome. Yeshiva students at times spend hours attempting to understand a difficult passage in the Talmud or its commentaries, or to resolve a certain difficulty, without success. Our tradition teaches that those efforts are inherently valuable, even if the question remains unresolved and the student is left with the same difficulty. The Greeks are described here as זדים – "cynics" – because they denied and ridiculed the concept of valuing unsuccessful scholarly endeavors. They could not accept the notion of study as an ideal unto itself, even if no practical conclusions are reached or if the material is not properly understood.

ולך עשית שם גדול וקדוש בעולמך
"You made for Yourself a great and sacred Name in Your world"

One of the central differences between Jewish and Greek ideology is the relationship between the sacred and the mundane. The Greeks believed that the two realms must remain separate, that there is no possibility of injecting spiritual significance into the ordinary, mundane areas of life. For the Jew, however, the entire purpose of human existence is to do just that, to elevate one's physical existence through loyalty and obedience to the Almighty. This is perhaps most clearly articulated by the *Shulhan Aruch*, in a remarkable passage of which few people are aware (*Orah Haim* 231):

Similarly, in all one's benefit from this world, he should intend not for his enjoyment, but rather for the service of the Creator, may He be blessed, as it says (Mishleh 3:6), "Know Him in all your ways". The Sages said, "All your actions shall be for the sake of Heaven" –

[meaning,] even optional matters, such as eating, drinking, walking, sitting, standing, relations, conversing, and all your bodily needs, should all be [done] for the service of your Creator, or for something that leads to His service. Even if one is thirsty or hungry, if he ate and drank for his enjoyment, this is not commendable. Rather, he should intend to eat and drink as needed for his sustenance so he can serve his Creator. Likewise, even sitting in the company of the righteous, standing among the sadikim and following along with the perfect ones – if one did this for his own personal enjoyment, to fulfill his wishes and desires, this is not commendable, unless he did so for the sake of Heaven. This applies to sleep, as well. It goes without saying that when one is able to involve himself in Torah and misvot he should not indulge in sleep to enjoy himself. But even when one is fatigued and needs to sleep in order to rest from his fatigue, if he did so for his body's enjoyment, this is not commendable. He should instead intend to give his eyes sleep and his body rest for health purposes, so that his mind will not be confused in [matters of] Torah because of his fatigue…

The *Shulhan Aruch* writes clearly that we are required to serve God even in the mundane areas of life, by engaging in mundane activities for the sake of Torah and *misvot*. The Torah famously tells us that Hashem is לכם לאלהים ("a God for you" – Bamidbar 15:41). He is our God even לכם, in our personal matters. Every area of human life is affected by our relationship with God, by our status as His faithful servants.

The Midrash teaches that the Greeks forced the Jews to write upon the horns of their cattle, אין לכם חלק באלהי ישראל ("You have no share in the God of Israel"). They wanted us to proclaim our rejection of the notion of לכם, the relevance of God and spirituality to the mundane areas of life. This declaration was made on the קרן, the horn of the Jews' cattle, because the word קרן is comprised of the letters קוף, ריש, נון. The final letters of these words are פ,ש,ן, which spell the word נפש. The term נפש refers to the lowest part of the human soul, the part which is involved in the physical, mundane aspects of life. The Greeks sought to force the Jews to deny the connection between the קרן, their physical and material pursuits, and אלהי ישראל, the God of Israel.

The victory over the Greeks glorified the Name of God בעולמך – here in this world. It demonstrated the eternal truth of the Jewish doctrine that Godliness is manifested here in this world, in the realm of the mundane, that *kedusha* must be infused into every area of life.

The numerical value of the word הטבע ("nature") is 86 – the same numerical value as that of the divine Name of אלהים, which signifies strict judgment. We "sweeten" and mitigate the judgment against us by introducing sanctity into nature, by engaging in our physical and mundane pursuits for the sake of Hashem. In *Al Ha'nissim* we say that the Hanukah miracle glorified the שם גדול וקדוש ("the great, sacred Name"). The שם גדול is the Name of אלהים, which is longer than the divine Name of הוי"ה, whereas the term קדוש refers to the Name of הוי"ה (as in the famous verse, קדוש קדוש קדוש ה'). The Hanukah miracle was a demonstration of the fusion between the שם גדול and the שם קדוש, between אלוקים and הוי"ה, between the sacred and the mundane.

This is why the central *misva* on Hanukah is the kindling of the lights outside our homes, symbolizing the need to bring *kedusha* outside, to the street, to the physical and material world. The candles are placed at the left side of the doorway, opposite the *mezuza*, at the side which is bereft of sanctity. It is precisely there, in the place which lacks inherent *kedusha* and spiritual significance, where the message of Hanukah must be expressed. Our response to the Greeks, who denied any connection between the body and the spirit, between the sacred and the mundane, is to commit ourselves to this fundamental Jewish precept of sanctifying the mundane, of bringing spirituality into every area of life.

The *menorah* in the Temple, which had seven candles, three on each side and one in the center, symbolizes Shabbat, which exerts its influence to the three preceding days and to the three days that follow it. Just as the six exterior candles of the *menorah* are turned facing the middle candle, similarly, as the *Zohar* teaches, the six workdays are subordinate to Shabbat and receive their influence and spiritual power from the observance of Shabbat. The day of Shabbat represents the sanctification of physical engagement. Specifically on Shabbat, the holiest day of the week, there is a *misva* to eat, drink wine, enjoy oneself, and engage in marital relations. Shabbat impacts upon the workweek by showing that *kedusha* is not divorced from physical activity, that precisely to the contrary, it means engaging in physical activity for the sake of God and in accordance with His laws. This, too, is the message of the *menorah*, which is structured like the week, and which shines its light and illuminates the darkness, symbolizing the need to bring spirituality and holiness to even the "darkest" and most mundane areas of life.

Similarly, the lighting of the *menorah* is done with a נר (lamp), פתיל (wick) and שמן (oil) – and the first letters of these words spell the word נפש. The kindling of the *menorah* represents the profound concept of נפש, the connection between the body and soul, a connection which we develop and cultivate by engaging in even our physical pursuits for spiritual purposes.

Ronnie and Meyer Safdieh

להצלחה
אליהו מנחם יוסף בן מזל

The Nineteenth Beracha
שִׂים שָׁלוֹם

An Indispensable Prerequisite to Blessing

The nineteenth and final beracha of the *Amidah* is the blessing in which we pray to God for שלום, peace. This is the final beracha of the *Amidah* for the simple reason that all other blessings for which we pray depend upon peace. Without the blessing of peace, all other blessings we receive are useless.

To understand why, we need just to imagine in our minds two families. The first is a well-to-do couple with everything they could have ever asked for in life. They have healthy children, a luxurious house, the finest furniture and chinaware, two luxury cars, and secure employment that allows them time to vacation around the world. All they are missing is שלום. They don't get along with one another, with their neighbors, or with their children. The family members constantly fight with one another, and they always seem to find themselves embroiled in bitter conflict. The second couple, meanwhile, lives in a small residence with only the barest furnishings. They can hardly afford food, but every night they sit down to a quiet, peaceful dinner eating whatever they could buy, and enjoying each other's company.

Undoubtedly, the second family is much happier than the first. They have less than the first family, but they enjoy what they have much more. Material assets do not help a person who does not have peaceful relations with the people around him. Hashem can give us all the luxuries we could ever wish for, but if there is no peace among our families and communities, we will always be miserable. It is only through the blessing of peace that our other blessings become blessings.

There are many indications in the Torah and in the teachings of *Hazal* that blessing cannot be received without the presence of שלום. The Sages describe peace as a כלי מחזיק ברכה, a "utensil that contains blessing". It is only through peaceful relations among people that we are able to receive and contain our blessings.

Yaakob Abinu, before his death, said to his children, האספו ואגידה לכם את אשר–יקרא אתכם באחרית הימים – "Gather, and I will tell you what will happen to you at the end of days" (Bereshit 49:1). The "end of days" – the final redemption – must be preceded by "gathering", by the Jewish people coming together in peace and harmony. The Temple was destroyed as a result of שנאת חנם, senseless hatred among Jews, and this unfortunate phenomenon must be eliminated for us to become worthy of its restoration.

The Rebbe of Rizhin commented that the blessing of rain is also dependent upon peace and unity among the Jewish people.

Hazal teach that on Shemini Aseret – the day on which we begin praying for rain – God tells *Am Yisrael*, קשה עלי פרידתכם, which is usually interpreted as, "Your departure is difficult for Me". On the surface, this means that we celebrate Shemini Aseret even though it does not commemorate any particular event, simply because the Almighty wants to spend another day with us, His children. After the lengthy, festive and emotional season of Rosh Hashanah, Yom Kippur and Sukkot, Hashem asks us to stay another day before returning to our normal routine. But the Rebbe of Rizhin explained this phrase to mean that פרידתכם, our divisiveness, is difficult for God. He warns us that our infighting makes it difficult for Him to answer our prayers for rain. He very much wishes to shower us with blessing and prosperity from the heavens, but our divisiveness prevents the blessing from descending.

The Rebbe added a beautiful insight to explain the connection between unity and rainfall. The Sages teach that after the death of Aharon, the miraculous clouds of glory that had surrounded *Beneh Yisrael* dissipated, thus exposing them to enemy attack. The Rebbe explained that during the lifetime of Aharon, the paradigmatic אוהב שלום ורודף שלום ("lover of peace and pursuer of peace"), the breath of all members of the nation blended together to form a hermetic cloud cover around them. The people spoke with another respectfully and courteously, and the air produced by their speech thus merged together. After Aharon's death, however, there were "cracks" in the clouds. The nation was no longer unified to the extent it had been during Aharon's lifetime, when he worked to bring people together and maintain peace and harmony. The cloud cover thus became porous, and exposed the nation to danger.

Similarly, the Rebbe explained, rainfall requires complete cloud cover, and for that to happen, we need to be unified and together; our speech must be pleasant and affable, so that it can blend together with the speech of the rest of the Jewish people to form the cloud cover needed to produce adequate rainfall.

Rain, like all blessings that come from the heavens, requires שלום. We cannot experience *beracha* as long as we are entangled in conflict and strife; and enmity and hostility prevail among the Jewish people. It is only when we enjoy peace and harmony that we are capable of receiving God's bounty.

Therefore, before we end the *Amidah*, we turn to God and pray for peace. Even if Hashem responds favorably to all our other requests, this will not help us if He does not bless us with peace. We must therefore pray for שלום so that all we are given will indeed be a blessing, and not the opposite, Heaven forbid.

"Its Ways are Ways of Pleasantness, and All Its Paths are Peace"

In numerous contexts, the Sages emphasized for us the importance of שלום and the great lengths we should be prepared to go to achieve it. The story is told (Vayikrah Rabba 9:9) of a woman who each week would attend R' Meir's lecture. One week, when she returned home, she found the door to her home locked. The husband resented his wife's weekly outing, and told her that he would not allow her home until she spits in R' Meir's face.

The woman certainly did not wish to spit at the great Rabbi, but she had no other choice. She entered the *bet midrash*, and as soon as she walked in, R' Meir, through his *ru'ah ha'kodesh*, realized what had happened. He approached the woman and told her that he was suffering from an infection in his eye.

"I need somebody to spit in my eye to soothe the pain", R' Meir said to the woman. "Would you mind spitting into my eye to help me?"

The woman, realizing that she had been given an opportunity to fulfill her husband's wish, obliged, and then returned home.

R' Meir's students, who observed the incident, were shocked. They asked their Rabbi how he could allow himself to be denigrated in such a fashion. He was one of the leading Sages of Israel. How could he have a woman spit into his eye?

"I simply followed God's example", Rabbi Meir explained. "The Torah says that if a husband suspects his wife of infidelity, he brings her to the *Bet HaMikdash* and determines her innocence or guilt through a special ritual that entails erasing the Almighty's Name. If God is prepared to allow His Name to be erased for the sake of repairing a strained relationship between husband and wife, then certainly I should be prepared to have somebody spit at me for the sake of marital harmony".

Rabbi Meir understood how much importance the Torah affords to peace, the extent to which God is prepared to forego on His honor for peace, and he therefore willingly waived his own honor for the sake of peace.

The Sages teach us that חותמו של הקב"ה אמת – the Almighty's "seal", so-to-speak, is truth. Truth is a paramount virtue, to the extent that it is considered God's "signature". Yet, even truth is superseded by the concern for peaceful relations among people. When Sara heard that she would bear a child, she chuckled, wondering if she could bear a child given her husband's old age (ואדני זקן – Bereshit 18:12). But when God relayed Sara's comments to Avraham, He quoted her as noting that she herself is old (ואני זקנתי – Bereshit 18:13). The Sages explain that God modified Sara's remarks so that Avraham would not hear that his wife called him "old". Our Sages teach us חותמו של הקב"ה אמת – God's "signet" is truth, and yet, nevertheless, He distorted the truth to ensure that Abraham would not feel even slightly offended by his wife's remark. It is permissible and appropriate to distort the truth even to prevent a slight degree of tension between two people. Just as God is prepared to have His Name erased for the sake of peace, similarly, He encourages foregoing on truth to maintain peaceful relations between people.

The Sages treated the value of peace with the same severity as they approached some of the most important *misvot* in the Torah.

The Mishna in Masechet Pesahim (49a) addresses the case of a person who, on Ereb Pesah, is on his way to slaughter his paschal offering, or to circumcise his son, or to celebrate his engagement with his bride, and remembers that he had not eliminated his *hametz* at home. Even though he is on his way to perform a *misva*, he must return home to eliminate his *hametz*, unless this would cause him to miss the *misva* in question, in which case he can just make a declaration of *bittul* (renouncing his ownership over the *hametz*). The Talmud Yerushalmi raises the question of why the Mishna included an engagement party along with circumcision and *korban pesah*. Circumcision and *korban pesah* are unique among the *misvot* in that one who fails to observe them is liable to *karet* (external excision from the Jewish people). Why would attending one's engagement celebration belong in the same list as these *misvot*?

The answer, as the Yerushalmi explains, is that maintaining peaceful relations between a bride and groom is as important as circumcision and *korban pesah*. Indeed, celebrating one's engagement with his bride bears as much significance as these fundamental *misvot*.

Elsewhere, the Sages noted that the Torah would not impose a *misva* that causes unpleasantness and distress. In Masechet Sukka, the Gemara briefly entertains the possibility that when the Torah requires taking on Sukkot an ענף עץ עבות, it refers not to *hadasim*, but rather to a certain prickly branch called *hirdof*. But the Gemara then immediately dismisses such a notion, citing the famous verse in Mishleh (3:17), דרכיה דרכי נעם וכל נתיבותיה שלום – "Its ways are ways of pleasantness, and all its paths are peace". Peace is so central and fundamental to Torah life that the Gemara could not entertain the possibility of a *misva* that involves a prickly branch that could cause distress. Torah observance must be pleasant and peaceful, and thus a prickly *hirdof* branch is quite simply out of the question.

In Honor of

Rabbi Eli J Mansour

Moshe Bennatar

Peace and Torah Study

Peace is unique among the *misvot* of the Torah in that we are required to not only maintain peace, but to pursue peace: בקש שלום ורדפהו – "Seek out peace and pursue it" (Tehillim 34:15). Generally, we must perform a *misva* when the situation arises, when we encounter a circumstance that requires a *misva*. When it comes to peace, however, we are bidden to actively pursue it, to constantly work toward establishing and maintaining peaceful relations with other people.

Peace shares this quality with the *misva* of תלמוד תורה (Torah study). One does not fulfill this *misva* by learning only when he happens to come across a Torah book, or happens to be in a place where words of Torah are spoken. Every person must pursue Torah knowledge; we must put ourselves in situations where we can learn Torah, rather than wait for these opportunities to arise. We are commanded - והגית בו יומם ולילה-to set aside time each day and night for learning. The Mishna in *Pirkeh Abot* exhorts, הוי גולה למקום תורה – one must "go into exile" to learn Torah. If the best Torah learning opportunity requires leaving the comfort and security of one's home and familiar surroundings, then he must do so and leave into "exile" so he could pursue Torah scholarship.

Indeed, a close connection exists between these two fundamental religious values – peaceful relations, and Torah. Thus, for example, the Torah writes that when *Beneh Yisrael* arrived at Mount Sinai, ויחן שם ישראל נגד ההר – "Israel encamped opposite the mountain" (Shemot 19:2). Rashi famously observed the singular form ויחן in this verse, as opposed to the plural form of ויחנו which the Torah normally uses in reference to *Beneh Yisrael*'s encampments in the wilderness. *Beneh Yisrael* arrived at Sinai כאיש אחד בלב אחד, as one person with one heart, united in bonds of peace, friendship and camaraderie. This aura of peace and harmony was indispensable for קבלת התורה. The nation could not receive the Torah as long as they were embroiled in petty conflicts and arguments. It was because they arrived at Sinai כאיש אחד בלב אחד that they were able to receive the Torah.

Similarly, Rabbi Haim Vital observed that the Torah does not issue explicit commands regarding מידות טובות, fine character traits. For example, we do not find a *misva* to be patient, to be forgiving, or to be courteous. Rabbi Haim Vital explained that the Torah does not issue such commands because their qualities must precede our acceptance of the Torah (דרך ארץ קדמה לתורה). We receive the Torah only *after* we develop the qualities of respectfiul and dignified behavior such that we can get along peacefully with one another.

Just as peace is a prerequisite for Torah, the reverse is also true: Torah enhances one's quality of שלום. The Sages teach,

תלמידי חכמים מרבים שלום בעולם – "Torah scholars increase peace in the world". Sincere, intensive devotion to Torah study leads a person to peaceful relations with other people, and therefore the presence of Torah scholars brings peace and harmony to the world.

Why is this the case? Why does immersion in Torah study enhance the שלום in a person's life?

For one thing, serious students of Torah are too preoccupied with their pursuit of Torah knowledge to be disturbed by the trivial matters that so frequently cause friction and discord. Yeshiva students are too busy worrying about a difficult comment of Tosafot, a perplexing ruling of the Rambam, or a complex analysis of Rabbi Akiva Eiger to pay attention to an insulting remark, or other petty "problems" that disturb most people.

We might compare a Torah scholar to a store owner who is having an exceptionally successful day, with streams of customers flowing into the store and waiting at the checkout counter. Throughout the day, the man frantically punches in the numbers, passes the credit card through the machine and packs bags. Not wanting to lose a single customer, he works nonstop to maximize his profits. He pays no attention to the fact that he hasn't eaten all day or that he's exhausted. The man's mind is focused exclusively on serving his customers so he could make money.

Suddenly, his wife calls. She tells him how upset she is because their friends did not invite them to their daughter's wedding.

The man, of course, does not care at all whether or not he is invited to this wedding. He is so intently focused on his business and the waves of customers rolling into the store that he is unaffected by his friends' snub.

This is true of Torah scholars, as well. They are working all day to accumulate knowledge and to understand every word of the Gemara and the poskim. They are thus incapable of being bothered by pettiness. If somebody says or does something offensive or inconsiderate, they just ignore it. They have too many other, far more urgent, matters to worry about – like the Gemara, Rashi, Tosafot, the Rambam, and so on.

Accepting Different Roles

But there is also another reason why engagement in Torah study leads to greater peace and harmony. Several times a day, we recite the famous prayer, עשה שלום במרומיו, הוא ברחמיו יעשה שלום עלינו ועל כל עמו ישראל – "He who makes peace in His high places shall make peace among us and among all Israel". We pray for the kind of peace that prevails in the upper worlds, meaning, the peace and harmony that exists among the angels in the heavens.

Why are the angels the models of the condition of peace to which we aspire?

The angels are very different from one another. In fact, they are opposites of one another. Some angels are made from fire, and others are made from water. The angel Gabriel is the angel of strict justice (the name גבריאל relates to the word גבורה, which signifies justice), whereas Michael is the angel of kindness (מיכאל originates from the words מי כאל, and אל is the divine Name that signifies the attribute of kindness). Yet, they all work together in perfect harmony. Each angel recognizes its God-given role and fulfills it, without giving any thought to the roles of the other angels. There is no strife or competition among the angels because they all realize that God assigned them their roles, that they are precisely in the position that God wants them to be in. It is therefore said about the angels, כלם בחכמה עשית (literally, "You made them all with wisdom" – Tehillim 104:24). The word חכמה may be read as כח מה ("What is this strength?") The angels recognize that their strengths, their talents and their capabilities are all given to them by God for a particular purpose. It is senseless to envy another angel with greater power in a certain area, because each angel is given exactly what it needs to fulfill its assigned purpose.

This is precisely the kind of peace that we pray for – peace that results from the recognition that we each have been given exactly what we need to achieve our assigned goals.

Am Yisrael is like an orchestra. The drummer does not envy the violinist, who does not envy the trumpet player, who does not envy the saxophonist. Each has its job to do, and each does it happily, to the best of his ability.

The more a person studies Torah, the more cognizant he is of this fundamental truth – that God gives each man and woman what he or she needs to fulfill his or her role. This recognition leads directly to שלום. When we all accept the fact that we are members of the same orchestra, that God has placed us in this world with just the right "instrument" that we need to play, there is no jealousy or fighting. We each do our job, and the result is magnificent music that fills the earth and enhances the lives of all its inhabitants.

This is why תלמידי חכמים מרבים שלום בעולם – because the Torah scholars are keenly aware of the different roles that different people play, that there is no sense in envying those who have been given different "instruments" with which to play their "music" in this "orchestra" that is the Jewish people.

R' Yehuda Hanasi, redactor of the Mishna, alludes to us this message through the structure of the Mishna. The first Mishna discusses the laws of the daily *shema* recitation, and the final Mishna concludes with the verse ה' עוז לעמו יתן ה' יברך את עמו בשלום (Tehillim 29:11).[8] Through the recitation of *shema*, the recognition of God's oneness, that He is the single Creator of all beings, we arrive at שלום. We understand that we are all members of the same team, working together to serve the Almighty, and there is thus no reason or cause for strife and conflict. By the same token, the section of the Ten

---

8. Incidentally, this verse itself alludes to the ability of Torah to enhance peace. The word עז refers to Torah study, and the verse thus indicates that once the Almighty blesses us with Torah, then we are consequently granted the blessing of peace, as well.

Commandments begins with the words אנכי ה' אלקיך, the declaration of God's oneness, and concludes with the word רעך ("your fellow"). Once we recognize that we are all created by and serve one God, we will then look upon each other as רעך, as our peer and friend, as somebody to work with, rather than work against.

"Kosher" Fighting

There is one final point that must be emphasized whenever we speak of the value and importance of unity, peace and harmony among the Jewish people.

A well-known Mishna in *Pirkeh Abot* (5:17) distinguishes between two kinds of fights: a מחלוקת לשם שמים – an argument waged for the sake of Heaven – and a מחלוקת שלא לשם שמים – an argument that is not waged for the sake of Heaven. The Mishna states that a מחלוקת לשם שמים "will ultimately endure", whereas a מחלוקת שלא לשם שמים "will not ultimately endure". The simple interpretation of the Mishna's remark is that when two people argue "for the sake of Heaven", out of a sincere desire to determine the truth, then this is a meaningful and valuable argument which will produce a positive result. But when people argue for selfish reasons, nothing valuable will emerge from such a fight.

There is, however, an additional explanation of the Mishna, whereby it warns of the dangers posed by arguments waged over matters of religion. When people fight שלא לשם שמים, over relatively trivial matters such as money and stature, the argument will, sooner or later, end. There is a limit to how far a person will go in fighting for such matters. But when it comes to a מחלוקת לשם שמים, a fight ostensibly waged "on God's behalf", it can never end. The parties will persist unrelentingly, as they see it as their duty and obligation to defend their religious principles. Backing down, they fear, will be tantamount to compromising their faith. This is why arguments waged over matters of religion are so dangerous, and so potentially destructive. When it comes to controversies of religious import, the parties will go to whatever lengths they feel necessary to defend their position and prove the other side wrong. Such controversies, as we know all too well, persist for far longer than they should, leaving in their wake painful wounds of mutual contempt and ill-will.

Of course, there are rare occasions when observant Jews must struggle to defend the Torah against its detractors. But such battles must be waged very delicately, and only under the guidance and direction of our Torah leaders. It is most unfortunate that so many people impulsively rush to fight when it comes to matters of religion, without first consulting with Torah authorities. Not everyone is qualified to certify a fight as "kosher". Fights against fellow Jews on religious matters are especially dangerous, and they therefore require the guidance of our *gedolim*.

Earlier, we cited the Sages' comment that God says to the Jewish people after Sukkot, קשה עלי פרידתכם - "Your departure is not easy for me". We noted that the word פרידתכם could refer to infighting among Jews. If so, then we could perhaps explain this remark to mean that the fighting among Jews עלי – "for God" – is especially difficult for God to accept. Although He always frowns upon conflicts and fighting, He is particularly distressed when Jews are entangled in bitter arguments because of Him, each claiming to have the correct path, the correct idea, the one and only way to serve Hashem. These fights are the most harmful, and the ones that cause the Almighty the most anguish.

As we have seen, fighting among Jews can sabotage God's *berachot*. When we pray שים שלום, asking God to grant us peace, we should also recommit ourselves to this central pillar of Torah life, to work toward peaceful relations with all Jews, of all stripes of colors, even with those with whom we strongly disagree with on important matters. This commitment, together with God's blessing of peace, will help ensure that we will be worthy of receiving His many other blessings, that will come from the heavens and fill the כלי מחזיק ברכה that we have built through our devotion to peace and harmony among Jews.

Peace with the *Yeser Ha'ra*

There is another kind of "peace" for which we must pray, and to which we must always aspire. The Ba'al Shem Tov commented that besides working to create and maintain peace among family members, friends and neighbors, and between us and the Almighty, we must also work to bring peace between ourselves and our *yeser ha'ra* – our evil inclination.

Why should we want peace with our evil inclination? Shouldn't our goal be to banish – or, even better, to eradicate – the *yeser ha'ra*? Is the evil inclination our "peace partner", a force with which we should pursue reconciliation?

The Sages (Pirkei Abot 4:1) famously teach, איזהו גבור? הכובש את יצרו – "Who is mighty? The one who captures his inclination". In ancient times, when a nation went out to war, its goal was not always to kill the enemy troops, but to do something even better – to capture them and make them servants, and this is our goal in our struggle against the *yeser ha'ra*. We don't want to "kill" it; we want to "capture" it, to harness the drives and tendencies that normally lead us to sin, and use them in our service of Hashem.[9]

We all have a natural inclination toward jealousy. Our objective in our ongoing battle against this *yeser ha'ra* is not to eliminate this tendency, but rather to use it for our benefit. Rather than envying people for their wealth and prestige, we should envy those who know more Torah than us. Lust should be used for marriage and procreation, to beget children and build a Torah home. If a person feels a natural impulse to spend money, he should donate to charities. People with a craving to shop can buy tickets

---

9. When Ribka was pregnant with Yaakob and Esav, she received a prophecy ורב יעבוד צעיר ("the older shall serve the younger" – Bereshit 25:23). On the simple level of interpretation, this means that the older twin – Esav – would be subjugated by the younger brother, Yaakob. Additionally, however, it refers to the subjugation of the *yeser ha'ra* and utilizing it as a servant of the *yeser tob*. The Sages teach that our evil inclination enters our beings at the time of birth, whereas the *yeser tob* develops later, at adolescence. The *yeser ha'ra* is thus "older" than the *yeser tob*. The prophecy of ורב יעבוד צעיר is thus an admonition to ensure that our "older" inclination serves the "younger" one, that our *yeser ha'ra* is at all times subservient to our *yeser tob*.

at Chinese auctions that benefit worthy institutions. If a person has an innate tendency toward wild, unruly behavior, he can use it in the *bet midrash* by learning with energy, passion and enthusiasm. Indeed, there was an incident where a person shouted אמן יהא שמיה רבה during Kaddish with unusual vigor, and in an exceptionally loud voice, to the point where it sounded bizarre and improper. Some congregants protested, so the Rabbi explained to them that this man had formerly spent his evenings in dance clubs. Since becoming religiously committed, he now utilizes that natural energy and tendency toward boisterous conduct, to pray with exceptional zeal and passion. This is how we "capture" the *yeser ha'ra*, and turn it into our servant.

In the daily *shema* recitation, we read the verse that commands us to love the Almighty בכל לבבך "with all your heart". The Gemara in Masechet Berachot (54a) noted that the word לבב, as opposed to לב, denotes two different "hearts". Meaning, the verse refers here to serving God with both aspects of our beings, with our *yeser tob* – our inclination toward good – and our *yeser ha'ra*. We are not commanded to eliminate our *yeser ha'ra*; after all, it is an integral part of the human condition which can never be eliminated. Rather, we are enjoined to "capture" our *yeser ha'ra*, to find ways to utilize all our natural tendencies – even those which we normally associate with sinful behavior – for noble purposes.

This is how we "make peace" with our *yeser ha'ra*. By using it for our own purposes, we make it into our "friend", we bring it to our side. The great challenge of religious life is to transform our sinful impulses from our archenemy to our faithful servant; from our dangerous foe to our devoted ally.

Elsewhere, the Talmud (Kiddushin 30b) comments, בראתי יצר הרע, בראתי תורה תבלין – "I [Hashem] created an evil inclination, and I created Torah as a spice". Torah serves as the antidote, so-to-speak, to our sinful tendencies; a person struggling to overcome his evil inclinations is encouraged to devote himself to Torah learning, which empowers him to defeat his *yeser ha'ra*. Significantly, though, the Gemara does not describe Torah as the "antibiotic" that kills the *yeser ha'ra*, but rather uses the term תבלין – "spice". Torah does not and cannot eradicate the evil inclination, but it most certainly can "enhance" the *yeser ha'ra*. It changes it into something beneficial and pleasant, into a force that can help us achieve our goals, rather than sabotaging our spiritual aspirations.

As mentioned earlier, the Talmud in Berachot begins with the laws of *shema*, and concludes in Masechet Uktzin with the verse, ה' עוז לעמו יתן ה' יברך את עמו בשלום. The first step is to understand and internalize the concept of לבבך, of serving our Creator with both our *yeser tob* and *yeser ha'ra*. By the time we complete the Talmud, as a result of our intensive learning, we achieve ה' יברך את עמו בשלום, peaceful harmony between the two different components of our souls. Once we devote ourselves to עוז (literally, "strength"), which refers to the Torah, we then earn the blessing of peace, complete reconciliation between our *yeser tob* and *yeser ha'ra*.[10]

This great blessing is also included in our prayers for peace. We pray that God assist us in making peace within ourselves, that we should enjoy inner peace, that instead of feeling conflicted and having to struggle and wage war against our internal enemy, we will be able to turn it into our ally and trusted servant. This, perhaps, is the most valuable kind of "peace" to which we must aspire.

---

10 . This concept is also alluded to in the שלש עשרה מידות שהתורה נדרשת בהן – the thirteen exetegical devices through which the Sages inferred *halachot* from the Biblical text, as we recite in our morning prayer service (ר' ישמעאל אומר בשלש עשרה מידות התורה נדרשת: מקל וחומר מגזרה שוה...). This list concludes with the phrase, וכן שני כתובים המכחישים זה את זה עד שיבא הכתוב השלישי ויכריע ביניהם. Meaning, the כן, the final מדה which culminates this list, is that a seeming contradiction between two verses is reconciled by a third verse. In some editions, however, the word וכן is spelled וכאן, or "and here". This has been explained to mean that by the time one reaches this point, after one has gone through and studied the various techniques required for understanding the Torah, he achieves ויכריע ביניהם – full reconciliation between the two otherwise contradictory forces within him, between his *yeser tob* and his *yeser ha'ra*.

שים שלום טובה וברכה
"Bestow peace, goodness and blessing"

Peace is what allows all of God's blessings to flow from the heavens; it keeps the "pipelines" of divine blessing intact so we can receive God's goodness. Therefore, we ask God to bestow peace upon us, as a result of which His "goodness and blessing" will naturally descend.

חיים חן וחסד צדקה ורחמים
"life, grace, kindness, righteousness and compassion"

חן stems from the word חנם ("gratis"), and thus refers to the gifts God grants us undeservedly, despite our unworthiness. חסד is the kindness which we have earned, and רחמים denotes God's willingness to grant us an "advance", paying us ahead of time, as it were, for what He foresees that we will earn in the future.

עלינו ועל-כל ישראל עמך
"upon us, and upon all Your nation, Israel"

According to some commentators, this *beracha* was originally recited only by the *kohanim*, immediately following the *birkat kohanim* blessing. After delivering their blessing, the *kohanim* would utter a prayer asking God that He grant His blessing of peace upon them, and upon the entire Jewish nation.

וברכנו אבינו כלנו כאחד באור פניך
"and bless us, our Father, all of us as one, with the light of Your countenance"

The concept of הארת פנים, God "shining His countenance" upon us, can be understood by considering the effect that a sincere, warm, friendly smile can have on other people. We have all experienced that sense of gratification, that jolt, of being received warmly and courteously by somebody. *Hazal* admonish us to greet all people בסבר פנים יפות, with a polite and pleasant smile, because such a greeting can profoundly impact upon the person's self-esteem and overall mood.

R' Yehuda Ha'nasi was a student of R' Meir, and he noted the inspiration he received by seeing R' Meir's back. Apparently, his seat in the yeshiva was positioned behind R' Meir, and he was therefore able to see only his great Rabbi's back. R' Yehuda remarked that if his seat had been positioned in front of R' Meir, such that he would have been able to see his face, he would have gained even more. This expresses the concept of הארת פנים, the power that a person has through the way he looks upon others. R' Meir was such a towering spiritual figure that he exuded this inspiration even behind him, without looking with his eyes.

This is what we ask from Hashem, that He look upon us at all times with love, warmth and grace. This alone is a source of great blessing.

כי באור פניך נתת לנו ה' אלהינו, תורה וחיים
"for it is with the light of Your countenance that You, Hashem our God, have given us Torah and life"

The height of הארת פנים was manifest at the time of *Matan Torah*, when God revealed Himself to the entire Jewish nation and gave us the Torah. At that moment, He lifted us all to the stature of prophets; in fact, every member of *Am Yisrael* achieved the prophetic level of Moshe Rabbenu. (The obvious difference between them and him is that they did not maintain this level after the experience of the Revelation, whereas Moshe, of course, did.) Rabbi Haim of Volozhin writes that at the time of *Matan Torah*, the people had a clearer perception of spiritual matters than physical matters. Thus, the Torah describes *Beneh Yisrael* as "seeing the sounds" (וכל העם ראים את הקולת – Shemot 20:15). Through their prophetic insight, they were able to perceive sound as though it were a visible entity.

We ask Hashem to always grant us His הארת פנים, which, as at the experience of Sinai, will elevate us and infuse within us all the qualities listed in the continuation of this passage.

אהבה וחסד, צדקה ורחמים
"love [for people] and kindness, charity and compassion"

The experience of *Matan Torah* turned us all into people of
אהבה וחסד צדקה ורחמים, people with a natural inclination to extend
genuine love and benevolence toward others. We need only to look at
the extraordinary sums of charity given by Jews today to recognize
this innate and distinctly Jewish quality, which was permanently
implanted within us at the time of the Revelation at Sinai. Jews
comprise an infinitesimal percentage of the population, and yet we
always find Jews spearheading campaigns on behalf of the victims
of oppression around the world. It is well-known that the medical
field is disproportionately inundated with Jews. Jews are naturally
inclined to pursue a medical career not only for the money (there
are easier ways of making a respectable living) but also due to their
natural drive to help people in need. At Sinai we became by nature,
רחמנים וגומלי חסדים – kind, compassionate, charitable and generous
people.

This also signifies the fact that our acceptance of and devotion
to Torah, must make us kinder and more sensitive people. Once
we receive the Torah, we must then develop אהבה וחסד צדקה ורחמים.
Being Torah observant must result in becoming a nicer person. King
Shelomo describes Torah devotion bereft of good character traits
with the expression נזם זהב באף חזיר ("A gold ring in a swine's nose" –
Mishleh 11:22). The Torah does not belong in a person who is selfish
and conceited, just as a magnificent piece of gold jewelry does not
belong on a hog. The acceptance of Torah must be followed by the
qualities of אהבה וחסד צדקה ורחמים.

ברכה ושלום
"blessing and peace"

The *Zohar* teaches that during the time of the *Bet Ha'mikdash*,
all the blessings in the world came by way of the Jewish people. God
showered His blessings upon *Am Yisrael*, and we then transferred
blessing to the rest of the world. In exile, however, we are dependent

upon the grace and goodwill of other nations. Today, for example, the United States is the greatest benefactor of the State of Israel. In the time of Mashiah, however, the Jewish State will be supporting the rest of the world, including the United States. When we are deserving, Hashem bestows upon us ברכה ושלום in abundance, and those blessings are then disseminated to the other peoples of the world.

וטוב בעיניך לברכנו, ולברך את כל-עמך ישראל, ברוב-עז ושלום

"and it is favorable in Your eyes to bless us and to bless Your entire nation, Israel, with abundant strength and peace"

Hashem wants to grant us His blessings of peace, but we must prove ourselves worthy of those blessings.

עז here refers to Torah. As mentioned, with Torah comes peace; our devotion to Torah serves to enhance the level of peace and harmony among ourselves and throughout the world.

In Honor of our mother

Miriam Naggar

In Memory of our father

Max M. Naggar

מרדכי משה בן שרה ע"ה

By their children
**Morris, Joseph, Sara, Carol
and Families**

Concluding Supplications

אלהי נצור

The Gemara in Masechet Berachot (16b-17a) tells that several Sages had the practice of reciting additional supplications after completing the *Amidah* prayer. Some of these texts, which are recorded in full in the Gemara, have been incorporated into our liturgy in various contexts. The prayer of אלהי נצור, which was added to the end of the *Amidah* by Mar Bereh De'Ravina, has been accepted as the concluding prayer of every *Amidah* which we recite.[11]

---

11. One possible reason for why this supplication was chosen over all the others mentioned in the Gemara is that it concludes with the verse יהיו לרצון אמרי פי, which, as will be noted later, is an especially significant pasuk that adds immense power to our prayers.

אלהי, נצור לשוני מרע
"My God, restrain my tongue from evil"

We ask God for help in our effort to avoid all forms of forbidden speech, such as slander and gossip. Of course, this effort is our responsibility, and not God's; the fundamental doctrine of בחירה חפשית, free will, establishes that we have the capacity to choose to act and speak properly or improperly. But this doctrine does not mean that we cannot or should not pray for the Almighty's assistance in mustering the self-control needed to do and say the right things. Praying to God for spiritual assistance is itself a proper use of free will, as we make a willed decision to try to act properly and ask God to help us succeed in this effort.

ושפתותי מדבר מרמה
"and my lips from speaking deceit"

The word מרמה refers to speaking in a misleading manner, in a way which misrepresents our thoughts and feelings, such as speaking kindly and flatteringly to people whom we actually dislike. This is why we make reference in this phrase to שפתותי – "my lips". We have two lips which are separate from one another, symbolizing the "split" that many people unfortunately make between what they say and what they feel.

The Torah describes how Yosef's brothers "were unable to speak to him peacefully" because of their negative feelings toward him (ולא יכלו דברו לשלם – Bereshit 37:4), and Rashi comments, מתוך גנותם למדנו שבחם שלא דברו אחת בפה ואחת בלב – "From within their disgrace we learn their praise, as they did not speak one way in their mouths but feel differently in their hearts". The brothers did not conceal their negative feelings behind a veneer of false flattery and staged admiration, and thus there is what to learn even from the inappropriate feelings of animosity they harbored toward Yosef.

We ask God to help us follow this example, and to always ensure to speak and present ourselves honestly.

ולמקללי נפשי תדום
"My soul shall be silent for those who curse me"

Hazal (Shabbat 88) speak in praise of הנעלבין ואינן עולבים שומעין חרפתן ואין משיבין – "Those who are insulted but do not insult, who hear their disgrace but do not respond". Great reward is promised to those who remain silent in the face of insults and degradation, who ignore those who offend them rather than follow the natural tendency to react angrily. The pasuk in Iyov (26:7) describes God as תולה ארץ על בלימה – he suspends the earth on nothingness – which the Gemara (Chulin 89a) explains to mean, אין העולם מתקיים אלא בשביל מי שבולם את עצמו בשעה מריבה – "The world is sustained only for one who stops himself during a fight". When we are provoked, insulted or wronged, our instinct is to shout in anger. It takes enormous strength and self-restraint to remain silent, and thus the reward for doing so is immense. We therefore turn to the Almighty for help in this regard, and pray for the ability to maintain our composure and remain silent when we are insulted.

The Rabbis teach us that when a person keeps quiet in the face of insult, that moment is an עת רצון, a favorable time for prayer, when our requests are answered. The story is told of a certain Torah Sage who advised a childless couple that if they ever see somebody hear an insult, they should urge that person to remain silent and to then pray on their behalf that they should have a child. Sure enough, they were sitting with some people and one person said something offensive to a woman who was with them. The childless woman urged the offended woman not to respond, and she remained silent. The woman then asked her to pray for her, and she did, and she soon had a child.

We pray here for help in restraining our natural tendency to respond angrily to insults, so we can be worthy of the immense rewards promised to הנעלבין ואינן עולבים – "Those who are insulted but do not insult". Additionally, ולמקללי נפשי תדום means that those who curse us should be made silent and unable to continue their verbal abuse.

ונפשי כעפר לכל תהיה
"my soul shall be like dust to all"

People "curse" and insult only those by whom they feel threatened. When we see impressive and accomplished people, this can arouse feelings of insecurity. This could then lead us to find some fault and offend them in order to protect our ego. We thus pray that we should appear to other people as insignificant as dirt so they do not feel threatened by us and will not insult us.

Alternatively, we pray here that we should reach the level where we do not even feel offended. In the previous clause – ולמקללי נפשי תדום – we pray for the strength to remain silent when we feel insulted, but now, we pray for an even higher level, where we are like "dirt", and are not affected at all by insults and slurs.

Tosafot, commenting on the Gemara, offers a different explanation. Just as the ground exists eternally, and will never disappear, similarly, we pray that our offspring shall endure for all eternity.

Others explain that this prayer refers to the fact that the ground always "triumphs" over those who abuse it. Nothing in this world is subject to greater degradation than the ground. People and animals step on it, spit on it, perform their bodily functions on it, and do whatever they please with it. The ground endures all this abuse, patiently waiting until the time when the human being or the animal perishes and is buried underneath the ground. During their lifetime, man and beast humiliate the earth, but eventually, the ground prevails and triumphs. We therefore pray for the wisdom and patience to respond to humiliation as the ground does, remaining calm and silent, knowing that in the end the victim always triumphs over those who abuse him.

פתח לבי בתורתך ואחרי מצותיך תרדוף נפשי

"Open my heart to Your Torah, and may my soul run after Your commandments"

The word בתורתך may be read as ב' תורתך – "Your two Torahs", referring to the Written Torah and the oral halachic tradition.

We pray that we not only observe the *misvot*, but "run after" them, with energy and zeal. One of the most effective tools the *yeser ha'ra* employs in trying to dissuade us from performing *misvot* is procrastination. "I'll do it tomorrow" is a very dangerous phrase, especially when it comes to Torah and *misvot*. As we all know from personal experience, "I'll do it tomorrow" is very often a convenient way of avoiding the responsibility altogether. The *yeser ha'ra* knows this as least as well as we do, and therefore when he cannot convince us to forgo on a misva, he convinces us to push it off – which often amounts to the exact same thing.

One night, David HaMelech was troubled by the thought that he lived in a glamorous palace, while the Aron Kodesh was being kept in a tent. He decided it was time to build the *Bet HaMikdash* so that the Holy Ark would be housed in an appropriately lavish building. God, however, determined that the time had not yet come for the Bet Ha'mikdash to be built, and that this would be done by King David's son, Shelomo. He thus appeared to the prophet, Natan, and instructed him to tell King David not to proceed with his plans, as the time for the *Bet HaMikdash* had not yet arrived. Natan beheld this prophetic vision in the middle of the night, and he figured he would wait until morning to convey the message to the king. But Hashem told him he must go to King David right away. Sure enough, Natan went to King David and saw he was already getting started on the project to build a Temple. As soon as the idea came to him, King David did not wait. He went to work immediately, and even after Natan relayed God's message, King David still devoted himself to making all the preparations for the Temple, such as purchasing the designated lot of land and drawing up plans.

Another remarkable example of תרדוף נפשי is King David's great-grandfather, Boaz. It was in the middle of the night when Ruth informed him that he was a relative of her husband and thus had the opportunity to marry her and redeem her husband's family's property. Boaz completed the entire process the very next day. We know how long wedding plans and property transactions can take, but Boaz did not want to risk squandering this *misva* opportunity, and thus he did it all in a single day. He married Ruth that day, and she conceived that night. As it turned out, Boaz died the very next day. Had he delayed the *misva* by even one day, he would have forfeited the opportunity to be the father of David Ha'melech and the Mashiah. Delaying a *misva* – even for just one day! – can cause us to lose its eternal benefits.

יהיו לרצון אמרי-פי והגיון לבי לפניך ה' צורי וגאלי
"May the words of my mouth be accepted, and the thoughts of my heart before You, O God, my Rock and my Redeemer"

The Shulhan Aruch (Orah Haim 128:2) rules that one should end the *Amidah* with this verse – יהיו לרצון... – which comes from Tehillim (19:15). Our custom is to recite this verse twice – once after the final beracha of the *Amidah* (המברך את עמו ישראל בשלום), and then again after Elokai Netsor, just before עושה שלום במרומיו. Those who recite additional supplications after Elokai Netsor (such as the prayer of Rav, which we discuss below) recite this verse a third time after their additional prayers, before עושה שלום.[12]

The scholars of Kabbalah spoke at length of the significance and power of reciting this pasuk, which has the ability to bring our prayers before the Almighty. Indeed, the Kaf Ha'hayim writes that one must recite this verse slowly, because of the depth and profundity underlying its words. The first and last letter of this verse is yod, which has the numerical value of 10, and there are ten words in the verse, alluding to a connection between this pasuk and the ten

---

12. It should be noted that many hazzanim unfortunately make the mistake of omitting יהיו לרצון when repeating the Amidah. This verse must be recited even after the hazzan's repetition (though it may be recited in an undertone, if the hazzan so wishes).

sefirot (emanations). The verse also contains 42 letters, representing the Divine Name of 42 letters.

In this verse we beg Hashem to accept not only אמרי פי, the words we recite – but also הגיון לבי, the thoughts of our heart. There are times when words are incapable of accurately expressing our thoughts and feelings, and this limitation of verbal expression makes it difficult for us to plead our case when speaking to other people. However, God sees the feelings in our heart just as clearly as He hears the words we articulate. We ask that He lovingly accept both components of our prayers, the spoken words and the silent emotions.[13]

Rav's Prayer

Many communities have also incorporated the prayer of a different Sage – Rav – into the daily *Amidah* recitation. This prayer, which is known as *Tefilat* Rav ("Rav's Prayer"), is recited by many after Elokai Netsor, before Oseh Shalom.

יהי רצון מלפניך ה' אלהינו ואלהי אבותינו, שתרחמנו ותחיינו חיים ארכים, חיים של שלום, חיים של טובה, חיים של ברכה, חיים של פרנסה טובה, חיים של חלוץ עצמות, חיים שיש בהם יראת חטא, חיים שאין בהם בושה וכלמה, חיים של עשר וכבוד, חיים שתהא בנו אהבת תורה ויראת שמים, חיים שתמלא כל משאלות לבנו לטובה לעבודתך, אמן [14]

ותחיינו חיים ארוכים
"and grant us long life"

The Shita Mekubeset to Masechet Ketubot (81) comments that Rav lived for over 300 years.[15] This may have likely been in the merit of his daily prayer for ארוכים חיים – long life.

---

13. One Rabbi quipped that the phrase והגיון לבי לפניך should give us incentive to concentrate properly while reciting the Amidah: we're asking that our thoughts, and not just our words, come before God – and we certainly do not want thoughts about our business, stocks or upcoming vacation being presented to God with our prayers!

14. As mentioned earlier, followers of this custom must recite יהיו לרצון a third time, before *Oseh Shalom*.

15. Rav Menaham Azarya of Pano wrote that Rabbi Abba, the famous student of Rabbi Shimon bar Yohai, was actually Rav. It thus turns out that Rav was a Tanna who lived until the time of the *Amoraim*. For this reason the Gemara comments on several occasions, רב תנא הוא ופליג – Rav had the status of a Tanna and thus had the authority to debate the positions taken by *Tanna'im* (whereas *Amora'im* were not given the authority to argue with *Tanna'im*).

חיים של שלום
"a life of peace"

When a person is beset by hardships and travails, Heaven forbid, his life progresses slowly; each year can seem like several years. But when a person enjoys peace and tranquility, his life seems to move quickly. In this prayer we ask for a life of peace, but which is also חיים ארוכים, a life that progresses slowly, so we can truly enjoy the time we spend in this world.

חיים של חלוץ עצמות
"a life of strong bones"

This refers to general physical wellbeing (Maharsha).

חיים של עשר וכבוד, חיים שתהא בנו אהבת תורה ויראת שמים
"a life of wealth and honor, a life when we have love for Torah and fear of God"

Why would a Rabbi – Rav – pray for "wealth and honor"? Is this what great Sages should aspire to?

The commentators explain that a Rabbi needs a degree of wealth and prestige in order to be effective. If a Rabbi lives in a small, rundown apartment and drives a beat-up car, many members of his congregation will look down on him and not take what he says seriously. When he admonishes a congregant for his wrongful behavior, that congregant will simply ignore it. Rav therefore prayed for עושר וכבוד so he would be taken seriously by the people under his charge and he would be effective in his efforts to uplift and inspire them. Moreover, a Rabbi who is poor and struggling to feed his family might be tempted to ignore the wrongdoing of wealthier congregants, as he depends upon them for his support. A Rabbi who enjoys "wealth and honor" will not be deterred by financial pressures from admonishing his wealthy congregants.

This is why the prayer for עושר וכבוד is linked to the request for "a life of love for Torah and fear of God". We ask for wealth and prestige not for our own enjoyment, but rather to assist us in our pursuit of Torah and spiritual greatness.

חיים שתמלא כל משאלות לבנו לטובה
"a life in which You will fulfill for us all our heart's desires for the best, amen"

We want God to fulfill our hearts' desires, but only לטובה – on the condition that it is "for the best". We do not always know what is best for us, and that which our hearts desire might not necessarily be in our best interests. A person might desire a certain job or position, but God knows that it is not good for him. A person might want to marry a certain girl, without realizing that she is not the best choice for him. Many people desire wealth, but wealth has ruined many people's lives, so we pray that God grants our requests לטובה, for our benefit and in our true best interests.

Notes

Notes

Notes